D0192810

Praise for *War and Peace and IT*

"War and Peace and IT offers a bold, insightful roadmap for building a company's digital capacity. With the pace of change in IT accelerating at such an unprecedented rate, I consider this essential reading for my entire leadership team."

—**François Locoh-Donou**, President & CEO, F5 Networks

"Having worked with hundreds of executives from large enterprises in my roles at AWS, it is clear to me that every CEO and CIO should read this book...together. As today's leader transform their organizations for the digital era, they invariably struggle with issues of cultural change, organizational change, and rigid legacy ways of working. If only they had had this book! It is the book they need to bring together IT and the rest of their businesses in the way that can overcome those hurdles. Mark's book is clearly informed by his executive leadership experience—both doing it himself and working with other enterprise leaders."

—**Stephen Orban**, General Manager at Amazon Web Services
and author of *Ahead in the Cloud*

"In *War and Peace and IT*, Mark Schwartz effectively highlights how the days of silo'd functions and delivering requirements like a *War and Peace* novel to IT are over. If you and your teams aren't out on the frontlines with IT fostering a new way of working together, your ability to succeed in the next era is likely over. If you want to learn how to embrace technology, respond effectively to ambiguity, and transform your business into an agile organization, then bring all your CXOs together and read this book with the CIO."

—**Chris Richardson**, Chief Operating Officer, Tru Realty

"This is the book I would want with me on a walk through the woods in a Russian winter. Mark's three books help to define how an organization should function as a whole, each approaching the question from a different angle and each as helpful in changing the organization. I am buying several copies of this book for my colleagues across all of our business operations...not business and IT."

—**Josh Seckel**, Head of Agile Practice at Sevatec, Inc

"War and Peace and IT makes a convincing case for change: its real-life examples and the evidence it presents are concrete and compelling."

—**Rodrigo Lobo**, Partner at PIPA Global Investments

"In an environment of chaos and uncertainty, there's opportunity, but only if you can recognize it and react quickly. This third book in the trilogy raises the most important issue—decisions need to be made and executed in real time. Outline a set of objectives, get out of the way, and allow the creativity to flow. Mark brings the reader through this journey, and having gone through it with him at the Department of Homeland Security, I can tell you it was one of most impactful initiatives we ever undertook."

—**Luke McCormack**, former CIO of the Department of Homeland Security

"Napoleon couldn't centrally manage his battles in real time, but today's leaders have no excuse. Independent cell-based teams using rapid hypothesis testing will win the battles against competitors who remain old-school. After explaining to IT leaders how to get *A Seat at the Table*, Mark Schwartz has advice for everyone else at the table."

—**Adrian Cockcroft**, VP Cloud Architecture Strategy at AWS

WAR

Business Leadership, Technology,

PEACE

and Success in the Digital Age

IT

MARK SCHWARTZ

IT Revolution

Portland, Oregon

25 NW 23rd Pl, Suite 6314
Portland, OR 97210

First Edition
Printed in the United States of America
24 23 22 21 20 19   1 2 3 4 5 6 7 8 9 10

Cover and book design by Devon Smith
Author Photograph by Gary Landsman

Library of Congress Catalog-in-Publication Data

Names: Schwartz, Mark (IT manager), author.
Title: War and peace and IT : business leadership, technology, and success in
the digital age / by Mark Schwartz.
Description: Portland, OR : IT Revolution Press, [2019] |
Includes bibliographical references.
Identifiers: LCCN 2018047857| ISBN 9781942788713 (trade pbk.) |
ISBN 9781942788720 (ePub) | ISBN 9781942788737 (kindle) |
ISBN 9781942788751 (pdf)
Subjects: LCSH: Information technology—Management. |
Technological innovations—Management. | Leadership.
Classification: LCC HD30.2 .S3878 2019 | DDC 004.068—dc23
LC record available at https://lccn.loc.gov/2018047857

For information about special discounts for bulk purchases or for information
on booking authors for an event, please visit our website at ITRevolution.com.

War and Peace and IT

To the leaders of finance, marketing, sales, operations
I have worked with, who have taught me much:

You! *Lecteur! mon semblable; mon client!*

CONTENTS

ILLUSTRATIONS

FOREWORD

Most Humble Readers:

I, Napoleon Bonaparte, Emperor of the French, King of Italy, Protector of the Confederation of the Rhine, First Consul of France, MBA,* do require and suggest that you read this book.

It is wrong in places, *bien sûr*, but what do you expect in the *brouillard de guerre*—this we forgive from an auteur who with insight describes how I, Napoleon, visionary and leader, brought transformation to France. Was it not I who persuaded all of France to use the metric system? I who created the Code Napoleonic?† I who dissolved the Holy Roman Empire and unified Germany? I and no other who legalized divorce, ended the Inquisition, and began the fashion for the felt bicorn hat, one of which—please note this, business readers—was sold for $400,000 this year of 2018? And was not it I who gave my name to a kind of pastry both frosted and filled?

Do you think all of this cultural change was easy? *Non*, impediments faced on every front: the British, the Austrians, the Italians, the Russians . . . that is, I mean the weather *horrible* in Russia—if you can overcome it, you will be more successful in your transformation, I tell you this.

I commend the *auteur*, M. Schwartz, who corrects the confused mutterings of that *espèce de vache sénile*, that *tête dodelinante*, Comte Leo Tolstoy and his *mille-feuilles* of *War and Peace* filled with nonsense and frosted only with ignorance. If only I had had this book of M. Schwartz—and vast quantities of *steak*

---

* I conferred on Harvard Business School the privilege to award me an honorary degree.
† It is, I assert, the finest specimen of bureaucracy—which, as the auteur says in Chapter 8, is the epitome of efficiency and effectiveness.

frites and well-made boots—I would surely have triumphed in Russia, despite the weather *horrible*.

This book teaches the successful tactics innovated by me, Napoleon. How *par example* I brought the technological *agilité* to my forces by making mobile the artillery, so can you learn to be masterful of technology. When the *auteur* says that speed is most important—*eh bien*, M. Mack surely observed this when I took Ulm from him by moving my troops from the English Channel to the Rhine even before he finished his *café au lait*. And in regards to the motivating of troops, as M. Schwartz observes, I engaged my finance department to invest in my troops coins rather than worthless paper money.

M. Schwartz further praises focus and risk-taking. I recall to mind when I defeated the Austrians at Austerlitz by deliberately weakening my flank, which provoked them to attack it, at which moment I focused all of my forces on the very center of their position. This lesson may be useful to you.

Bon. Let us then boldly take up the banner of digital transformation and cross the Nieman River into the fray of competition and disruption. We will together make war on outdated ideas, aim our mobile artillery at the old guard, innovate to found a digital era, and make *foie gras* of the British. For as I have said in my memoirs, also required and recommended reading (*Paris: Beaudoin Frères*, 1821, available on Amazon.com), "Lead the ideas of your time and they will accompany and support you; fall behind them and they drag you along with them; oppose them and they will overwhelm you."

Napoleon Bonaparte
Sainte-Helene, 2018

PREFACE

May the Sheniu officials, who make the conditions of the lives of men, not cause my name to stink.

—The Egyptian Book of the Dead

But what does it really matter to me how So-and-so expounds his text? The main thing is that I should get some sleep.

—Epictetus, *Discourses*

In my role at Amazon Web Services (AWS), I meet with executives of large enterprises who are leaping to "transform" their organizations but are stumbling over cultural patterns, organizational issues, rigid processes, and implacable bureaucracy. They know that their organizations have a history of brilliant innovation, a leadership position in their markets, a passion for serving their customers . . . but somehow, despite their feeling that change is urgent, despite their worries about disruption, despite the innovation they see around them, their troops are not advancing.

I have seen a pattern to these cases. While everyone can see that digital transformation has something to do with digital technology, many don't see that it also has to do with digital technologists—or, more have precisely, the role technologists play in their companies. Ever since IT departments have existed, companies have developed ways of working with IT that actually hold the whole business back as it attempts to enter the digital age.

Having experienced both the CIO and CEO roles, I wanted to write a book about how *non*-IT leaders in the enterprise can work *with* IT to succeed in the digital world.

My last book, *A Seat at the Table: IT Leadership in the Age of Agility*, was written for IT professionals. In it I discussed recent changes in IT practice and what those changes mean for the CIO and other IT leaders. As I was writing it, I realized that these new ways of managing IT—the technique known as DevOps, in particular—were thoroughly inconsistent with the way IT has traditionally been incorporated into the broader enterprise of which it is part. At the same time, studies have shown that these new IT practices lead to vastly better business outcomes. So, I said, the CIO must change this relationship, accepting responsibility for business outcomes and taking a seat at the business strategy table.

The feedback I received from the IT community regarding the book was flattering: they loved the illustrations and my references to obscure kinds of pasta, although there were some objections to my controversial remarks on strozzapreti. But when it came to my main thesis—that the business-IT divide must be dissolved—they suggested that someone needed to inform the business community of this. Sensing another opportunity to lock myself in my room for long hours with coffee and a word processing program, I promised them that I would write something for the non-IT folks they interacted with, looking at the same questions but from the business's point of view.

Guess what? It finally hit me that I was really looking at the same problem from two sides. Enterprises are filled with technologists who are trying to bring their companies into the digital age and who are focused on achieving business value with technology. And they're frustrated trying to do so. Enterprises are also filled with non-technology business leaders who are trying to bring their companies into the digital age and achieve business value with technology. And they are just as frustrated in doing so. And here I am, a former CIO and CEO armed with a keyboard sitting between warring parties in violent agreement.

———

Digital transformation exposes a number of tensions that have existed within organizations. The tension between those who, according to stereotype, get pleasure from accomplishing business outcomes and those who find it in working with technology, is one. But there are also tensions between moving quickly and retaining control, between improvising and following a plan, and between the creation of new competitive advantages and the destruction of old ones. These opposites seem impossible to reconcile; it is war, with brief periods of peace as temporary accommodations are reached.

It reminds me of something I experienced back when I was CIO at Intrax Cultural Exchange. One day my IT organization received a helpdesk ticket request from an employee that read, "Please solve Israeli–Palestinian problem!"

I was proud that they thought so highly of my IT organization that they would send us a request like that, and my team was eager to help. It only took us a moment to figure out what the ticket writer had really meant—there was a database issue that made it hard to record the biographical data of certain applicants, but no one wanted to fix it because of the sensitive politics. It was what the IT world would call a *reference data* problem. The employee just wanted us to fix the database.

I must admit that we never did fix the Israeli–Palestinian problem. But organizational oppositions I've described are a far more tractable problem, especially with the tools available to us today. We merely need to stop using old mental models to manage the new realities of the digital world.

Throughout history, philosophers, scientists, authors, and religious thinkers have noted tensions between opposing forces. Yin and yang in Chinese philosophy, the forces of good and evil in Zoroastrianism, creation and destruction in Hinduism, thesis and antithesis in Hegel's dialectic. In each of these cases the great thinkers identified these tensions as the forces that drive the world forward—that account, in other words, for transformation and change.

If heads around the company are nodding yes to digital transformation, we should take advantage of all the head bobbling and get going. The route to digital wonderfulness can best be explained, I tell you, through references to Napoleon and early warfare, to Krishna driving a chariot between the Pandavas and Kauravas, to the toys with shaking heads that one finds across cultures and geographies, and to dead ancient Egyptians. You can trust me on this.

INTRODUCTION

Because technology is the negation of any definitive truth—and to dominate the transformation of things it must be this negation—the destiny of the West is radical anxiety.

—**Emanuele Severino**, *The Essence of Nihilism*

Nothing is more damaging to a new truth than an old error.

—**Goethe**, *Maxims*

Today, across industries and geographies, executives of large enterprises are struggling to transform their organizations. They have a sincere desire to "become digital" but are getting stuck along the way. They know that their enterprises are special—they have a history of brilliant innovation, a market leadership position, a mission they're passionate about. They look at companies like Amazon and Apple, innovating at high speed, getting products to market in nanoseconds, and creating new types of business value that no one has ever before conceived. They wonder, why can't their enterprise do the same?

It's easy to blame cultural patterns, organizational issues, rigid processes, risk aversion, and implacable bureaucracy for their inertia. But the real obstacle is something different and harder to see. It's the relationship between IT—the company's organ of technical expertise—and the rest of the enterprise. The digital age demands leadership from those responsible for digital technology. But the conventional ways in which the "business" part of the enterprise and the IT part work together make that impossible.

What do enterprises want from IT? They want business outcomes. They want IT to help improve the company's competitive positioning. They want IT to drive technology-inspired innovation. They want IT to deepen relationships with customers and promote repeat business. To streamline operations and help make better use of their employees' time and mental capacity. To manage risk—particularly in information security. As the business world becomes digital, technology becomes central not just to the mechanics of running a company, but to the company's ability to compete and survive.

What do enterprises actually ask and incentivize IT to do? To deliver projects on time and according to plan. To reduce IT costs. To provide good customer service to the company's own employees. To take in requirements from the business units and deliver IT capabilities to fulfill them precisely as stated. To control risk by not allowing scope to creep and managing to deadlines.

What we *ask* of IT isn't what we *want* of IT; it's at best dimly related.

As the cliché has it, the pace of change is accelerating. That's nothing new to technologists—for decades, changes in technology have come faster and faster as startlingly inventive people join the technology world; as software, hardware, and IT service providers pour resources into growing their markets; and as demand for features, scale, security, and resilience drive innovation. A software developer, for example, must constantly learn about and experiment with new programming languages, new practices, and new mental models for architecting and designing IT systems.

The increased pace now applies to business and product strategy as well, largely because technology is so much at the center of everything an enterprise does. Why are executives on email twenty-four hours a day? It's not just because email is available; it's because they actually feel a need to make decisions while eating pasta, watching reality TV, and emerging from REM sleep. We feel that urgency in our stress levels. Lowered barriers to entry let disruptive companies transform industries in the flick of an eyelid. The cloud, the pliability of well-written software, the unmediated access to customers globally over the internet, the availability of venture capital, an incoming workforce that has an intuitive understanding of younger markets—all of these raise the risk that a company that was once comfortable will wake up one day to find itself dead or delisted, or at least no longer welcome on the S&P 500 index.

It's not just startups that threaten established enterprises. Other traditional enterprises have found ways to draw on the magic of today's technology to pull new products out of a proverbial hat, to make costs disappear, or to transform red financials to black. According to a Boston Consulting Group (BCG) study, companies are dropping from top-three positions in their industries faster than ever before, and once they do, are also likely to drop from the top ten rankings within five years.[1]

There is simply no way an enterprise can feel comfortable with its status quo, or move slowly and tentatively toward a vaguely glimpsed future; urgency and clarity are the demands of the day. Forty-seven percent of CEOs report feeling pressure from their boards to digitally transform[2]—whatever they might mean by that—and sixty-two percent already have some such transformation underway.*[3] Companies that move too slowly are destroying business value every nanosecond.

In their book *Accelerate: The Science of Lean Software and DevOps: Building and Scaling High Performing Technology Organizations*, authors Nicole Forsgren, Jez Humble, and Gene Kim identify four areas where organizations must accelerate:

- delivery of goods and services to delight their customers
- engagement with the market to detect and understand customer demand
- anticipation of compliance and regulatory changes that impact their systems
- response to potential risks, such as security threats or changes in the economy[4]

To accelerate, enterprises must find a way to bring technology to the heart of their work, for just as technology is causing this disruption, it is technology that provides the solution. It's the internet that lets them quickly reach customers across the world, it's the cloud that lets them instantly acquire the

---

* Also 42% say "digital first" or "digital to the core" are their company's default digital postures.

infrastructure they need, and it's the changeability of software that lets them continuously innovate and transform to meet emerging demands.

Ironically, enterprises often consider IT to be a hindrance—a frictional force that slows them down as they grind forward to deliver value for their customers. But it's IT departments, which have lived with change and uncertainty for their entire existence, that have developed ways of coping with the constant pressure to adapt. The IT folks have quietly been streamlining their processes and finding ways to figure skate delicately at high velocity; what remains is for enterprises to put on their skates and get comfortable gliding on the digital world's slippery surfaces.

Leaders of digital transformations often look around their organizations and see heads nodding. Everyone seems to agree that change is needed to survive in the digital age. Everyone understands that it's urgent and that there is a risk of being disrupted if the company doesn't transform quickly enough. Capital markets are demanding growth and innovation, while the board wants management to invest in becoming future-ready. Executives are aware that competitors are learning how to build closer digital relationships with customers. Frankly, it's rare to so easily arrive at consensus.

But nothing seems to be happening. Heads are bobbling yes-yes-yes, plans are being discussed, priorities are being set . . . but the digital prince remains an analog frog. It's easy to blame the lack of progress on corporate culture, a lack of up-to-date skills among employees, rigid bureaucratic processes, lack of cohesion across business silos, heavy compliance requirements, accounting rules, or inflexible auditors. For any large enterprise, those are indeed important factors. But many of them are within the company's control and others, as I'll show later, are outputs of successful transformation—not prerequisites.

If you want to unlock your enterprise's digital transformation, you must change not only its relationship with technology, but its relationship with its technologists. Conventional wisdom has settled on a way of integrating IT into the enterprise that hasn't been very effective up to now and remains much less likely to be effective in the digital future. IT and the business face each other across a daunting chasm of stereotypes and perceived risk like rows of bobblehead dolls, bobbling and smiling at each other with goodwill and mutual respect, coupled with a formality that precludes intimacy. The key to digital transformation is to change the way IT and the business interact.

———

Over the decades that IT has been part of the corporate landscape, it's been regarded as a sort of arms-length contractor serving the rest of the business. A business unit decides what IT capabilities it needs, writes a requirements document, negotiates an understanding with IT about scheduling and costs, then tosses its requirements over the wall for delivery. IT is then responsible for fulfillment, delivering what was requested on the schedule it agreed to. We speak of "IT and the business" as if we're referring to two different things, and we encourage IT to treat the business as its customer. It's as though IT were an outside service provider full of people who just happen to be employees of the same company.

Digital transformation, on the contrary, means making technology central to the way an enterprise defines itself, rather than a utility or support function that can just as easily be outsourced. But this can only happen if the technologists are as much a part of the business as employees in marketing, finance, and operations.

Changing this relationship can be uncomfortable for both sides. On one hand, business employees have gotten used to being treated as IT's customers, whether the customer service they received was tip-worthy or not. This contractor-like model has given the illusion of control to the business—the feeling that even when they don't understand the technological details, they can at least hold IT accountable to some performance standard. They can feel like they've shifted the burden of technical uncertainty, complexity, and change onto the IT folks, and thereby gained predictability and simplicity for themselves. As long as IT said a project would be completed by a certain date, uncertainty had been managed away, or at least could be overseen by way of conventional risk management practices.

On the other hand, IT departments have never had to take responsibility for business outcomes. Someone else always decides which technology capabilities will create business value; someone else works to harvest the business value from the products IT delivers. IT has been able to say, "We can't do anything until we get your requirements," while enforcing policies and standards that might constrain business operations. By pushing the burden of value determination to the business, IT can feel like it's free of the biggest uncertainties and complexities in its activities.

As we move into today's digital world, uncertainties and complexities are becoming an everyday matter for everyone—IT and non-IT alike. We can no longer separate technology risk from business risk, or technology opportunity from business opportunity. The business must accept the risk and uncertainty that comes with technology, while IT must accept the risk and uncertainty that comes with business.

It's not just IT that finds itself distanced from the core strategic activity of the enterprise—there is a deeper and more general issue at play. As business and technical functions became more complex and specialized, organizations came to structure themselves into functional silos. Finance was expected to focus on finance, marketing on marketing, and IT on IT. Each area was assigned goals specific to its functions, which were then further subdivided and passed down to subspecialty areas. In this way, the reasoning went, each functional area could be held more accountable for things that no one outside completely understood anymore. But organizations are now paying the price for this fracturing as they try to develop a coherent strategic approach to the digital world.

The chief financial officer (CFO), for example, has often wound up focused on cost reduction and the operational efforts of seeing that the books get closed on time. According to a McKinsey study, two-thirds of CFOs think they should spend less time on traditional finance activities and more on strategic leadership.[5] About 30% of the finance department's effort is invested just in the mechanics of assembling data and resolving inconsistencies.[6]

The digital world, however, demands that the CFO play more of the role of strategic business advisor—the custodian of shareholder value or mission delivery.[7] In a digital organization the CFO drives competitive advantage by applying capital to opportunities as they arise, turning data into actionable business insights, and managing risk strategically. In place of cost reduction, the digital CFO focuses on making processes leaner, thereby removing waste and increasing the enterprise's velocity.

Among chief marketing officers (CMOs), the story is similar: 74% say their role doesn't allow them to have the impact on the business that they should.[8] Today, marketing must handle more countries, more customer segments, more media, more distribution channels, and more price points than ever before—as many as twenty million price points per year for a consumer products company, according to a McKinsey study.[9] But despite the complexity, what the CMO really wants is to deepen relationships with customers, develop the company's brands, and work with colleagues in other functional areas to grow the business.

Boards of directors now find they must take a more proactive approach to ensuring that their companies survive digital disruption—particularly by overseeing decisions that balance risk and opportunity. They need to make sure the company is building a sustainable position, which, as I'll show, largely depends on building agility and nimbleness into assets and processes. Given the increased pace of competition, they need to find leading or current indicators they can use to assess their company's performance in place of the trailing metrics of traditional financial reporting. Audit committees must ensure that controls are effective despite the increased pace of change, the new risks of the digital world, and the increasing stringency of compliance frameworks.[10]

The pattern is that each of these specialist executives must participate outside of their area of specialization by working with colleagues on strategic issues that cut across the enterprise as a whole. The CFO is not just in charge of finance and the CMO is not just in charge of marketing—both are responsible for bringing their functional expertise to bear on *all* of the company's activities and working across silos to accomplish business outcomes. So too for the CIO, who can no longer be responsible solely for running the technology function, but must bring technology expertise to bear on companywide strategy.

The task is harder for CIOs than for the rest of the executive suite, as I'll show in the next chapter. IT was suddenly injected into the enterprise landscape only five or six decades ago and has yet to find its place. As McKinsey reports, "There is little awareness of or agreement on how IT can meaningfully shape a business's future."[11] But, the report continues:

> . . . the results suggest one clear element of high-performing IT organizations: active CIO involvement in the business. Where respondents say their CIOs are very or extremely involved in shaping enterprise-wide strategy, they report much higher IT effectiveness than their peers whose CIOs are less involved.[12]

As we move into the digital era, it's IT that can help the CFO, CMO, and the board realize their objectives, supporting them as they move to the strategic role they were meant to play—and indeed *must* play for the digital enterprise to succeed. IT can make the other CXOs superheroes.

As a former CIO, I can tell you that IT needs to be held to higher—but different—standards, and that it will be pleased to step up to them. Engineers are builders—the joy in being a technologist is the joy of creation and of making a difference.

Here's one lesson I learned when I was CIO at Intrax Cultural Exchange. Intrax runs international cultural and educational programs such as work and travel, internships, high school exchange, English schools, and au pair placement. My first large initiative as its CIO was a very successful project to bring our au pair business online. The second project was to do something similar with our high school exchange program; it was a resounding disaster. For that one, IT had received a set of business unit requirements that seemed misguided and contradictory. We were convinced they made little sense from a business perspective. But the business unit was in charge, so in the end we gave in.

We were right, dammit—it was a mess. Employees who had to use it found that it slowed them down. Scrambling to fix it, we made it more like what IT had initially visualized. The CEO called me in and essentially said, "You screwed up." I protested that we had faithfully implemented the requirements and that it wasn't our fault that those requirements were wrong. To this he replied, "You're missing the point. I trusted you with spending our IT budget and getting good returns. That's not what I got."

He was absolutely right. A CIO is responsible for investing in technology to achieve business outcomes. It was my failure.

I could have argued that he hadn't set a context in which it was OK for me to disagree with the business unit and reject their requirements. As we saw it then, IT's job was to provide good "customer service." Taking orders and executing them was what the business unit leader expected. But now as a senior executive, I've come to believe that a CIO has to fight battles when necessary, to use influence and leverage to make sure that the right outcomes are achieved.

Enterprises face pressure to find new ways to grow. Since existing business lines are in danger of being disrupted or lost to competition, companies need to stimulate innovation to protect their markets and forge deeper relationships with customers, finding new opportunities to serve them. KPMG's study of

CEO priorities found that the majority believe growth is more important than finding cost efficiencies, while one-third said their companies weren't taking enough risk to meet their growth objectives.[13]

Geoffrey Moore, author of *Zone to Win: Organizing to Compete in an Age of Disruption*, points out that when a firm enters a new high-growth category, investors price its stock dramatically higher—often to ten times projected revenues or more. Once the category matures, however, valuations stabilize around one- or two-times current revenue. The only way to make the share price move again is to enter another emerging growth category at significant scale.[14] In other words, businesses must be consistently catching the next wave.

In business school I was taught that companies need to develop sustainable competitive advantages (care of the writings of business theorist Pankaj Ghemawat, for example). But sustainable advantages are rare these days. The cloud, the internet, and the globalization of markets have conjoined to reduce barriers to entry. Resource advantages? All companies have access to the same technologies. Locking up a distribution channel is far less sustainable now that new competitors can disintermediate the channel. Firms can build core competencies, as C. K. Prahalad and Gary Hamel have said they must,[15] but who's to say whether their competencies will continue to be of value?

In the digital world, competitive advantage must be constantly renewed. Successful companies continually innovate, harvesting the advantages of each innovation, then moving on to the next when the advantage is competed away. Our economy is largely the one Joseph Schumpeter envisioned in 1942 when he introduced the term "creative destruction."[16] Growth is driven by innovation, whether it's innovation in products, in building customer relationships, or in improving processes to reduce costs.

The only way to sustain continuous innovation is to reduce the cost and risk of trying new ideas. The good news is that today's IT techniques give companies the agility, nimbleness, and speed they need to do just that. Enterprises using the cloud, along with the set of practices known as DevOps, can deploy IT capabilities to customers and employees hundreds of times a day—rather than once every six months—and can do so reliably, securely, compliantly, and at a high level of quality and usability.

The bad news is while today's technology supports innovation and business agility, the way enterprises *use* it remains based on mental models from decades ago. The challenge is not in the technology, but in realizing the business value it can deliver. To gain and maintain competitive advantages, stimulate innovation, delight customers, and react quickly to changing market circumstances, a company must change its way of making technology decisions, overseeing its technology initiatives, budgeting and accounting for its technology . . . and most of all, change its way of interacting with its technology group.

As Stephen Denning says in *The Age of Agile: How Smart Companies are Transforming the Way Work Gets Done*, "Trying to exploit technology and data with the management practices that are still pervasive in many big corporations today is like driving a horse and buggy on the freeway. To prosper in the very different world that is emerging, firms need a radically different kind of management."[17]

The harsh truth is that the C-suite has often not felt comfortable with IT as a business function. How can technologists be held accountable for their work? They're always late with projects. The systems they create are buggy. Equipment suddenly stops working or is too complicated for employees to use. IT always says no. IT costs are too high; benchmark organizations do IT better and cheaper. IT people overcomplicate everything and speak technical jargon that makes everyone else feel dumb.

The problem is serious. In *Leading Digital: Turning Technology Into Business Transformation*, George Westerman and his coauthors report: "Many executives told us that, given their IT units' poor performance, they were going to find a different way to conduct their digital transformations. The business executives were going to move forward despite their IT units, not with them."[18] Particularly disturbing to me is the finding from the CIO Executive Council's 2015 *Power of Effective IT Communication Survey* that only 3% of business stakeholders consider IT to be a game changer, 11% think of it as a peer, while 58% think of IT only as a cost center or service provider.*[19] Although organizations view digital *technology* as a game changer, many apparently don't think of the stewards of digital technology—the IT folks—as game changers.

In a survey of 800 global business and IT executives, 34% of the business and 31% of the IT respondents characterized their relationship with each

---

* Note that this is based on a survey of CIOs—that is, CIOs believe that this is the way business leaders think.

other as combative, distrustful, or siloed.[20] It is war, in other words, but a war within a single dysfunctional family. And those of us who drive our chariots between the two warring armies feel as bad about it as Arjuna does at the start of the Bhagavad Gita.*

Given this disconnect, it's no surprise that enterprises have thought of bringing a new member into the C-suite: a chief digital officer (CDO). Gartner has proposed that business technology needs to move at two speeds: slow for the legacy, backoffice, and low risk-tolerance systems; fast for customer-facing, innovative systems.[21] If they're right, then it makes sense to have a CIO who continues to dispiritedly plod along with slow-moving IT and a CDO who's responsible for prancing joyfully about with systems of speed and flexibility.

I don't think much of this two-speed idea. Today's best practices suggest that *all* of the technology in the enterprise should move fast, and that *all* of it should align with the way the company competes in the market and serves customers. Separating IT into CIO and CDO roles is likely to increase the obstacles to nimbleness and innovation I describe in this book.† It would be much better to heal the divide between IT and the remainder of the organization.

But recognizing that organizations have different needs and that some prefer to separate these roles, when I speak of the CIO, please interpret it in the sense of "head of digital technology"—whether that person is a CIO, CDO, or Emperor of Bits and Bytes and First Consul of Computing. In the digital world, an organization will need to learn how best to work with its technologists, whether they're working for a CIO or CDO.

———

Imagine an enterprise leadership team, who, upon seeing their competitors evolving quickly around them, plops themselves down in a conference room

---

* In the opening scene of the Bhagavad Gita, the armies of the Pandavas and Kauravas, many of them related to one another, face each other before battle in the Kurukshetra War. Arjuna, a Pandava prince, despairs, seeing his friends, relatives, and teachers on the other side, and asks Krishna for advice.

† Note that my point is only about the C-level position. Digital products should probably have their own product management hierarchy, just like any other product. I would also argue that the C-level leader should act as an advisor/consultant to the C-team on technical opportunities—this also makes more sense if it is a single person.

and proclaims, "We need digital transformation!" They hire a consulting firm or talk to companies that are already enjoying successful transformations. They gather ideas about how leading technology companies move at high velocity. Then they reconvene in the conference room.

"We can't do that! We're too bureaucratic. We don't have the right skills! We have too many compliance constraints! There's no security if you move so fast! There's no way to control that kind of IT! Good ideas, but our company is different. It won't work here until we radically change our culture. But we do *need* to transform!"

Yes, but. . . . Yes, but. . . . Yes, but. . . . This is the leadership team's impression of bobblehead dolls, heads bobbing in the wake of the fast-moving companies around them.

The bobblehead model is not an effective business strategy.

Now is the time to start transforming, because it's both low risk and urgent. You might be surprised that I say it's low risk, but I insist. Enterprises may feel like they should move slowly and cautiously, stepping onto the digital path only after they've checked the traffic coming from all directions. But the very point of digital transformation is to *reduce* risk. Digital enterprises set risk-mitigating guardrails* in place, then use their speed as a way to quickly adjust course when new risks appear. And the transformation can be undertaken incrementally, one reversible decision after another. Think: big vision, small execution. This is no time for cautious head-bobbling. You can use the ideas in this book to move quickly and limit your risk.

Maybe it has occurred to you to ask, "What can I do differently to get better results from my technologists?"

Donuts.

It's worth a try. But maybe that's just me. My point of view is that of someone who has a background in IT but has seen the divide from the outside as well, having helped senior leaders move their enterprises into the cloud and overcome their cultural, bureaucratic, organizational, and skills barriers. I have been a CEO as well as a CIO, a former software developer (I shall claim to have

---

* More about risk-mitigating guardrails in Chapter 6: Risk and Opportunity.

been one of the great stylists of the COBOL language—*take that, William Shakespeare!*). I've worked in the private sector, the nonprofit sector, and even in government as the CIO of US Citizenship and Immigration Services (USCIS). When it comes to telling hawks from handsaws,* I can train an artificial intelligence "machine learning" program to do it well. I know what as a CIO I wanted my colleagues in other functions to know about IT, and what as a CEO and as an independent advisor, I wanted the CIO to know.

Our goal here is to overcome the IT/business duality so that the enterprise—the business and IT—can enter the digital world, smiling and nodding happily just like bobblehead dolls. Why bobbleheads? To me, there is something endearing about them; they are agreeable and don't take themselves too seriously. They appear across different cultures—the head-nodding ox called akabeko in Japan; the dancing dolls of Thanjavur, India; Victorian era "nodders"; not to mention today's bobbleheads that play such an important role in the sacred American ritual of baseball.[22] As agreeable as they are, you can't really tell whether they are bobbling empty-headedly or wisely. A digital transformation, I want to say, means going from a state of agreeable head bobbling to a different state of agreeable head bobbling—one that is filled with wisdom and effective practice. Culture, bureaucracy, risk management, investment oversight—all will continue to be there, just as they always have been.

Throughout this book, you'll find cycles of creation and destruction—innovation that requires doing away with legacy ideas, bureaucracy and culture that need to be nudged repeatedly in a new direction, Napoleon defeating Russia only to find that Russia has defeated him. But through it all, the bobbleheads bobble. Their smiles will just mean something different at the end of your transformation.

A few themes run throughout:

- For historical reasons, businesses have adopted a model for working with IT that is holding them back.
- This model is deeply connected with a flawed way of thinking about risk and opportunity.
- IT practitioners have long accepted and even reinforced the model, but have recently come to their senses.

---

* That's Shakespeare, who had no abilities whatsoever in machine learning. Touché!

- An environment of high risk, uncertainty, and change requires different mental models than does an environment of predictability.
- Software and cloud infrastructure are pliable. Despite some of our preconceptions, they're actually the easiest things in the enterprise to change, and therefore ideal allies in coping with uncertainty.
- Agility is an asset, even if it isn't recognized on the balance sheet.

Part I, "Principles," discusses why the traditional relationship between IT and the rest of the enterprise won't support digital transformation. Part II, "Particulars," breaks down some of the typical concerns the enterprise has about working with its IT organization, and how these can be given a new foundation so as to equip the enterprise for the digital world. "Prescriptions," Part III, is an action plan for moving forward—immediately and with a sense of urgency—into this digital world.

———

Who this book is for:

If you're a CEO, you are likely to be focused on growth and innovation. If so, you should be thinking hard about how to integrate IT with the rest of your organization. Or perhaps you're thinking about how to nimbly respond to uncertain circumstances while avoiding disruption by startups, competitors, and hackers. I'll show you how to use IT as a strategic component of your organization, yielding results from it that will shape your company's performance.

If you're a CFO, then we need to talk. You're in a difficult position today. You face the challenge of growing your company and finding new sources of value while also safeguarding your company's core business. You have probably recognized that you need to shift your focus from analyzing the past to forecasting and planning for the future. On one hand, you're responsible for control and risk management—you are at the front lines where compliance bureaucracy meets innovation and are the steady hand that manages the company's financial resources and investments. On the other hand, you recognize the need for speed and sense that finance should be a competitive weapon.* IT has always been a problem area for you—one that resists effective controls. I'll

---

* By the way, Napoleon did too. See Chapter 11: The Leadership Team.

address issues around capitalizing versus expensing IT costs, about new ways of establishing auditable controls, and about selecting investments and managing their risks. How do we measure IT success? What I have to say will, I hope, improve your life.

If you're a non-IT CXO, then this book is about how to let the CIO help you accomplish your objectives. You may be frustrated by the relationship between IT and the rest of your organization, or you might simply have lowered your expectations. But IT is there to accomplish your company's goals. You should be able to rely on its expertise in areas where you've spent less time becoming an expert, but you might need to learn how to help them be more effective. This book should help.

If you're a CIO or IT leader, then you may have begun rolling out Agile development along with Lean and DevOps practices, but have hit organizational impediments in trying to extract their full value. If you read my previous book, *A Seat at the Table*, it may have given you ideas about how to play a more consequential role in your company. Now you need to have a conversation with the rest of the leadership team about it. This book is that conversation.

If you're any other category of business leader, then this book is the missing manual about how to work with IT to be successful. Your performance will be judged largely on what you're able to get from or with IT.

For others in the business and IT community, I hope this book will open up a discussion on the economics and strategic impact of organizational agility through technology. The promise of DevOps was to create a more humane work environment by putting operations and development people on the same team. This book furthers that mission by putting technologists and non-technology business people on the same team so that their heads all bobble together.

PART I

Principles

THE BUSINESS AND IT

On the day of cutting off the hair Set and the Company of the Gods fastened my head to my neck, and it became as firm as it was originally. Let nothing happen to shake it off again!

—*The Egyptian Book of the Dead*

A picture held us captive. And we could not get outside it, for it lay in our language and language seemed to repeat it to us inexorably.

—**Ludwig Wittgenstein**, *Philosophical Investigations*

Once upon a time, businesses ran fine without computers. They had pencils; they had paper. A secretarial pool typed documents on typewriters, adding machines added numbers on paper strips, telephones and the postal system provided communications, and the most influential technologies were paperclips and staplers. It all worked—your company didn't feel like it was missing anything. But suddenly digital technology erupted.

Computers were not like a new kind of stapler or adding machine. The difference—the critical one—was that they could only be managed by specialist knowledge workers. The company had to hire computer programmers, computer operators, and . . . well, other technical folks who required big paychecks. They were experts, but not in your company's business—they were experts in some kind of a science. And soon they became critical to everything your company did. Enterprises suddenly had to find a way to work with these outsiders, to realize business value from their presence. But how?

Imagine we're back in the early days of IT, say 1975 or so. Your company has just bought its first computer: a DigitalWhiz 1000 XPZ (Extreme Processor Zippiness). The DigitalWhiz has its own room, air conditioned to igloo settings. The computer room door has a window that you and other employees can look through as you pass by on your way to the lunchroom. Inside you see refrigerator-sized tape drives jerking in one direction then another, then spinning exuberantly. In the middle of the room is a hunk of machinery you assume is the DigitalWhiz, with a stack of punched cards clack-clacking through its card reader. Paper is jetting out of a fast line printer—the pride of the Computer and MIS (management information systems) Department.

And through that window you can see a few technicians wearing white lab coats, perhaps to keep warm as they thread tapes into the tape drives. They look concerned. One of them you recognize—Gerald, said to be the brainiest of the computer programmers.

You remember the last conversation you had with Gerald. The payroll system had stopped working and employees across the company weren't getting their paychecks. It was urgent, so you found him sleeping under his desk and woke him up. "Gerald, the payroll system is down!" He blinked under his thick glasses, frowned, paused for a moment or two and muttered, "Mmm, interesting." He then moved aside a Star Trek model on his desk, found his M&Ms, and busied himself with them.

"Gerald, it's not *interesting*. The payroll system is down. People aren't getting paid!"

"Ah. Probably the emphatic byte munger I wrote last month. Very interesting. No one has ever munged B++ plackets with Kim-Poppenlooper cyclical nascency before. I was able to integrate a recursive maxicode initializer algorithm into randomized bit-swapper proxy . . ."

"Gerald, this is an emergency."

"Mmm, yes. Would you like me to fix it?"

"Yes! Gerald! Fix! Soon!" You turn and leave him frowning at his desk.

The problem still hasn't been fixed a few hours later when you see Gerald staring deeply at the floor in the hallway. Why, you wonder, had he been spending his time on all those cyclical nascency things when there were bugs in the accounts receivable system, the new inventory system was behind schedule, and the computer department was over budget?

Aside from a few details (I made up the Star Trek model on his desk), this is a true story. As an intern, I worked with "Gerald" during summer college breaks.

Exaggerations aside, there were several lessons in those early IT encounters. It was clear that he and the other "computer people"—the scientists—didn't care much about the business. What they wanted was to spend their time fooling around with boxes of hardware that looked like B-movie props, writing and rewriting . . . and rewriting . . . Kim Poppenlooper algorithms. They were odd people and spoke a funny language. They kept spending money to get the latest new equipment, but never delivered what they promised.

They weren't bad guys (Gerald tried to be helpful), but how could you get them to focus on what the business needed—the reason you were paying for their cyclical nascency in the first place? How could you hold Gerald and his peers accountable when they were the only ones who understood this new IT domain? And every time you talked to him about payroll, Gerald changed the topic to byte-mungers.

So enterprises began hiring IT managers, and later CIOs, who could speak both tech and business. Their goal was to get this new IT *thing* under control; to manage its costs and translate between what had been a fully functioning company before and the new troop of technologists who were suddenly essential.

The stereotypes went both ways. To the IT people, the business was filled with suit-wearing folks who were clueless about technology, were obsessed with organizational politics, were overly demanding, and showed poor judgment in the way they used the software and computers they were given. What they asked for made no sense, and all code had to be protected against their mistakes ("idiot-proofed" was the term they used). It was flabbergasting that the business people couldn't figure out how to do obvious things, like pressing Ctrl–Alt–Del when the system stopped responding.

A working relationship evolved. The stakeholders specified precisely what they wanted the geeks to do by writing "requirements," and they set up a "governance" process to rule over IT investments and make sure that IT "stayed aligned" with the business. They had IT prepare Gantt charts and status reports to stay focused on the schedule. With that schedule pressure, IT would no longer be able to waste time on emphatic byte-mungers and dongle fabulators. For its part, IT insisted that the business write down and commit to its requirements so that IT could always prove it had done what it had been asked, no matter how insane.

The relationship was an arms-length, us and them, contractor-like relationship, where something called The Business was the customer of a service provider called IT. The Business described what it wanted, IT gave a quote, The Business placed its order, and IT reliably failed to deliver on it at the quoted price.

It became natural to think in terms of "The Business and IT" as if they were separate things—the people who tried to get things done to bring shareholders joy, and the technical people who found joy in algorithms and routers. The "and" in "The Business and IT" was more of a wedge between the two—IT people, though they were company employees, weren't *part* of the business.

Both IT and business folks expressed the hope that someday IT would learn to run like a business, with the CIO as its CEO. Some organizations went as far as setting up a chargeback model, where IT billed each business unit based on the amount of IT it had consumed. IT was expected to provide good customer service to its clientele—the company's employees. Increasingly, IT resembled an external contractor.

This model let the business feel comfortable that IT investments, expensive as they were, were under control. For IT, it seemed like a way to satisfy the demanding, fickle customers they supposed the business folks to be. Perhaps it was a bit strange that the arms-length service provider group and its customers were actually employees of the same company. Well, not for long; it was an easy step to think about outsourcing IT, since it was already, well . . . outsourced, albeit internally.

The stereotypes solidified and went unquestioned, reinforced by these processes and a bit of confirmation bias. It was easy to catch the geeks doing something that didn't seem relevant to the problem at hand, or the business folks using their CD drive trays as cupholders. This manner of working "together" became the norm, inscribed in each company's sacred copy of *The Book of Processes*.

I believe that if you look around today with fresh eyes, these stereotypes no longer hold. Most of the IT geeks I know are very business- or mission-focused, even if they still wear cryptic T-shirts. They love technology—yes—but they are problem solvers more than anything, and love to solve them on behalf of the business. They speak less like geeks and more like post-millennials—because that's often what they are. The reality is more like that described by Menlo Engineering: "What we have tried to do at Menlo is to emancipate the heart of the engineer, which is to serve others. We engineers exist to produce something that the world will enjoy, something that will delight people."[1]

And the clueless business folks are not clueless. They've become accustomed to IT and the consumer technology they use every day; in fact, their expectations are constantly rising for the technology they're forced to work with. They can make Excel do fancy tricks while the geeks are still pecking with one finger and trying to find the menu option that turns the text red. The business folks, for the most part, have an idea what the cloud is, how many megapixels their camera records, and how to use a computer that doesn't require them to hit Ctrl–Alt–Del. They can tell big data from puny data and sometimes they don't even wear suits.*

Though the stereotypes no longer hold, the processes by which enterprises work with IT are descended from them. But here is a little secret—the stereotypes were never really accurate. I know that when Gerald heard that the payroll system was down, he was immensely concerned. He reacted by going deeply into thought, trying to figure out what had changed that could have caused the problem. And he hadn't been working on his Kim-Poppenlooper algorithm just because it was fun. Kim-Poppenlooper was going to speed up a critical part of the payroll system that was becoming a bottleneck as the company grew, threatening that employees wouldn't get their paychecks on time. In a sense, Gerald knew better than anyone else what was important to the business.

This contractor-like way of working with IT has never been effective. As we all know, projects tend to run behind schedule, IT is generally backlogged and unable to address critical business concerns, systems break down, and employees and customers have to find painful workarounds.

It's more than that. Now that we're in the digital era, technologists— natives of the digital world—should be driving innovation, leading and inspiring the enterprise to make the most of its digital potential. But how can they do so from their arms-length position? How can the non-IT parts of the business change this relationship to get the results they want, all the while managing risk, pleasing the capital markets, accomplishing business outcomes, and seizing growth opportunities? How can they do so in a way that holds IT accountable, provides predictability and transparency, and controls costs? These questions become increasingly critical as the enterprise tries to refine its digital posture.

---

* JP Morgan now requires all of its employees to take coding classes. "Coding is not for just tech people, it is for anyone who wants to run a competitive company in the 21st century," according to Mary Callahan Erdoes, head of Asset Management.[2]

What I called in my previous book the contractor-control, or traditional, model for working with IT went something like this: something called "The Business" decides on a new set of IT capabilities it needs. It assembles a requirements document, puts it through an approval process, and signs off on it as a definitive specification. It hands the requirements document to IT and asks for an estimate. After some back and forth, both parties agree on a schedule and budget. IT initiates a project to deliver the capabilities, with agreed-upon milestones for items such as completing a requirements analysis, designing the system, programming the components it will comprise, testing its code, and deploying it to The Business. The Business performs a user acceptance test (UAT) before code is released to make sure its original requirements have been met. And finally, business value happens.

As an IT delivery process, this set of practices is known as the waterfall model, so-called because of how it appears on a Gantt chart. Task follows task and phase follows phase linearly, with milestones in between. Driven by a fixed set of requirements and a project plan, its success is measured by adherence to that plan—"on time" and "on budget" delivery, where "on time" means "as planned before the effort started."

One seeming advantage of the waterfall is that it holds the technology team accountable. In particular, it's held accountable for delivering the scope of required capabilities, in accordance with the agreed-upon schedule, and within the agreed-upon budget. Unfortunately, this also forces IT to divide its creative work into separate, ordered phases—each of which must be deemed complete before the next phase starts.

But it turns out that a much more effective way to complete IT work is to perform it iteratively and incrementally, mixing the phases together to get quick feedback from the product users. So what used to seem like a good way to control the IT process turns out to be costly and burdensome to those executing it.

Having observed that the waterfall process wasn't working, the IT world started to produce books about how to do it better. IT conference sessions discussed how to do a better job of estimating schedules, eliciting requirements, and managing the work so that all phases of projects could be completed according to schedule. Strangely, the result was just more large failures. That is, until around 2001 when a consensus began to form around a new way of thinking about IT projects—the Agile approach, which I'll describe in a subsequent chapter.

Unfortunately, the old model of interacting with IT isn't likely to lead to the business results you're after. Even if it did what it was intended to do—that is, give you a way to control IT's performance—it would still work against the best interests of your business. This is because the plan-driven waterfall approach depends upon locking in the project scope ahead of time through a requirements document. Since projects are often long-lived, say anywhere from six months to five years, that amounts to deciding in advance what your company will need over that timeframe (actually much longer than that, since the system will continue to be in use for a long afterward).

The more uncertainty there is in the business environment, and the more change that's expected, the less likely it is that the plan accurately captures what will be most important to the company over that period. Rather, today a company should expect that its competitive situation will change, that new technologies will be introduced, government regulations will be amended or rewritten, and new employees will come onboard with fresh ideas. So the company is likely spending a good deal of money to ensure that it'll wind up years behind where it needs to be.

For the plan-driven approach to work, it must avoid *scope creep*—the addition of new requirements after the requirements document is finalized. This is because if the requirements change, then the plan is no longer valid and IT can't be held accountable to deliver on schedule. But as Jeff Patton, an IT thought leader, says in *User Story Mapping*, "Scope doesn't creep—understanding grows."[3] If the company's needs change, or if requirements are discovered to be incorrect—which they will be—then what is truly best for the business? To let the scope creep, or to proceed with the original—and wrong—set of requirements?

The real enemy isn't scope creep, but rather "feature bloat"—that is, unnecessary requirements. It's really feature bloat that results in higher costs and causes the work to take longer than it should. This negative effect is then compounded by the cost of maintaining those extra features coupled with their added complexity. Unnecessary features might even open potential security holes (IT folk say that they increase the *attack surface*).

And yet the waterfall process actually *maximizes* feature bloat by its obsession on eliminating scope creep. Stakeholders are instructed that they must include everything they think they'll need—for the duration of the project through commencement of the next—in the requirements document. Since there is uncertainty about what they'll need, they include every business improvement they can dream of. A Microsoft study found that only one-third of ideas actually accomplish their intended objective; another one-third have the opposite result, and one-third don't have either effect.[4] Yet a requirements document includes all three thirds.

The bloat problem has been confirmed by studies showing that more than half of the features in IT systems are rarely or never used.[5] We've probably all had the reaction, "I didn't know it could do that!" when we see someone use an application's more esoteric features.*

Even entire software applications can go unused. One study showed that across the US and UK, about 28% of the installed software on desktops hadn't been used in the last ninety days, and that the cost of unneeded software amounted to $7 billion in those two countries.[6] Since we tend to add features to our systems over time but never remove any, we carry this costly maintenance burden forward year after year.

Companies sometimes admonish requirements writers not to "gold plate" their requests. But in an environment of uncertainty, it's difficult, even impossible, to know in advance which requirements will truly turn out to be valuable. Requirements writers sincerely believe that their requirements are the right ones, at least at the moment in which they are written.

You might think I'm suggesting that companies have been wasting more than half of the money they spend on IT capabilities. You're right—I am suggesting that. Perhaps more to the point for the digital age, imagine how much more quickly you could get products to market if you could avoid all of that feature bloat!

The best way to avoid feature bloat is to start by deploying a minimal product, then adding capabilities only as necessary until the project's objectives have been accomplished. One principle from the *Manifesto for Agile Software Development* says, "Maximize the amount of work not done."[7] In other words, any work that turns out to be unnecessary—even if it was in the original requirements—should be avoided.

That's to say good technologists add value by *not* doing things. It sounds like cheating, right? Let's say that the project is running behind schedule, but the project team finds a way to get back on plan by not doing some of the

---

* Did you know that Microsoft Word will let you draw mathematical equations by hand or that it will score your writing based on either the Flesch Reading Ease score or the Flesch-Kincaid grade level score? Maybe you did.

work laid out in the requirements. Should that kind of behavior be rewarded or punished?*

If you think that not meeting some of the requirements is cheating, then you may be possessed by the evil spirit of the IT-as-a-contractor model. The right question to ask is whether the *business objectives* have been achieved, not whether all the requirements have been delivered. Yet when we continue to think of the relationship between the business and IT as a contractual relationship, with IT committed to delivering the agreed-upon scope on a particular schedule, then maximizing the amount of work not done is a breach of contract.

***

The very idea of assembling business needs into a requirements document has a cost to the enterprise. During the time it takes to accumulate enough needs to declare them a project, assemble the requirements, document them, debate them, and approve them—well, three startups were founded, funded, floundered for a moment or two, found their way, and forever stole your market. Or maybe a competitor's star programmer just built the same IT capability in a few minutes, didn't tell anyone, and snuck the new feature into production.

During all of that prep time the company doesn't see any delivered benefit. Just as there is a time value of money, there is a cost of delay (a metric promoted by Donald Reinertsen in his book *The Principles of Product Development Flow*) in not getting the capabilities into users' hands. One reason we spend a lot of time planning is that we have always thought of IT as expensive. Planning time, on the other hand, seemed more or less free. But implementation costs are lower today and the cost of delay is higher. That's not to say that planning is bad, only that each incremental moment of planning must be balanced against its cost—including the cost of not having the completed work soon enough.

From a risk perspective, the waterfall model dramatically increases the company's exposure compared to the alternatives. It poses the risk that our original requirements and plan won't meet our needs as circumstances change. It raises the risk that some of the requirements are wrong, and since the plan is inflexible,

---

* In government IT we had a process called Independent Verification and Validation (IV&V), which evaluated the results of each project by going requirement by requirement through the original scope, checking to make sure every one of them had been implemented, thus ensuring that the project team had done its entire job. IV&V, in other words, was making sure that the government had wasted more than half of its money.

IT will be building the wrong thing. And then there is delivery risk; money keeps going into the initiative and results don't come until the end.

———

Does the waterfall, in fact, give the enterprise predictability and control over its IT investments? Is the pope Zoroastrian? Does a bear shave in the woods?

The waterfall tries to make sure the project stays on schedule by conducting status meetings. IT reports on its progress relative to the Gantt chart with—you know—those little red, yellow, or green circles to indicate whether it's on track. I've seen too many of these; they're all the same. The current work is always somewhat behind schedule, but yet the remainder of the schedule is still on track. The delays are temporary and later work will make up for them by taking less time than planned.

Suddenly, one week the little yellow balls turn red! The project team, grilled on the cause of the "delay," draws some ill-founded conclusions about why it's behind schedule, promises to fix the underlying problems, and guarantees that it will get back on schedule.

Well, of course they say that. They're already committed to the original schedule, right? Note that the best, most logical explanation for what is happening is that the original estimates were too low. And yet the team promises, against all evidence, that those for the next phase are too high!

This is a consistent pattern in cases where uncertainty is manifest. The original plan was known to be subject to uncertainty (a true estimate really would include an attached confidence interval, and a large one at that), but when the uncertainty actually manifests itself, "reasons" are found and blamed. The truth is that those reasons are statistical noise—we already knew there would be variances.

Here's a game. I show you ten boxes, each containing a bobblehead. I tell you that seven of them contain bobbleheads of Blaise Pascal and three contain nodding images of Reverend Thomas Bayes. I point to a box and ask you to guess who is inside. You, very intelligently, guess Blaise Pascal, but when I open the box, there—grinning and bobbling—is Reverend Bayes. Do you then blame yourself for the mistake, try to figure out the "reason" it was Bayes rather than Pascal, and vow not to make the same mistake again?

Many businesses believe they need *predictability* in the delivery of IT capabilities—defined as conformance to the original project schedule. You might want to think carefully about whether or when you do need it. How important is predictability to you, relative to business agility and effectiveness? And to what extent can it be achieved in a complex and uncertain environment?

I can imagine some cases where predictability is very important. For example, the company might be preparing an IT system that has to be ready by a certain date, as was the case with the Healthcare.gov fiasco that was timed to coincide with a political initiative. Or it may be a situation where other company plans—perhaps marketing activities—must be coordinated with the launch of an IT system.

Unfortunately, the waterfall doesn't actually offer predictability, since complexity and uncertainty often don't cooperate with any plan milestones. And as we've seen, project teams are incentivized—required, really—to deny the reality of schedule changes until it's too late to maintain the fiction of being on schedule.

If predictability is important because other activities need to be coordinated with the completion date, then it's best to have the team constantly re-estimate and re-baseline the schedule based on their progress. How often should they be allowed to do this? As often as possible. The more often they re-baseline, the better predictability you'll have. This isn't predictability in the sense of knowing before the project starts how long it'll take; rather, it's predictability that acknowledges the reality of change and uncertainty.

But predictability isn't really the issue here, is it? A demand for it is often a way to try to enforce control over a project, to insist that the project team deliver on its "commitments." It's a way to hold IT accountable, not a way to gain predictability. This is my point—many of us have become trapped in a mental model that has become so ingrained that we barely notice it is there.

It sounds strange to say, but what you want from IT is not delivery *on schedule*. You want it *as soon as possible*. This is very different. If it can't be delivered as scheduled, then you don't really want it to be. But if it can be delivered ahead of schedule, then that's what you want. You really want urgency. You want delivery ASAP. When you think about it, ASAP delivery means the same thing as delivering with the shortest possible lead time, which is the goal of Lean manufacturing. You can take out your Lean playbook and ask, "What are the steps in the delivery process? Which of them can be shortened? Where can we eliminate waste in the delivery process?"

That—precisely—is what you want to hold IT accountable for: the leanest, most waste-free, shortest lead-time delivery of needed capabilities. And if it turns out that some of the waste in that delivery is outside of IT, or within the interactions between IT and the rest of the business, you want to eliminate that as well. Spoiler alert: some of it is.

―――――――――――

The classic view of IT is not just about enforcing control through pre-planning and milestone adherence: as we've seen, the contractor-control model also encourages IT to treat the other business employees as its customers, further distancing IT from non-IT. George Westerman and his coauthors describe and dismiss the customer service model in *Leading Digital: Turning Technology Into Business Transformation*:

> In the long-distant past, we were taught that IT was the keeper of technology and that IT leaders were service-providers to the rest of the business. Their job was to stay aligned with business strategy, taking orders from the business and delivering new systems. If they kept the systems running and delivered new projects on time, then all was good. That time is over, and has been for many years.[8]

That time is over, because merely keeping systems running and delivering projects on time is both too much and too little to ask of IT. Too much, because there is too much uncertainty in the IT world. Too little, because even if IT could deliver these things, it wouldn't necessarily be delivering business value. It could easily be delivering the wrong things on time, or overspending on keeping systems running. In the digital world, you don't want IT to be a service provider—you want it to deliver business outcomes.

When IT has functioned as an order-taker, it has predictably wound up with too many orders to manage. To paraphrase blogger Pascal van Cauwenberghe, IT winds up with a "vomit of requirements" that it must then clean up.[9] Too much demand means long wait times to get important work done, and because IT is jerked from one demand to another, it cannot formulate a meaningful IT strategy or plan an overall architecture for the company's systems.

The contractor-control model also disincentivizes some of the behaviors you seek from IT. To keep the company's infrastructure secure, you need IT to be an enforcer, sometimes making its customers unhappy. Depending on budget decisions you make, IT may need to say no to tasks or devices its customers want. If employees have misunderstandings about how to use technology, IT should set them straight. And when requests are impractical or against the best interests of the business, IT should refuse. This is customer service without the smile. In Westerman and Hunter's words:

> Saying that "the business is IT's customer, and the customer is always right" seems like a good idea. . . . But over the long term, this value trap sets up the IT unit for failure, because customers are often wrong (especially about matters in which they are not expert), and calling colleagues "customers" puts a wedge between IT and the rest of the business.[10]

Customers are the people outside the enterprise who pay for its products. IT people and non-IT people within the enterprise are *colleagues*.

———

With no better model for what success looked like, IT leaders often took the position that they would "run IT like a business." They would look for efficiencies and benchmark IT against outside organizations. They would institute a chargeback model, where lines of business were charged based on the amount of IT service they consumed. Geoffrey Moore, usually a more insightful writer on IT subjects, explains this model's presumed benefits by saying that "it puts the service-providing organization on notice that program work is not an entitlement but rather must be earned, potentially in competition with an external supplier."[11]

This places the IT organization—employees of the company, note—on notice that they could be replaced by an outside supplier. Honestly, doesn't that sound like an unpleasant way to treat employees? How have we come to think of this as normal?

The idea is a poor one for other reasons. While the chargebacks are supposed to reduce demand, they inevitably fail to result in an equilibrium where supply matches demand. Of course, there is a way to achieve such a balance, and that is to let IT's prices go up until the market-clearing price is reached. It would be a price unrelated to actual costs, and the IT group would show a profit at the expense of the other budget holders . . . who would not be happy.

If IT really were an independent business, it would be able to scale as needed to meet demand. It would be able to hire freely and set salaries optimally. It would be able to choose its customers, only taking on new ones when it had available capacity. No, IT is not a business, and we would not want it to be.

It would be curious if an internal IT department lost a benchmarking competition against an outside organization. An external contractor must earn a profit. It has transactional costs that it must pass on: the costs of negotiating a contract, legal fees, and administrative fees, along with sales and marketing costs. It has costs in coming up to speed on its customer's business and its organizational dynamics. When changes must be made to requirements, not only does the contractor add fees, but the company suffers administrative costs in communicating those changes and authorizing the extra charges.

Nor is the argument convincing that the outside organization is better or more cost-efficient; IT most likely uses similar delivery practices, and it can pull from the same labor markets to hire similar people. Yes, economies of scale can give the outside provider an advantage, but only for services that actually have economies of scale. Cloud infrastructure, for example, can be obtained at a higher quality level and lower price because of scale. But the usual functions of IT as a service provider—basically the provision of human effort—do not lend themselves to such economies.

In an apples-to-apples comparison, there is simply no way an outside service provider can provide *the same services* at a lower cost. The IT department can only come up short if the benchmark is comparing rambutans to durians. The internal IT group may have a better sense of what will actually be required, while the external contractor will wind up adding to their charges when the enterprise later submits change requests. The external contractor might compromise quality or not pay as much attention to making the system easily maintainable or secure. Or maybe your development work is a loss-leader for them and they plan to profit through subsequent system maintenance work.

Treating IT as a contractor can unnecessarily impose many of these costs on the enterprise. CIOs are sometimes told they must market their services across the enterprise and demonstrate that they're adding value. This is waste—IT should focus all of its resources on actually adding business value. Back-and-forth negotiations between IT and business stakeholders are also a cost that the enterprise shouldn't have to bear. And chargebacks to business units—while they might be valuable for cost accounting—add administrative costs and frustration. Avoiding these should be an advantage to keeping IT inhouse!

All of this is beside the point in the digital world. Treating IT as an external service provider sacrifices its biggest advantage as an internal entity: the fact that it can have closer contact, more touch points, and more involvement in running the business itself. An internal IT department cares about the company's mission, absorbs its culture, and participates in defining what the company is.

To compete in a digital world, you must engage the IT department in determining and fulfilling business objectives. IT cannot be accountable merely for producing IT products as "required," but instead must be given, and must assume, accountability for business outcomes. Your IT technologists are your colleagues and allies in times of digital disruption.

COMPLEXITY AND
UNCERTAINTY

Many neckless faces sprouted, and arms were wandering naked, bereft of shoulders, and eyes were roaming alone, in need of foreheads.
—**Empedocles of Acragas**, *On Nature*

Life can only be understood backwards; but it must be lived forwards.
—**Søren Kierkegaard**, *Journals*

In *War and Peace*, Tolstoy writes of the battle of Borodino, in which Napoleon (sort of) defeats Russia and wins the opportunity to watch Moscow burn, though not much more. The day before the battle, he walks the battlefield and gives his commanders orders for the disposition of the troops—orders which are, for the most part, ignored. During the battle, he stands in the nearby redoubt of Shevardino—which he has unexpectedly captured the day before— observing the battle and issuing instructions. Or trying to, because he's about a mile away and the battlefield is covered with smoke and mist and gullies which block his view.

> While an adjutant was riding the mile or more that separated him from Napoleon, the circumstances changed, and the news he was bringing became incorrect. Thus an adjutant arrived from the viceroy with news that Borodino had been taken and the bridge over the Kolocha was in the hands of the French. The adjutant asked Napoleon if he ordered the

troops to cross it. Napoleon ordered them to form ranks on the other side and wait; but not only as Napoleon was giving this order, but even as the adjutant was leaving Borodino, the bridge had already been retaken and burned by the Russians.[1]

When Napoleon is able to get orders out in time, he often issues them assuming that his previous orders have been followed, which . . . *um* . . . is a bad assumption.

The marshals and generals who were closer to the battlefield . . . gave their own instructions and orders . . . without asking Napoleon. But even their instructions were carried out as rarely and to as small a degree as Napoleon's instructions. For the most part, what came out was the opposite of what they had ordered.[2]

This is Napoleon, famous for his skill in commanding armies! In an environment of great complexity, uncertainty, and rapid change, neither following a preset plan nor giving direct orders from a distance is effective. And the environment Napoleon is in has all three of those characteristics:

- Complex, because many people, with many different interests, are all giving orders, and the orders interact in complex ways.
- Uncertain, because the results of any order depend on what the enemy does and its intentions, with its capabilities being only partially understood.
- Rapidly changing, since, for example, by the time a messenger tells Napoleon what is happening, text messaging has practically been invented.

In *On War*, Carl von Clausewitz says, "War is the realm of uncertainty; three quarters of the factors on which action is based are wrapped in a fog of greater or lesser uncertainty."[3] Napoleon isn't really in control, according to Tolstoy, except in his own mind and in those of historians as they retrospectively assign credit and blame. Napoleon's problem is that his decisions during the battle have a long lead time, even though circumstances are changing with a much shorter lead time. In an environment of rapid change and uncertainty, lead time for decisions and execution must be shortened to align with the pace of change. It is the troops, those who can rapidly decide and act, who can respond at the necessary tempo.

Another example of complexity is given by Atul Gawande in *The Checklist Manifesto: How to Get Things Right*, in which he describes the dynamics of a hospital's intensive care unit. Patients exhibit myriad symptoms that are constantly changing—malfunctions in one bodily system suddenly lead to malfunctions in others—and a team of doctors interferes with that progression by trying to reverse it.[4] An average patient in an ICU requires 178 individual actions per day, "ranging from administering a drug to suctioning the lungs," with each of those causing a variety of only somewhat predictable effects.[5] Just lying motionless in an ICU can cause additional problems, such as muscle atrophy, blood clots, and pressure ulcers.[6]

This is what we mean by a complex environment. It's different from something that's merely complicated—complexity means that the interrelationships, feedback loops, uncertainty, and lack of knowledge are so great that it's impossible to understand the complete state of affairs and to know what will happen next. Leaders in a complex environment are mistaken if they think they're free to give orders: when they try to, the result is that France becomes a republic once again.

It might seem like a stretch to compare the business environment to a battle,* but a set of common characteristics seems to exist between war, ICUs, business in the digital era, and IT. Each of these, including the business enterprise, is an example of a *complex adaptive system* (CAS)—a self-organizing system (a concept that draws from evolutionary biology) in which individuals pursue their own objectives and interact in complex, ever-changing ways.

John Henry Clippinger Jr., in *The Biology of Business: Decoding the Natural Laws of Enterprise*, lists seven characteristics of a CAS:

- aggregation; that is, that the whole is greater than the sum of its parts
- non-linearity; that a small change can have a big impact
- flows, or networks of interactions
- diversity

---

* Here I must admit that I have never served in the military and so have no direct experience with the military ideas I describe throughout the book. There is a danger in comparing military to business situations: I don't want to trivialize the very real risks and challenges faced by those who serve their countries.

- tagging, or naming that gives significance to actions
- internal models, which are simplified representations that anticipate future events
- building blocks, or components that can be recombined[7]

"The behavior of such complex organisms is typically neither deterministic nor linear; rather, living systems continuously reorganize themselves in unexpected ways," Clippinger says.[8]

Businesses are filled with people who pursue their own objectives and who are then combined into teams and larger organizational groupings that also pursue their own objectives. No one has complete knowledge, and information is delayed in making its way from one employee to another. Initiatives in one part of the enterprise affect those in other parts of the enterprise. Upper management layers don't directly know what is happening on the ground, and line employees don't know what conversations are taking place behind closed boardroom doors. The more that companies decentralize authority into teams—the hallmark of the digital age—the less direct control they have over the teams' actions.

As CIO at US Citizenship and Immigration Services and a member of the government's Senior Executive Service,* I was considered high up in the federal hierarchy. And as a change agent, I was frequently challenging my organization with . . . unusual requests. In an assessment of one large IT initiative, feedback from independent advisors let me know that there was often a disconnect between what I thought I was asking for and what the technologists thought I wanted. Apparently, when my requests descended through the hierarchy, each middle manager subtly altered them based on his or her own understanding and interests. By the time the message reached the technologists, it had changed significantly and was sometimes close to absurd. Fortunately, they ignored my requests, and the project was going fine. I was Napoleon, leading from Shevardino, thinking I mattered.

---

* Technically, as an SES I was the civilian equivalent of a flag officer; that is, a one or two star general or admiral. Had Napoleon been around I'm sure he would have been a four star, and I would have reported to him and ignored his orders like everyone else.

If the business itself is a complex system, the complexity just gets worse when you consider it in its market context. Let's say we have a bobblehead company that decides to produce a new line of Albert Einstein dolls and projects its likely revenue and profit. But will a competitor release an even better Einstein bobblehead? If they do, how will it affect our revenues and profits? When will they get theirs to market? Will a researcher discover next week that Einstein loved gefilte fish* and, as a result, contributed to their impending extinction—causing environmentalists to picket stores that sell Einstein bobbleheads?

Will someone from the Nobel Prize Committee see our fine Einstein bobblehead, become nostalgic, realize that Einstein never received an award for his theory of relativity, invent a new prize, award it posthumously to Einstein, and as a result create a new market for Einstein memorabilia? Did we perhaps neglect those events in our revenue and cost model?

Uncertainty overwhelms our calculations. Yes, it's unlikely that Einstein will win another Nobel Prize (especially since it's never awarded to the dead), but it is likely that *some* unpredictable event will interfere with our plans, and with unpredictable consequences. One need only step back a few decades and think, from the point of view of a manager at that time, how little they would have known about the forces that would eventually affect their business. The internet? Social media? A book in which Malaysian fruits, *War and Peace*, and Hindu gods† feature prominently?

Many of our mental management models—those tools we're taught in business school—assume a reasonable degree of predictability, an orderly march back toward equilibrium whenever it's disturbed, and a business environment that rewards careful planning and conscientious execution of plans. We prioritize investments based on their business value—generally some notion of expected returns. As long as the environment is reasonably predictable, then doing so may be effective. But the more uncertainty, complexity, and rapid change we introduce into the picture, the less informative our predictions can be. And the more we insist on sticking to any plan as the world changes around us, the more of a liability that plan becomes.

What if uncertainty were such that an honest business case would have to say something like, "This will cost $1M (± $3M to be within a 60% confidence

---

* OK, I know it's not a real kind of fish.
† Spoiler alert.

range), and will return $2M every year for the next six years (±$4M, with a 60% confidence interval)?" It wouldn't be all that effective for making decisions, but might be a more accurate assessment of the information we typically have today when making an investment decision.

Even if the future could be known, the present is still a challenge. Do we really know what our customers want today? Do we know which hidden security vulnerabilities in our software will be exploited tomorrow by a hacker? Do we know now whether hackers are plotting to break into our systems? Do we know which of our employees is thinking of quitting?

I love these scientific-sounding formulae from IT leadership writers—which I believe express the traditional way of thinking about IT investments:

> The first question to be answered in assessing a proposed initiative is this: exactly how, and how much, will the investment affect and improve business performance?

> One way to assess how IT-savvy your firm has become is to perform the following calculation for each major IT project: ROI business case – [minus] ROI post-implementation review. Total the results for all of last year's major projects. In IT-savvy firms, this total sum approaches zero.[9]

But it does not approach zero—that's about as likely as a bobblehead becoming president. For one thing, last year's projects probably wouldn't have yielded their ROI yet. I'm certain that if this calculation could actually be performed, it would turn out that not a single company was IT savvy. When assessing a project, we cannot know exactly how much that investment will improve business performance. If we want to run our company responsibly, we must find a better way to make decisions under uncertainty than pretending certainty exists.

Nevertheless, someone is paying us to be transformational leaders, expecting we'll do something more than stand around in Shevardino issuing inconsequential orders. Given the complexity, uncertainty, and rapid change of the digital world, how can we direct the enterprise to the right outcomes? Clippinger gives us some clues as to how to lead a complex adaptive system:

> The complexity of a CAS is not chaos—as an evolutionary system a CAS can be directed toward a set of outcomes by setting the conditions for

the survival of the fittest—in a business context, by setting incentives and communicating vision . . . management cannot, and need not, have perfect information; the challenge of management is to create the conditions and contexts that select for a range of desired outcomes as in the processes of natural selection.[10]

The task of CAS leaders isn't to issue orders, but to put in place conditions that will cause independent actors within it to choose behaviors that will lead to the right outcomes.[11] The enterprise leadership team sets the vision that, in effect, defines what delivering business value will mean.*

The military, notwithstanding Napoleon's prowess, has realized that it deals with complexity as well. As A. M. Gray states this challenge in *Warfighting* (the manual of Marine Corps doctrine), "We must therefore be prepared to cope—even better, to thrive—in an environment of chaos, uncertainty, constant change, and friction."[12]

To respond to that complexity, the Marine Corps has put agility at the center of its doctrine. The idea is to operate in small teams, each of which acts independently and makes decisions based on the situation it finds on the ground. At the same time, all teams share principles and values that are part of their training and culture, and all understand the *commander's intent*—the goal for which they were sent into action and the parameters that should drive their decision-making. Since Napoleon, in his redoubt, cannot effectively instruct the troops what to do, they must be trained and empowered to make good decisions, as Napoleon presumably would make if he were among them.

No matter how much data we collect, we still can't know the future. Yesterday's results do not predict tomorrow's performance. Any extrapolation into the future—the realm of our strategic decisions—requires assumptions to be made.

Nevertheless, we like to believe that great business leaders are visionaries who can see the future—a myth perpetuated by the media. Yes, good leaders can spot trends and extrapolate from them, but a huge part of the future is

---

* You'll find a deeper discussion of why the definition of business value depends on how executives set the parameters through which the business evolves in my book *The Art of Business Value*.

truly uncertain. Being a great leader cannot be about knowing what number will come up when the dice are rolled. In retrospect, though, the person whose prediction turns out to be right is considered a genius. Like the account of Kutuzov in *War and Peace*:

> "However, they say he's a skilled commander," said Pierre. "I don't understand what is meant by a skilled commander," Prince Andrei said mockingly. "A skilled commander," said Pierre, "well, he's one who has foreseen all possibilities . . . well, who has guessed the thoughts of his adversary." "That's impossible," said Prince Andrei, as if the matter had long been decided.[13]

Here's a way to make a bagful of bucks (illegitimately—don't do this). It is known as the Sure-Shot Investement Scam. Send an email to 100,000 people declaring that you can predict the direction of the stock market. For half of them say it will go up tomorrow; for the other half, say it'll go down. The next day, determine which prediction was right, and to the 50,000 people to whom you sent the correct prediction, send another one. To half of them predict an increase, to half do the opposite. Repeat this process over seven days. You'll be left with 1,500 or so people for whom you've now correctly predicted market direction seven times in a row. To those people, offer to sell them your secret to predicting the future.

Someone is always a genius in retrospect. But the truly great leader is the one who adapts nimbly to whatever happens, not someone who happened to guess right when the outcome was actually uncertain.

In *On Grand Strategy*, John Lewis Gaddis weaves together Tolstoy with Prussian General Carl von Clausewitz to explain why a leader doesn't have direct control over outcomes, yet often seems to have such control:

> What Tolstoy means here—I think—is: (a) that because everything connects with everything else, there's an inescapable interdependency across time, space, and scale—forget about distinguishing independent from dependent variables; (b) that, as a consequence, there'll always be things that can't be known . . . (c) that owing to what we can't know, we'll always retain an illusion of agency, however infinitesimal.[14]

Strategy in conditions of uncertainty, complexity, and change has a very different look to it. On the one hand, strategy must lay out the vision and incentives that determine the evolutionary direction in the enterprise—a complex adaptive system. On the other hand, it must allow for constant learning and updating of models and plans. It's about experimenting and testing hypotheses. It's about deliberately collecting actionable information—not once a year, but continuously. And it's about having the humility to step back and learn, rather than rashly charging forth with a plan based on untested assumptions and hubris.

Agility increases the value of whatever information we do have when we make a decision, as Paul Drnevich and David Croson explain: "While flexibility is a substitute for perfect information about the future (which, if possessed, would obviate the need for flexibility), it becomes a complement for, and increases the marginal value of, imperfect information about the present."[15]

Learning only helps if we're adaptive enough to make use of what we learn. Unfortunately, many of our business processes are designed for a more predictable world. We codify our beliefs in *The Book of Processes*—in bureaucratic rules, in corporate culture, in governance processes and controls—then continue to apply them despite changes in the environment. Today we are optimizing for yesterday, even though it's already tomorrow.

The Agile approach I describe in the next chapter was created to address this problem. It proposes a way of constantly shifting course, all the while maintaining a focus on objectives. It's a way of building flexibility and nimbleness into processes while still adhering to a guiding vision. In the Agile paradigm, decision-making power is pushed to semi-autonomous teams. They learn and adapt; rather than trying to plan uncertainty away, they use rapid feedback cycles to reduce it. And the enterprise benefits by being able to direct its efforts toward what really matters.

Some IT complexity follows from the complexity in the business, for, after all, the company's IT systems mirror the company's operations. But to this IT adds the complexity of technology systems and technical practices.

Let me take you inside that black box of IT for a quick look.

You've probably already realized that IT is complex: entry to the profession is only available to certified propeller-heads. But I'm not referring to that kind of complexity; I'm referring to organizational complexity, administrative complexity, and gajillion-factors-to-consider-in-making-a-decision complexity. IT history has largely been about finding ways of dealing with such complexity. Each time an advance is made that reduces complexity, IT practitioners simply add another layer.

Imagine that your software application has millions of lines of code. Code is generally retained as a set of computer files, so think of it as any number of Microsoft Word documents totaling millions of lines of text.* Now imagine you have many developers working on that codebase at the same time—anywhere from a handful to dozens, hundreds, or even thousands. At any moment they have hundreds of work items—creating new features, changing existing ones, fixing bugs. A single change made to any of the millions of lines of code can have unpredictable—or let's say *surprising*—impacts on any of the other millions of lines of code. The developers are bouncing from one part of the codebase to another to make changes, depending on which tasks they're assigned. They are under time pressure.

Now mix in the technical complexity. Perhaps a developer adds a new feature, but—*OOPS!*—it suddenly slows down a function that was working speedily before. Now the developer has to dig through code that perhaps was written by another coder, attempting to ascertain all of the interrelationships between it and the millions of other lines in the codebase, all to create a new design that will fix the speed problem. The changes are made and—*YIKES!*—suddenly another feature stops working! Meanwhile, another developer has made changes that accidentally overwrote the changes the first person made. Then someone calls a meeting and all developers drop what they're doing. When they return they've forgotten where they were in the codebase. By this time the code may as well be in one of Atul Gawande's ICUs.

Technologists deal with complexity by layering their solutions. A solved problem becomes a layer on top of which future problems can be solved. When you're working on a particular layer, you don't have to worry about the complexity of all the layers underneath: someone has already solved them. There is sort of a leveling effect—technologists keep the complexity of their jobs more or less constant, at the limit of the complexity they're able to handle, by ignoring the complexity below and above the layer they're working on.

---

* Actually, programmers use a different type of document editor called an IDE, or Integrated Development Environment.

Electricity makes its way to each of your AC outlets at home only because scientists figured out you can power appliances by making electrons flow through a set of wires. They had to discover the relationship between moving magnetic fields and electricity, then devise practical devices that could generate electricity by moving magnetic fields around. And they had to invent transformers that could step voltage up and down so as to move electricity over long distances.

But you don't have to worry about any of that—you just plug in your toaster. So it is with the layers of computing. Someone has already figured out how to encrypt data, and they in turn relied on mathematical principles that had been developed by those who came before. We don't have to deal with getting all computers to communicate with one another—the internet and its protocols already exist. We can focus our energies on building upon what already exists.

But things can go wrong in any of those layers. Of course, the lower the layer, the harder it is to find and fix the problem. IT people can wrap their heads around complexity because of layering and the tools they've developed. But the complexity remains.

Today, technology departments break down software systems into small components, each responsible for a small segment of functionality. The components communicate with one another, delegating and coordinating each piece of work. For example, when an online shopper clicks a buy button, one component locates the shopper's account information, another obtains their credit card data, yet another sends the transaction to the credit card processor, the next receives the authorization response, still another deducts the item from inventory, and the last one notifies the warehouse to pull and ship the product. Each of these may be further divided into more granular subcomponents. Individual components may run on disparate hardware and they might access multiple databases.

The resultant complexity makes it hard to even imagine what kinds of things might go wrong. As a result, a new discipline called *chaos engineering* is emerging, pioneered by the Netflix engineers. Their idea was to simulate major failures in live systems to make certain such failures are gracefully handled. They started by randomly turning off servers, as if someone had stumbled over a power cord and accidentally unplugged it. Later they moved to more sophisticated failure modes. They wanted to learn what would happen. Would one failure cascade into another?

Once you make a computer system available over the internet, you take on an enormous amount of additional uncertainty. Web applications can be accessed by anyone, anywhere, at any time, and are consequently subject to vast, instantaneous swings in their scale of usage. Hackers will try to find their way into any system as soon as it's connected. And picky users are no longer willing to accept a website that apologizes that it's "Down for Maintenance" or "Under Construction."

Handling such uncertainty requires true artistry. The most difficult aspect of creating applications for internet scale is the need to manage *concurrency*. Because IT systems are simultaneously handling the activities of many customers, unexpected coordination problems arise that can't be easily reproduced or diagnosed. What if two shoppers buy the same unique artisan bobblehead at the same moment? As the number of system users increases, the likelihood of timing-related problems arise. If you find Gerald in a bad mood, it's probably because he's trying to diagnose a concurrency problem.

As enterprise change agents, we must understand that we're dealing with a complex system, where changes in one location might have unpredictable effects in another. In his article "Responsible Change," Christopher Avery talks about "provoking and observing" as the way to cause change within a complex adaptive system:

> We can never direct a living system, only disturb it and wait to see the response. . . . We can't know all the forces shaping an organization we wish to change, so all we can do is provoke the system in some way by experimenting with a force we think might have some impact, then watch to see what happens.[16]

To work effectively in the digital world, you must first accept complexity and uncertainty, for they demand a very different approach to carrying out initiatives. A predictable world rewards advance planning and rigid plan execution. But a complex and uncertain world rewards an empirical cycle of trying, observing, and correcting. This was the insight behind the development of Agile and Lean IT, as I'll show in the next chapter.

AGILITY AND LEANNESS

If you wish to make Pythocles rich, do not add to his store of money, but subtract from his desires.

—**Epicurus**, *Fragments*

You can't play Thersites and Agamemnon at one and the same time. If you want to be Thersites, you must be humpbacked and bald; if Agamemnon, you must be tall and handsome and love your subjects.

—**Epictetus**, *Discourses*

The digital age demands that we get new ideas to market quickly to ward off disruption by competitors. It requires that we cope with uncertainty and complexity by staying nimble, by learning how to observe and react, and by reducing the cost and risk of making changes to our products, processes, and even our business model. It encourages us to innovate and grow, to deepen our relationship with customers, and to seize opportunities as we find them.

The problem is that being agile and rigidly sticking to a plan are opposites, yet sticking to a plan has been the enterprise expedient for achieving control and managing risks—and, in particular, for trying to gain control over IT investments. In this chapter I'll show that there are better ways to control those investments without sacrificing agility.

What makes it possible to achieve this synthesis is a suite of techniques IT practitioners have come up with over the last few decades, and refined over the last few years. I'll show how the enterprise can take advantage of these new ways of doing IT—Agile delivery, Lean IT, and DevOps—to speed products to market, drive innovation, respond quickly to changes, reduce risk, and reduce costs—all while satisfying the need for responsible financial stewardship.

⁂

In 2001, a group of software development gurus met at Utah's Snowbird Mountain ski resort to assemble a set of principles for a new way of delivering software. Like Nietzsche's Zarathustra descending from his mountain, or Moses and Mohammed before him, they returned to IT society with a revelation that was both startling and visionary in its coherence and completeness. The four values and twelve principles of the *Manifesto for Agile Software Development* have guided IT delivery ever since. Simple, perhaps obvious, these principles undermine the contractor-control, plan-above-all model that was so ingrained in corporate IT.

The essence of the Agile model is to manage complexity and uncertainty by continuously learning and adapting. As we've seen, similar principles were emerging at the same time in domains outside of IT. This has been particularly true in the military, which—following the destruction of the World Trade Center—was faced with the challenge of fighting an enemy that was constantly reconfiguring itself and could be hiding anywhere. "As the situation changes continuously, we are forced to improvise again and again until finally our actions have little, if any, resemblance to the original scheme," says A. M. Gray in *Warfighting*.[1]

To maximize learning, Agile IT works in short cycles, finishing small pieces of work and gathering feedback. The feedback might come from users and managers, or it might be observations or data collected as people use their product. As feedback is incorporated, the product develops as a series of increasingly better approximations to perfection.

Work is done in small teams, because small teams can communicate easily among themselves, sharing learnings and observations, passing work back and forth, and helping each other. The team members take on joint accountability for delivering results. They meet daily—briefly—to synchronize their activities, then gather again periodically to assess and improve their process. Again, the idea parallels military theory: "First and foremost, in order to generate the tempo of operations we desire and to best cope with the uncertainty, disorder, and fluidity of combat, command must be decentralized," Gray says.[2] Despite

Napoleon's futile attempts to command, it is the troops themselves who can react quickly enough to make good decisions.

That is exactly the Agile IT idea. Decisions are decentralized, but—importantly—controlled through a shared and well-understood "commander's intent." They're also continuously adjusted through leadership participation and oversight.

***

You can contrast the Agile way of thinking with the traditional plan-driven waterfall approach. Instead of locking in requirements and setting a rigid plan at the start of a project, Agile IT establishes clarity about its goals, creates a tentative list of features ("stories") that will accomplish those goals, then has developers and users of the software work together to refine features as they're delivered. By working with users, technologists make sure the code they're producing actually satisfies those users' needs and accomplishes the organization's goals. The enterprise is free at any time to reprioritize the features that haven't yet been developed, change them, or eliminate them.

Back in the waterfall world, a complete set of requirements was assembled and the system designed as a whole. It was then divided into technical components, each of which was independently built. Only in the end was it all put together to create features people would use; and only then would the whole system be tested.

Instead, with the Agile approach each feature is developed, start to finish, as an independent entity. (The original Agile writers described it as a slice of sashimi, perfect and complete on its own.) Developers are able to start building and delivering results almost immediately—feature by feature—testing and delivering each before moving on to the next. That there is no waiting for the remaining features to be completed is the trick that changes everything. The work can be modified or reprioritized, allowing the company to change direction at any time. This business agility is what gives the practice its name. Note that the goal of the technique is *business* agility, not just technical flexibility. The nimbleness and speed it provides are precisely what an enterprise needs in the digital world.

But here is a catch. When organizations that are used to the old way of working begin to adopt Agile techniques, they tend to spend a lot of time preparing their tentative list of features. They over-specify each one, rather than letting users work with the technology team to refine them. Rarely do they step back to reevaluate what they need and then freely change the requirements. In other words, they reintroduce inflexibility into a process that is meant to maximize flexibility. To transform, you accept the gift of flexibility and thank the Snowbird gurus.

Since Agile IT is based on *completing* work items quickly and frequently—that is, reducing the lead time to delivery—it's logical to apply Lean manufacturing principles, such as those of the Toyota Production System, to the IT delivery process. We can think of each work item—a requirement—as a unit that must make its way through a series of process steps. Each step takes time, some of which might be waste.

In the Lean sense, waste is any activity that doesn't add value to the finished product, or, as some experts phrase it, activities that a customer wouldn't be willing to pay for. I like to refine this definition a bit—to me, waste is any activity that doesn't add *enough* value to justify its cost in dollars or additional lead time.

According to Lean, the sources of manufacturing waste are inventory, extra processing, overproduction, transportation, waiting, motion, and defects. In their classic work, *Lean Software Development: An Agile Toolkit*, Mary and Tom Poppendieck show how the traditional sources of manufacturing waste have equivalents in an IT process.[3] Defects are a source of waste in IT as well as in manufacturing, as is extra processing (process steps that can just as well be eliminated—for example, testing twice for the same error condition). Waiting, a classic source of waste in manufacturing, might, for example, correspond to the time from when a programmer has finished coding a feature to when a tester is available to test it, or the time a document sits on someone's desk waiting for a signature.

Overproduction corresponds to feature bloat. Transportation waste is replaced by task switching: the time it takes to bring an IT person's attention to the work, rather than the other way around. Motion corresponds to the movement of documents from one organizational silo to another, or the effort it takes a developer to get answers to questions that inevitably arise.

Large batch sizes are an important source of waste according to Lean thinking. Their IT equivalent is a large group of requirements processed as a single deliverable. Lean IT teams, therefore, carefully limit the amount of work in process (WIP). Reducing batch sizes reduces cycle time, variability in flow, risk, overhead, costs, and schedule growth. It also accelerates feedback, improves efficiency, and increases motivation.

By reducing lead time, developers and requirements writers can quickly get feedback that lets them know whether they're accomplishing the organization's goals and whether their code is usable. And they can get product to market more quickly.

Since IT delivery is typically a constraint in executing new business initiatives and responding to market events, it's IT lead time you need to consider when conducting a digital transformation. If you look closely at the IT delivery value stream, however, you'll see that much of its lead time occurs in the interactions between IT and the rest of the business. That's why I say that changing the way we fit IT into the enterprise is the largest factor in increasing organizational agility.

For example, the arms-length contractor relationship between IT and the business demands that the requirements document be perfected and formally approved (signed off on) by the business stakeholders. But face-to-face communication is much more time efficient; it also leads to better outcomes because it allows questions to be answered, possible approaches to be discussed, and variations to be considered.

To give you a sense of how much overhead sneaks into the IT process at the interface between IT and the rest of the business, let me describe a scenario from my days in government. Though the government all too often provides extreme examples, no doubt you'll recognize your own organization in the following description.

A critical mission need is recognized and an IT capability must be deployed to meet it. The first step in government IT . . . is to wait. That is, to wait until enough needs have accumulated that they can collectively be turned into a project. After all, a single mission need is too granular to be put through an investment management and governance process. Only with enough proposed tasks can a project be initiated, documented, and a business case prepared.

At the Department of Homeland Security (DHS), the IT oversight process required the preparation of around one hundred documents, each of which had to be signed by a collection of senior agency people. The process required thirteen gate reviews, including a review of the mission need, the project plan, the requirements, and so on. Each review entailed a formal meeting and required convening about twenty people with busy schedules. (Note that lead time refers to calendar time, not effort time. Although the meeting only took an hour, it could take months to schedule.)

When the business case was approved and funding was secured from the capital markets—that is, Congress—a contractor would be engaged through a formal procurement process (virtually everything is outsourced in the government). This generally took between six months and three years.

Next, computer hardware was ordered, received, placed in a datacenter, and configured. Eventually software design and development took place. The resulting IT capabilities were tested and the problems remediated. Then the security team analyzed the product for potential vulnerabilities, which would also be fixed. When everything was ready to go, a change management process was initiated to make sure that any other IT systems that would be affected were ready, that users had been trained, and that the process for deploying the capabilities was bulletproof. *Et voilà*, business value.

It's no wonder that government IT capabilities can take years or even decades to be deployed. Though it may differ in its precise steps, the process in most organizations follows a similar pattern. Relatively little time is actually taken up by technical product development; much more time is spent on handoffs and coordination between IT and the business, or in preparing documents for those handoffs. Business or mission needs (note that word—*needs*) in my opinion should be met in hours or days. But what can make the process take years are the risk-reduction activities intended to make sure that the IT work stays aligned with business needs.

Risk reduction and alignment with business needs are indeed important goals. But they can be accomplished far more effectively and with far less waste. To accelerate and meet the demands of the digital age, we must systematically find ways to reduce the time this process requires without sacrificing the controls that reduce our risk.

———

Agile and Lean IT come together in the set of practices called DevOps. It's the technical approach I recommend you follow in digital transformation, and is used successfully today by enterprises across virtually all industries—Capital One, Nike, Target, John Deere, Disney, to name a few. It's based on cross-functional teams (to avoid handoffs between IT specialties) and heavy use of automation to streamline processes and make them repeatable. DevOps is powerful for businesses because of its approach to speed and control—it effectively does away with the tradeoff that formerly existed between the two.

The impact of DevOps on business results has been studied by DevOps Research and Assessment (DORA) and written about by Dr. Nicole Forsgren, Jez Humble, and Gene Kim in their book *Accelerate*. In their research, they found that the companies making the most use of DevOps practices were 1.53 times as likely to meet or exceed their organization's goals—including, for example, profitability, market share, productivity, units sold, and operating efficiency.[4]

Their employees were also 2.2 times more likely to recommend the organization as a great place to work, which in other studies has been correlated with better business outcomes.[5] For those companies that are publicly traded, high performers in these IT practices had 50% higher growth in market capitalization than low performers.[6]

DevOps is practiced in small teams, say five to nine people. Small teams can communicate among themselves face-to-face, thereby avoiding the overhead of passing around and perfecting documents. Each team is cross-functional, with skills in software development, testing, infrastructure engineering, operations, and security.

These functions are not necessarily represented by different people. In fact, DevOps organizations prefer what they call T-shaped people:[7] employees who have a broad set of skills but go deep in one area. They're generalists who have a specialty; for example, a particular team member might be able to develop software and engineer infrastructure, but is especially good in performance optimization. Teams of T-shaped employees are very agile because they can pass work back and forth as needed, and yet draw on deep expertise when necessary. You may recall that in Chapter 1 I discussed the problem with fracturing skill sets into silos; the T-shape is a solution to the problem of needing deep specialization, but wanting people with diverse skill sets.

DevOps teams rely heavily on automation (in geek speak they say, "Automate all the things!"). They automate their testing, as well as their infrastructure setup in the cloud. They automate controls that monitor for security and regulatory compliance. And they automate the process of merging code from developers and resolving conflicts.

What is most remarkable about DevOps is its emphasis on deploying code to users very frequently. The movement entered the IT community's consciousness in 2009 when Flickr, the photo sharing site, announced it was regularly performing ten deployments every day. By today's standards that's nothing—Amazon.com is probably the current leader at over fifty million deployments per year. In fact, how often they're able to deploy valuable changes or new capabilities has become something of a point of pride with DevOps practitioners.

From a Lean point of view, DevOps is . . . well, very lean. There are no handoffs to external groups because the cross-functional team has all of the skills it needs to do its work. Features are completed and immediately deployed, so there is little work in process. Automation reduces the work the team must do to produce each feature. There are fewer defects and less rework because the automated tests find problems quickly.

Back to deployment. It might sound risky or chaotic to deploy changes to users so often, but it's actually the opposite. In the past, IT teams have made large, infrequent deployments that invariably *did* cause chaos for the rest of the business and for themselves. But with DevOps, each deployment is small and therefore unlikely to fail; if it does, the problem can be quickly found. In addition, the deployment process itself is well-tested because it's used so often.

DevOps, you may have noticed, is attuned to the speed of the digital age—a fast process for fast times. Forsgren and her coauthors write:

> Our analysis of high, medium, and low performers provides evidence that there are no tradeoffs between improving performance and achieving higher levels of tempo and stability: they move in tandem. This is precisely what the Agile and Lean movements predict, but much dogma in our industry still rests on the false assumption that moving faster means trading off against other performance goals, rather than enabling and reinforcing them.[8]

The DORA study* used cluster analysis to separate companies into cohorts based on their IT performance. To measure this they used a construct they called SDO (software delivery and operational performance) that brought together measurements representing throughput, stability, and system availability. As proxies for throughput they used the frequency of IT feature deployments and the lead time from when a developer finishes coding an IT capability to when it's deployed. To represent stability they measured the change failure rate and the mean time to repair (MTTR) problems. Based on SDO, they were able to cluster companies into four performance groups: low, medium, high, and elite performers.

Comparing the elite performers (who use DevOps best practices most extensively) to the low performers, they found that the former are able to deploy features 46 times more frequently, show 2,555 times faster lead times from the point of finishing code to deploying it, are 2,604 times faster to recover from downtime, and are only one-seventh as likely to have a change fail.[9]

It's not surprising that DevOps practices are correlated with good business results. For one thing, these practices reduce many types of risk. Security risk is reduced both through frequent testing and fast response to vulnerabilities when they are detected. While a waterfall project risks virtually its entire budget by not delivering results until the end, a typical Agile project risks only the cost of the increment under construction. And DevOps, with its fast, frequent deliveries, risks only the tiny increments between deployments.

DevOps practices also reduce costs. By quickly deploying a minimal product and then adding to it incrementally, your organization is able to stop wasting effort on unneeded features, or features that customers don't actually want. Costs also decrease as the company finds ways to make the delivery process leaner. Since DevOps reduces defects it also reduces unplanned work.[10] And finally, it seems to allow the size of delivery organizations to scale without diminishing returns.[11]

---

* For their 2018 report, they surveyed 1,900 professionals about their IT practices and business outcomes. Thirty-eight percent of the respondents worked for organizations of more than 10,000 employees, so large enterprises were well represented.

You can control a DevOps initiative through continuous involvement and feedback, rather than by simply approving a plan at the beginning of an effort. Instead of checking on the project through periodic status reviews, you get to see and use completed work throughout—a much better way to gauge progress. You can continually adjust priorities and reallocate resources, as well as evaluate the quality of the work by seeing business results, rather than through a few weeks of user acceptance testing at the last minute.

In short, you trade perceived control for actual control. In my view this means your expectations for technologists should actually be higher (and these expectations will be satisfied, because technologists are happy to be judged this way). You should expect that technologists will quickly and frequently finish and deliver results. That they will be of high quality. That technologists will work to reduce lead times, thereby becoming more responsive to business needs and reducing waste in processes. And that they'll bring their creativity and passion to solving business problems, rather than waiting for requirements to be tossed over the wall to them.

<hr>

In his book *The Lean Startup*, Eric Ries draws out some of the business implications of being able to deliver products in a streamlined, lean way by showing how successful startups use an iterative approach to defining themselves. A startup begins with an idea and a vision for a product that it thinks will be attractive to customers. As Ries puts it, the company has a *value hypothesis* about which product attributes will be valuable to customers, and a *growth hypothesis* about how that customer value will translate into increasing revenues for the company.[12] It then tests these hypotheses through marketplace experiments. Based on what it learns, the startup can continue with the two hypotheses as they are or "pivot"—discard them and formulate new hypotheses. This, according to Ries, is how startups succeed.

Ries summarizes the Lean startup process this way:

> Identify the beliefs about what must be true in order for the startup to succeed. We call these leap-of-faith assumptions. Create an experiment to test those assumptions as quickly and inexpensively as possible. We call this initial effort a minimum viable product. Think like a scientist. Treat each experiment as an opportunity to learn what's working and

what's not. We call this "unit of progress" for startups validated learning. Take the learning from each experiment and start the loop over again. This cycle of iteration is called the build-measure-learn feedback loop. On a regular schedule (cadence), make a decision about whether to make a change in strategy (pivot) or stay the course (persevere).[13]

The goal of a startup, then, is to achieve validated learning through experimenting, to maximize learning while minimizing investment. It does this by creating a series of *minimal viable products*, or MVPs—the smallest, cheapest versions of a product that will help the company learn and adjust course. MVPs can be surprisingly simple: perhaps at first, they're onscreen mockups that can be shown to users to get their feedback. This could be followed by *concierge products*—that is, services having a *Wizard of Oz*–like "man behind the curtain" who performs the function that will later be automated.

The Lean startup approach is also used by established enterprises developing new customer-facing digital products, or IT systems for use within the enterprise. Instead of building from requirements, an Agile team should work from hypotheses: "We believe that if we create this particular feature, we'll get this specific business result." They can then test their hypotheses by creating MVPs. Testing ideas leads to better outcomes than asking users what they need. As Ries says:

> The reason to run experiments is to discover customers' revealed preferences through their behavior. In other words, don't ask customers what they want. Design experiments that allow you to observe it. . . . [Minimum viable products] are real-life products, no matter how limited, that create maximum opportunity for us to be surprised by customer behavior.[14]

***

Putting all these pieces together—DevOps, Agile, Lean Startup—we see a very different model emerging for how companies use IT. Instead of writing a requirements document based on what they think will be a good investment, they start with a business objective, generate ideas about how to achieve it, and run small tests to see if those ideas seem to advance the objectives . . . or, if not, how they can be improved. Small tests are possible because the IT team is using a DevOps practice that lets it quickly get features into users' hands and gauge how effective they are.

———————

In the past we've talked about making sure that IT is aligned with the business. But this is where the enterprise might want to align with IT. To gain the business benefits of DevOps and Agile practices, it must streamline all of its organizational processes, of which IT work is a part. Investment oversight, procurement policy, requirements formulation, and risk management are areas where companies can vastly reduce waste and lead times while actually improving controls. Until they do so, they'll be sacrificing the speed and fast feedback that DevOps brings.

Think carefully about what success looks like. In the digital world, it looks like speed, flexibility, controls, and leanness—not like making plans and following them. It's these new IT practices that will bring you those benefits. They have already brought them to the many other enterprises that have started down the path and, in some cases, disrupted industries.

SIDE GLANCE:
GRAPHS

And indeed, all limits to human action, once laid down as absolute laws—God's law, natural law, moral law—are now falling before the onslaught of technology's productive-destructive capabilities.

—**Emanuele Severino**, *The Essence of Nihilism*

Mundus vult decipi: the world wants to be deceived. The truth is too complex and frightening; the taste for the truth is an acquired taste that few acquire.

—**Martin Buber**, *I and Thou*

Although technology might be complex, the laws of IT—the business and process principles used in working with that technology—are surprisingly straightforward, or perhaps straightforwardly surprising if you haven't tried overseeing an IT initiative yourself. Our intuitions are often wrong; the contractor-control model makes it hard for us to accept some of the basic principles that evidence shows guide IT. The old mental model encouraged us to—essentially—assign IT the blame (we usually called it "accountability") for the uncertainty and inevitability that are inherent in business and technology. A few graphs may help.

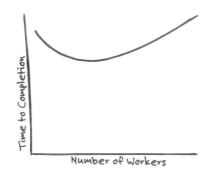

Figure 1: Time versus Number of Workers[1]

Figure 1 is a classic graph in IT theory. In his 1975 book, *The Mythical Man-Month*, Fred Brooks argued that you can't speed up a project that's behind schedule by adding more engineers to it. There is at first a diminishing return from adding incremental developers, and then the return becomes negative. The explanation is that the more engineers you add, the more complicated their interactions and communications become. This is why modern IT is done in small teams.

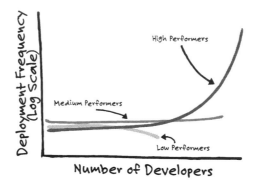

Figure 2: Deploys per Day per Developer[2]

Figure 2 is a very recent graph from *Accelerate*, showing that when we use DevOps, the number of deployments per day per software developer—the best productivity measure we know of—actually goes up as you add more developers. In other words, with DevOps—which streamlines interactions between engineers—productivity can actually go up as you add developers (perhaps showing that Brooks's Law no longer applies).

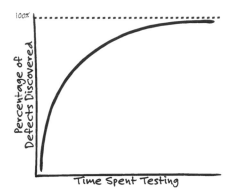

Figure 3: Diminishing Returns for Testing

Figure 3 illustrates this concept of diminishing returns on manual testing effort. In a waterfall project, the more time you spend manually testing a system, the fewer incremental bugs you find. You must decide on the optimal point for releasing the product, knowing that you'll still have some defects but can't spend an infinite amount of time looking for them. DevOps changes the equation because tests are automated and run in minutes. Each release is tiny and incremental, and all tests, including old ones, are run every time a change is made.

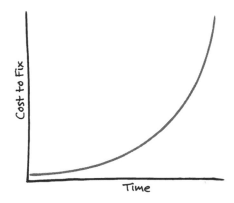

Figure 4: Cost to Fix a Defect versus Time to Discovery[3]

Figure 4 shows the cost of fixing a defect as a function of how long it took to discover it. In other words, the x-axis is how much time has elapsed since the defect was introduced, and the y-axis is the cost to fix it. There is a huge penalty for not finding and fixing a defect immediately. If the defect is not found until users discover it, the cost to fix it is orders of magnitude higher. DevOps provides very fast feedback: new code is immediately tested using automated scripts, code is merged with that of other developers to quickly discover conflicts, and feedback comes quickly from monitoring usage after code is released.

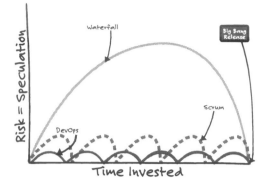

Figure 5: Risk Increases Based on Time Without a Release[4]

Figure 5 shows value delivered and risk levels over time for a waterfall project, an old-style Agile project, and a DevOps project. Any money spent on the project is at risk until code is released to users and the business can verify that it is adding value. For waterfall projects, the result is "speculation buildup"—money keeps flowing into the project on the speculation that it is adding value. The total amount of risk is the integral under the curve. Agile and DevOps initiatives maintain risk at a low level by constantly releasing software whose value can be ascertained, and capture considerably more value—especially given the time value of money.

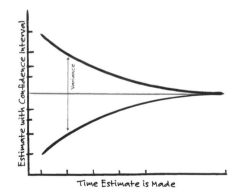

Figure 6: The Cone of Uncertainty

Figure 6 is another classic, called the Cone of Uncertainty. If you estimate a project before it starts, your estimate should have a very large confidence interval. The further into the project you get, the more information you have, so the confidence interval decreases. Early estimates should never be relied on—they are (legitimately) always wrong.

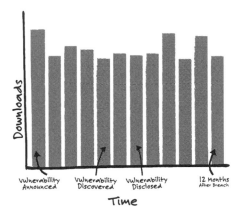

Figure 7: Vulnerable Downloads per Month[5]

Figure 7 illustrates something important to understand about security. Even though we know that certain pieces of software have security vulnerabilities, we're still using them. This graph shows that businesses continued to download and use a piece of open-source software even after its vulnerability was apparent. One reason for this is that we're afraid to patch our software because something might break. DevOps helps solve this by incorporating automated tests that quickly tell us whether that risk is real. To generalize the message of Figure 7: simple hygiene can considerably improve our security postures.

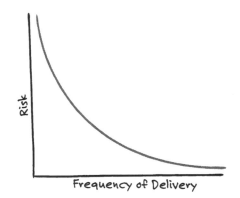

Figure 8: Risk versus Frequency of Delivery

Figure 8 shows delivery risk versus frequency of delivery. The more frequently you deploy, the better you become at it. And the smaller your deployments are, the less risk you have in each one.

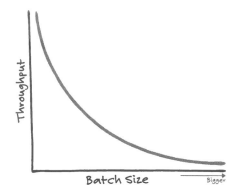

Figure 9: Throughput versus Batch Size[6]

Figure 9 is a standard Lean graph that shows throughput deteriorates quickly as batch size increases. Think of an IT initiative as a batch of requirements (they sit in inventory, then they're processed and completed). This is one reason why large projects fail. It is a good reason for limiting work in process—working a small number of requirements to completion, then moving on to the next ones.

———————

Some takeaways: Work in small teams, create fast feedback cycles, reduce requirements-in-process, improve security hygiene, deliver small pieces of work frequently.

4 THE BUSINESS VALUE OF IT

Very often when we have found ourselves forever separated from what we had intended to achieve, we have already, on our way, found something else worth desiring.

—**Goethe**, *Maxims*

If I were to wish for anything, I should not wish for wealth and power, but for the passionate sense of the potential, for the eye which, ever young and ardent, sees the possible. Pleasure disappoints, possibility never.

—**Søren Kierkegaard**, *Either/Or*

In 1995 the Standish Group released a report, known as to as the *Chaos Report*, with the spectacular claim that only 16.2% of software development projects are fully successful, finish on time, and stay on budget. They said that 31.1% are cancelled before they finish, and 52.7% cost 189% of their original estimate.[1] Standish has since repeated the study, tracking projects from 2003–2012, this time finding that only 6.4% were successful.[2] Compared to that, an IBM study was positively encouraging—it found that 41% of projects meet schedule, budget, and quality goals.[3]

Standish's startling results set off spasms of anxious rethinking regarding IT practices. The initial reaction was to double down on the classical project management principles. Organizations had to do a better job of documenting requirements, planning more carefully, estimating schedules more precisely, reporting more frequently on the status of each project, and being prepared to cancel projects ruthlessly if they appear to be going out of control.

Shocking as Standish's results appear, there is a very different way to interpret them. Perhaps they're really just a confirmation of uncertainty, telling us that early estimates are invariably unreliable, that success can't be measured by reliance on an estimate made before enough information is available. In this interpretation, the *Chaos Report* is simply a confirmation of Figure 6: The Cone of Uncertainty in the prior chapter. Standish's study errs in imposing a value judgment on neutral data.

But another set of studies raises different and more serious concerns, since they aren't about schedule adherence but about value delivery. According to a KPMG study, "50 percent of respondents indicated that their project *failed to consistently achieve what they set out to achieve*."[4] A McKinsey study found that "17 percent of large IT projects go so badly that they can threaten the very existence of the company."[5] McKinsey also said that large IT projects deliver 56% less value than predicted.[6]

Again there is a question of how to interpret these results, though another set of studies gives a clue. Apparently, 75% of project participants lack confidence that their projects will succeed[7] and 70% have been involved in a project they knew would fail from the start.[8] In other words, people knew their projects weren't going well but were unable to change course. Well, of course they couldn't—the plan was already locked in! To be successful, a project team needs to make course correction an everyday part of its activities.

In 1995 Tom DeMarco, one of the more provocative early IT thought leaders, published the book *Why Does Software Cost So Much?* We can all probably understand his question. Software is intangible; in a sense, it's just a simple translation of a desired computer behavior into a language the machine can understand. Yet creating it usually takes teams of highly paid developers, testers, and database administrators. It can take months or years. It is never finished, and always costs more than expected.

Accepting DeMarco's insinuating premise, we might indeed be tempted to say that software indeed costs too much. And taking the Standish findings at face value, we would have to conclude that most IT projects fail, while the rest are highly challenged. Yet we know very well that businesses—rational actors on the whole—keep investing in IT. You're reading this book because you believe in the power of IT to drive business outcomes. So why invest in guaranteed failure?

The answer is that technology *is* delivering business value, and boatloads of it—despite the fact that IT *projects* seem to fail. Projects have a fixed scope and schedule and are driven by a plan, but IT's value is primarily in the operational use of the capabilities it delivers. As DeMarco says, the flip answer to his question (and one that he rejects as being too simple) is, "Compared to what?"[9] Software is what runs our businesses today: it's what lets us compete in markets. Surely the value of *that* is high.

The real question for those leading digital transformations is how to maximize the business value they get from IT, not how to make projects finish on time. Here we run into a number of tricky issues and misunderstandings. This chapter will look at what exactly business value means and what it means for IT to deliver it, and how that might change as we enter the digital world.

DeMarco's cynical answer, by the way, is that IT isn't really expensive—just as it isn't really failing. Asking the question, he says, is a way of trying to put maximum pressure on the technology organization to lower costs.[10] I see it more as a way that enterprises have wishfully tried to gain control over highly variable costs they felt powerless to manage.

Imagine going to a crafts market in a country where bargaining is the norm. You're uncomfortable with bargaining and unfamiliar with prices in that country. You spot an artisan bobblehead you really want to buy. The vendor assures you that it's a particularly fine specimen, undoubtedly worth the one hundred Napoleonic livres* he says it'll cost you. You're sure that this price is absurd because, after all, you're a tourist and the vendor can see that.

But what is the normal price, you wonder? After turning the bobblehead over a few times, frowning at it, and trying to look like you're no fool, you offer half—fifty livres. After some back and forth you finally wind up bargaining a price of seventy-eight livres. No doubt you're being ripped off, but what else can you do?

---

* For history buffs: the French franc was created in 1794, before Napoleon's campaign in Russia, but livres continued to be used until the 1830s.

Now imagine The Business early in its encounters with Gerald and his platoon of technologists. How much will it cost to fix the ephemeral ramifier, Gerald?

Here is a sample conversation I've actually had to this effect:

CEO: Did you get the requirements from the Bobbling Bear business unit?

CIO: Yes, and I had my staff review them.

CEO: How long will it take?

CIO: Well, my team put together an estimate. But it's only an estimate.

CEO: Yes, of course. How long?

CIO: We think that if we can simplify a few things in the requirements, it'll be about sixteen months.

CEO: What? Sixteen months? That's way too long. We need this to respond to the Evil Empire's new competitive product. We can't go sixteen months without a Bobbling Bear!

CIO: How quickly do we need it?

CEO: We have to have it in eight months.

CIO: That's impossible. The Bridge at Borodino feature alone will take six months.

CEO: OK, well let's say ten months, then. But no later! If your team can't handle it, then outsource it.

CIO: Well . . . if we can simplify the Borodino Bridge feature and if the Bobbling Bear business unit sets aside a team of three people to help us, maybe we can do it.

CEO: Very good. That's good, creative thinking. OK, then, it'll be done by next June, right?

I didn't say whether I was the CEO or the CIO in this scenario. I've been both. This conversation is natural when no one has a good basis for predicting the cost. They might as well be arguing about the number of grains of sand on the beach in a science fiction novel that takes place in an invented universe.

Notice how the exchange moves subtly from an estimate to a commitment. An estimate is an estimate—you can't negotiate an estimate. But that's exactly what happens here. Both parties implicitly take the estimate to be a plan, and then the planned time is negotiated to a lower number. But that doesn't change the *estimate*, which is still the CIO's best educated guess as to how long the project will take. The CIO believes the project will take sixteen months, but is now committed to doing it in ten. If it winds up taking fourteen months, is that good or is it failure? In Standish's definition, it's failure.

Also notice that the original estimate is a point estimate. If we were honest with ourselves, we would give our estimates with confidence ranges, something like "I'm 60% confident that it'll take between twelve and twenty-four months." We don't like to admit to the uncertainty and therefore hide it by giving a point estimate. In this case, the CIO probably feels like it's part of his job to know how long an IT project will take, and the CEO expects a precise estimate (is that perhaps an oxymoron?) for planning purposes. How much uncertainty is there? Much. That's what Standish's IT project failure rate tells us.

What are some of the uncertainties? First of all, every IT project is different—there is no applicable historical data. Technology often doesn't work the way you expect: interactions between one part of the system and another surprise us. No matter how careful the business unit is when writing the requirements, they will change significantly. In short, this is a complex and uncertain endeavor.

The requirements begin at a high level of abstraction and later, when the details are known, it'll become clearer how much time is actually required. An IT project is a journey from abstract to concrete—while the project starts with a high-level vision, code is its concrete and detailed interpretation. When the requirements finally have become concrete—in other words, when the code is already written and tested—it will become easy to estimate how long the project has taken, so a point estimate with 100% confidence is appropriate. But at any earlier time, an estimate should have a wide confidence interval. That's the message of Figure 6: The Cone of Uncertainty in the prior chapter.

———

Business leaders were once tourists in the crafts market when it came to IT spending. It's natural when a tourist, having no idea what the right price for a traditional bobblehead might be, turns to another tourist and asks, "How much did you pay for yours?" But the problem is that there is no "right" price—prices depend on the workmanship, the vendor, the buyer, and the moment.

Similarly, some businesses try to benchmark their IT spending against that of other companies to determine how much they "should" be spending—

often comparing the percentage of revenue spent on IT. But IT spending really depends on what the company is trying to accomplish; that is to say, it depends on the company's strategy. It depends on how the industry and its customers' tastes are changing; whether the company is planning for an IPO, an acquisition, or another exit; and what ideas the CEO, CFO, CMO, and COO have that require technology support.

Even if you buy into the idea of benchmarking your IT spending, what is the right target? Spending at the average rate? Is the company's goal to be average? Using this type of benchmark suggests that the company considers IT to be only an unavoidable and unfortunate cost of doing business rather than an element of competitive strategy.

On the other hand, not all IT spending is good spending. An enterprise that wants to get the most value from IT must distinguish good spending from bad. What we really need to know is, given a particular intent, is our IT spending cost effective for realizing that intent, or is it wasteful?

You can set any IT spending target you want. If it seems that spending at the industry benchmark percentage of revenue is a good idea, then there is no reason why you can't hit that number. Virtually any CIO can cut the IT budget by 15%, 35%, or even 75% by doing less IT work or reducing its services to the rest of the company. But what is the impact of doing so? It's probably a feeling that IT can't meet the company's needs. It might mean cutting corners and incurring technical debt, which will then make it harder and costlier for the company to accomplish its IT objectives in the future. That doesn't mean it's wrong; just that it will have consequences, particularly in the digital realm.

It's important to look at *marginal* impact: an incremental one hundred livres of spend in IT might increase revenues or decrease costs in another part of the business. IT spending affects the whole of the business, even if the budget and capital plan are specific to IT.

I would rather reframe the IT spending discussion this way: Is there waste in the IT costs? If so, it should be located and eliminated. If there isn't any, then budget cuts will have an impact on the IT estate, the capabilities produced, and consequently on the rest of the organization (which may or may not be acceptable). If the IT organization is running leanly and the budget is boosted, then the increase will have the optimal positive impact. It's then a matter of choosing what impact you want IT to have.

IT should be measured by the amount of business value it creates; its initiatives should be prioritized based on the amount of value they are expected to return. Ummm . . . but what exactly do we mean by business value? I'm not sure this is clear to everyone—I've seen the definition shift as employees try to make the case for what they believe is most important.

At USCIS, for example, I had a team working with the Service Center Operations (SCOPS) business unit. I had appointed a lead from the IT side, while the head of SCOPS appointed a lead from the business side. Together the two had created a list of priorities to guide IT work. I periodically checked in and was assured that the business case for each listed item was sound.

One day I was in a senior leadership meeting where there was worried discussion about the growing backlog on processing I-90 forms (the application for green card renewal or replacement). This was deeply troubling to the agency and, it turned out, a major concern of the head of SCOPS. I knew that there was plenty IT could do to help. But when I asked the two project leads about it, they told me that it wasn't in their plans. Yes, the leads answered me, they were working on things that would produce the highest business value: improving I-90 processing just wasn't one of them.

How was it possible that they were prioritizing the work that would yield the highest business value, yet weren't doing anything about the agency's highest priority? This was a puzzle that drove me to a deeper inquiry regarding business value.

Authors Jeanne W. Ross and Peter Weill, in *IT Governance: How Top Performers Manage IT Decision Rights for Superior Results*, raise the question of how to measure business value:

> Enterprises have struggled to understand the value of their IT-related initiatives because IT cannot always be readily demonstrated through a traditional cash flow analysis. Value results not only from incremental process improvements but also from the ability to respond to competitive pressures . . . [and] it can be difficult to determine in advance how much a new capability or additional information is worth.[11]

Discussions of IT prioritization often refer to return on investment (ROI) or internal rate of return (IRR) as the basis for decisions. It's true enough that ROI is often used as a simple way to make capital investment decisions, or at least to compare investment options. But there are a number of problems with

ROI, beginning with the vagueness of its definition. ROI is certainly a return divided by an investment. But which return should be used in the calculation?

Typically, it's incremental profit. But profit, as we know, is a financial accounting concept, not an economic one. It may depend on factors such as how inventory is valued and how capital assets are depreciated. And how many years of profit should you include? Are future years discounted?

If you're trying to make decisions about which individual features to include in a product or in the maintenance activity flow for a system, then ROI becomes especially difficult to assess. How much will profit increase if we let users sort a data table by any column they want? In theory, we can measure these things,* but now that we can deliver IT capabilities at high speed and low cost, it becomes harder to justify spending the time.

We also have to admit that we don't actually know ROI when we're making investment decisions—we can only project it. Perhaps when IT was primarily a way of reducing costs, we could reliably project returns. But in the uncertain digital world, where technology is the enterprise's basis of competition, revenue generation, compliance, and customer service, returns are difficult to project. Can you estimate the return on an analytics platform, the purpose of which is to discover which product changes might increase consumption? Or estimate revenues from a product that a competitor might quickly copy?

I'm not saying that it's impossible to create business cases, just that estimates have a high cost to prepare, a very low precision, and a high expected variance—to the point where basing decisions on them can be misleading. Yes, enterprises need to make the best capital investment decisions they can, but I'll show later that there are better ways to do so than relying on low-fidelity estimates. IT now has surprisingly few of the typical capital investment characteristics.

Some Agile writers suggest using *cost of delay* as a way to prioritize features. For each proposed feature, they say, calculate how much the enterprise is losing by not having it (in terms of revenues foregone or costs not avoided). Then select the feature that has the highest cost of delay. That's not bad as a way to foster agility, but unfortunately it still depends on very uncertain projections and is subject to the same lack of clarity when we try to estimate cost.

---

* See, for example, Douglas Hubbard's *How to Measure Anything*. I think many of us are inspired by Hubbard's book but then sheepishly have to admit that we don't actually have the time or energy to actually measure everything.

What is the cost of delaying an information security initiative? How can you compare the cost of delay of a feature that would help prevent malaria with one that would reduce operational costs?

Remember too that incremental profits are not necessarily what an organization values. Sure, for a publicly traded company, we can agree that profit is a goal. There are about 5,000 publicly traded companies[12] out of about twenty-seven million businesses in the US—that's 0.02%. Or to be more reasonable, make that out of about six million businesses having more than one employee—let's say .08%.[13]

What are the others? Family run businesses are 70%–90% of global GDP and one-third of the global 500.[14] According to Associate Professor Belén Villalonga of NYU Stern School of Business, "Most companies around the world are controlled by their founders or founding families, including not only private firms but also more than half of all public corporations in the US and Europe, and more than two-thirds of public corporations in Asia."[15] Add to that the number of other businesses that are closely held private companies. In all of these the owners decide what is business value—and it's not necessarily related to profit. Business value is simply . . . what the business values.*

How about the 3,500 companies funded each year by venture capitalists (VCs)?[16] Private equity investors also have their own priorities as owners. Perhaps the most valuable result for a series A investor is that series B financing be raised at a high valuation. That often doesn't depend on profit. A VC's idea of what is valuable might also depend on where they are in the lifecycle of their fund.

There are 1.5 million nonprofits in the US, accounting for 5% of GDP.[17] What is business value in a nonprofit? Or in a government agency? Business value in DHS probably has something to do with averting terrorist incidents in America. How would you measure ROI? Even if you could, how would you make value judgments, such as whether saving ten lives is worth spending $100 million?

The point is that there is no universal currency in which business value is measured, or at least no currency that is helpful in deciding how to prioritize or fund IT investments. If there were—say ROI—then we would be able to

---

* Long story—I learned my lesson on this. Don't advise owners to divest a business unit that they like but that is losing lots of money. You heard it here.

translate all proposed investments into that currency and compare them. But there is no preordained way to compare the investment in a security device, such as a firewall (a device that protects a network), to an investment that will save ten people from malaria.

<hr/>

Actually, let's look more closely at that firewall investment. To estimate its ROI, we would have to make assumptions about:

- the probability of a hacker attack,
- the likelihood that it could be stopped by the firewall,
- the value of whatever data and system availability might be compromised by the incident,
- the possibility that some other security technique already in place wouldn't have already stopped the attack,
- the value of data that might be added later to the systems but isn't there yet,
- the cost to the company if *that* particular data is compromised,
- . . . and, well, other stuff.

It's especially hard to calculate ROI for technical IT investments such as a firewall because IT touches so many other business areas, and because it's so deeply affected by uncertainty. To make matters worse, organizations often think of such an investment as addressing one of IT's needs, rather than a business need (because IT isn't the business, right?).

Interestingly, ROI doesn't really capture the value of agility itself. If we build a first tranche of capabilities with an initial investment installment, then we have the option (but not the requirement) of investing future tranches if we later decide they have value. That is, we've bought a *call option* on the remaining tranches.

Furthermore, in developing IT capabilities we can often create latent value—the potential for value that can be harvested later. If we build capabilities that enable others, even if we have no immediate plans to follow through, we have also bought an option. If we build or buy a flexible, reusable piece of technology, even if we don't know exactly how else we might use it in the future, we've bought agility—again, an option. If we design agility into our systems, making them cheap and fast to alter, then we have purchased an option that can reduce future costs.

Drnevich and Croson discuss the economics of IT options:

> Real options is the strategy concept perhaps most directly applicable to the valuation of IT investments under uncertainty. . . . Like financial call options, for example, a real option may give the firm the ability to acquire a rent-generating resource (such as a new technology) if the resource were to become valuable, without needing to commit fully to the resource before its value-creation potential is fully known. Like financial put options, a real option may give the firm the ability to discontinue an unprofitable activity, divest a losing technology investment, or recover money invested in a past technology resource even though its current market value had dropped below its historical cost. Both options substitute for the organization's imperfect ability to predict the future when it must make strategic decisions such as market entry, positioning, or value chain configuration.[18]

Another hard-to-identify, intangible source of value is information. Agile teams deliberately structure their efforts to maximize learning; the Lean startup approach carefully makes hypotheses explicit and tests them. Every bit of learning improves our ability to cost-effectively deliver the outcomes we want, and in the process reduces our risk. In the traditional waterfall world this value was negligible, as learning wouldn't be used to change the plan, but today information value is vital.

When we consider investing in an analytics or business intelligence (BI) system, or a data warehouse or data lake we'll use for analysis, rather than painfully trying to compute a vastly imprecise ROI, we would be better off seeing the return as a combination of information value and options made possible by having that information.

What if we put resources into improving the internals of an IT system to reduce technical debt (see Chapter 5)? Perhaps we can value it as an investment to reduce future costs of development, though that will be hard to model since we don't know what we'll develop in the future. We could instead think of it as creating options (it will make us more Agile later) or mitigating risk (it will reduce the likelihood that any change made later to the system will break it). And how about the value of compliance controls? Perhaps some of the value is in the form of a risk reduction, while some of it may be seen as a portion of spending on a compliance program that in total will increase revenues or reduce costs.

A common theme runs through these alternative value sources: they become more valuable the more uncertainty there is in the environment. The value of an option increases with uncertainty. The value of risk-mitigating investments—including security investments—increases with uncertainty. Information value is higher under uncertainty. The ROI-based-on-profit approach, I'm suggesting, is progressively less applicable as we move into the digital age—an age dominated by uncertainty.

Many of these problems spring from setting up IT as an order taker, which in turn requires that the value of proposed projects be compared. But there is a different way to frame the business value discussion. Enterprise-wide objectives can be set by senior leadership, then IT can work with other business leaders to translate them into specific initiatives. They would need little business case justification, since they're based on those high-level objectives.

This cascade of objectives may be the only practical way to interpret business value, given that we can't translate different types of investments into a single currency of value. The senior leadership team turns the enterprise's ultimate goals—increasing shareholder value or curing malaria—into a set of concrete objectives in the strategy-setting process. These then become the organization's definition of business value—that is, what is valuable to the business—to be used when making lower level prioritization decisions.* By cascading objectives in this way, the enterprise helps make IT, alongside the rest of the business, responsible for business outcomes.

In the earlier SCOPS example, this was precisely the missing element. The projects being considered were dreamed up by the software users; none of them advanced the objectives of senior leadership. Nevertheless, each had a business case that demonstrated "business value" by some definition of the term. Perhaps it would reduce costs or eliminate time-wasting activities for the employee who proposed it. Each appeared to be individually justified. But

---

* See *The Art of Business Value*, where I make this case in greater detail.

because all of the available IT capacity was being used up on those work items, the organization couldn't accomplish what really mattered to it.

———————

IT investments don't just produce operational capabilities. As you embark on the digital transformation, it's important to consider their strategic benefits as well. This is difficult if you consider only the immediate cash flows the investment generates. IT investments made to cultivate new growth opportunities, for example, will be hard to fund because they'll never seem to have as good a business case as those that increase profit in existing business lines.[19] Clayton Christensen shows in *The Innovator's Dilemma: When New Technologies Cause Great Firms to Fail* that the traditional best-practice approach to valuing investments has resulted in the demise of a number of leading companies by causing them to miss the emergence of new market categories.[20]

To Drnevitch and Croson, IT adds value by changing the tradeoffs between different possible strategies:

> Our premise is that investments in IT and complementary (digitally connected) organizational capabilities fundamentally alter the set of business-level strategic alternatives and value-creation opportunities that firms may pursue, as well as change the relative attractiveness of pursuing those options on both a risk and reward basis.[21]

They note that IT's contributions are not only (in some cases) balance sheet assets, but also enablers of capabilities; they only become actual when combined with other unique capabilities of the company.[22] As a result they are difficult to copy, and through them the company can gain competitive advantages.

Ultimately, IT can provide us with the strategic value of flexibility to respond to opportunities that arise by letting us react quickly, try out innovative responses, and reconfigure our business activities.[23] It is precisely this strategic use of IT that we must focus on in our digital transformations.

PART II

Particulars

SIDE GLANCE:
HUMILITY
AND HUBRIS

How is it that someone becomes wise all of a sudden when Caesar appoints him to take care of his chamber pot?

—**Epictetus**, *Discourses*

I have so many ideas that may perhaps be of some use in time if others more penetrating than I go deeply into them someday and join the beauty of their minds to the labour of mine.

—**Gottfried Wilhelm Leibniz**, *Letters*

I have realized that as a manager, I've learned a set of behaviors that resists innovation. What does a manager do when an employee comes with a new idea? I know what I do. I say things like, "Well . . . have you thought of this? Have you thought of that? Did you talk to Gerald about it? How do you know it'll work?"

I talk like that because my superior experience adds value (I'm the manager, right?); I can often spot things that might go wrong. New ideas are risky and it's my job to protect the enterprise. I think I'm not unusual in this. An employee with a new idea is immediately on the defensive. While trying to encourage employees to be innovative, we quickly get in their way when they try to be.

I could be wrong sometimes. I don't feel bad about that. After all, an early reviewer suggested to Herman Melville that *Moby Dick* would be better without the whale.[1] Walt Disney was fired from the *Kansas City Star* because "he lacked imagination and had no good ideas," and Einstein was rejected from the Zurich

Polytechnic School.[2] Prediction is tough, especially when it's about the future, as Yogi Berra* once pointed out.

—————

There is a better way to handle innovation. Since it's now possible to try out ideas quickly, cheaply, and at low risk, I can simply encourage the employee. Instead of trying to think of things that can go wrong, I can work with the employee to design the smallest possible experiment that will give us good information as to whether the idea will work. I can help the employee interpret the data we gather and decide whether the idea will work as is, might require changes, or should be abandoned. We can decide *together* whether the idea is worth pursuing.

My job is not to be right or to know more than any employee. It's to help an employee design a data-driven approach to assessing new ideas and to develop intuition, judgment, and market intimacy skills. This doesn't mean encouraging a free-for-all where anyone can do what they want—it means building accountability for good decision making based on data and hypothesis-testing, in addition to coaching employees about how to manage risk themselves.

This is possible if I have the humility to accept that testing an idea is better than making decisions based on what I think I know.

—————

Writing a requirement is an arrogant gesture. Requirements spring from a business need. To think that we know precisely how to fill that need in an environment of complexity, bursting with uncertainty, is hubris. It's to assume we know our customers well enough to decide for them what features they desire. And to turn a business objective into a specification that, when later implemented and used, we claim will precisely satisfy that objective, is . . . well, not only arrogant but risky. To issue a command (after all, a requirement is a command) to colleagues in a business organization is presumptuous.

Of course, that's what we've been doing for decades in the IT context. And there may be valid instances; perhaps, say, within the realm of fast-moving consumer goods. Here a product manager may have such a deep grasp of the

---

* Baseball player and coach famed for his unique aphorisms. Available as a collectible bobblehead doll on eBay.

market, born of long experience with subtle toothbrush tweaking variations, that he or she can predict market activity to within a bristle or two. But will adding a "notes" field to a screen give call center reps the information they need to improve customer service and thereby increase repeat business? Requirements of this sort are exactly what we find in requirements documents.

Requirements are risky. Every time we turn an objective into a requirement we add the risk that it won't actually meet the objective, even if it's perfectly implemented. How much of a risk is it? You won't be surprised when I say it depends on the amount of uncertainty in the environment and the complexity of the process surrounding it. Hubris in our digital world has a real cost.

———————

A thought experiment—I hold in my hands a deck of cards, each with a picture on its face. I tell you that two-thirds of the cards depict Napoleon, and one-third Kutuzov, his opponent at Borodino. You have to guess, before I turn over each card, whether it's a Napoleon or a Kutuzov, and you win a livre every time you're right. What's your strategy?

Perhaps your strategy will be to guess Napoleon about two-thirds of the time. If you're really talented at the game, you'll anticipate which cards have which general and take a bunch of livres from me. At least, this is the approach of the arrogant player, who believes he has special insight that lets him know which cards feature Napoleon. He does not. The correct strategy is to admit to uncertainty and choose Napoleon 100% of the time. The expected return from this is sixty-six livres, while the expected return from "intelligent" guessing—naming Napoleon two-thirds of the time and Kutuzov one-third of the time—is only fifty-five livres. Admitting that you don't know leads to a better outcome.

This is difficult for a player to do, especially a manager or senior leader. After all, they're being paid to have special insight and make "right" decisions that lead to the best outcomes. Confidence is valued; we've been taught to proceed with our wild guesses—insights, I mean—with conviction. The prevailing culture in many organizations doesn't allow leaders to hesitate or change their minds,[3] for to do so would be wishy-washy. As Eric Ries says:

> One of the hardest assumptions to dispel is the idea that the leader is the supreme expert: The leader makes the plan, and subordinates execute it. When there is uncertainty, the leader provides definitive answers. And

if any subordinate fails to deliver, the leader metes out appropriate punishment—because failure to execute the plan is a sign of incompetence.[4]

When leaders make decisions under uncertainty that later turn out to have good consequences, we praise them for their insight. All the more so if all indications would have suggested a different course of action, but they boldly chose the path that rational actors wouldn't have taken. In retrospect, their decision seems prescient and the outcome inevitable.

But in conditions of true uncertainty, those decision makers should not be our role models. If the leader incorrectly chooses Kutuzov rather than Napoleon, there is still a one-third chance that he or she will be proclaimed a genius. And when the weather forecaster assures us there is a 90% chance it will rain tomorrow, there is still a 10% chance it won't. If it doesn't, does that mean that those who left their umbrellas at home are geniuses?

What people call requirements are actually—let's be honest—hypotheses. When a product manager dreams up a capability that customers will certainly love, this is certainly only a hypothesis. When someone decides that an IT capability should be developed for company employees to use, that person has a hypothesis that it will be valuable—specifically, that it will lead to the business outcome they desire. We must have the humility to accept that the hypothesis may turn out to be false, along with a willingness to accept evidence that it is. Arrogance, we know, leads to confirmation bias—that is, to only noticing evidence that confirms the hypothesis and discarding all else.

If we invest many livres in a hypothesis without first confirming it, then we have risked many livres. In the waterfall model, where entire IT systems were delivered in a single shipment at project's end, we had to take that risk. Agile practices now let us quickly deliver partial capabilities so we can test a hypothesis before committing to it too deeply. Based on what we learn, we can alter the hypothesis, discard it all together, or continue investing in it with more commitment.

If I'm not sure whether an Isaac Newton or an Albert Einstein bobblehead will be more popular in the market, but I can place ads on Google for both to see how many people click on each one. *A/B testing* is also a common marketing technique that's been adopted for user interface (UI) design today. If I want users to click a button and I am not sure whether it should be green or blue, I can test which one gets more clicks.

Such testing leaves room for experimenters to be surprised. With arrogance, I "require" that the button be green. With humility, I test both colors and prepare for surprises.

———————

At USCIS, our Transformation project tried to speed up the adjudication of immigration benefit requests by eliminating all paperwork—permitting applicants to file applications electronically and adjudicators to then process them in the same manner. The system designers thought deeply about how to create a UI that would speed up the entire process as much as possible. When we launched the first part of the project after a long design and development effort, we found that what used to take adjudicators fifteen minutes (when they were working with paper) was now taking an hour and a quarter. We had already built the application; it was too late to change plans. The users had surprised us.

This happens all the time in the IT world. Instead of designing screens that seemed (to us) to make sense, we could have first mocked up a few, then watched the adjudicators use them. We would have quickly discovered that some of our most basic assumptions were flawed. For example, adjudicators could flip through a pile of papers very quickly, especially if they marked key pages with sticky tabs. Scrolling through information on a screen took them longer.

More importantly, we'd assumed an adjudicator would focus on data that was most relevant to the adjudication—in particular information that had changed since the last time the agency had encountered an applicant. What we didn't realize was that because policy held the adjudicator responsible for validating all information related to an application, they preferred to step through every bit of the form and review it. This took them longer on the screens we'd built than on paper.

———————

When you adopt a Lean perspective, you have to think carefully about what it means to manage employees. In IT, for example, it's the line employees who have their hands on the technology and deliver business value—the software developers, infrastructure administrators, testers, and security engineers. Not only are they the ones who directly create value, but they're the ones who see opportunities as they arise, know what has worked and what hasn't, and have an intuitive feel for what is possible and is likely to be effective.

Managers and leaders, on the other hand, are waste. Napoleon added no value during the battle of Borodino. More precisely, managers are useful only to the extent that they facilitate the delivery of value. Their job is to create conditions in which the executors can go about their value creation, to remove impediments when they arise, and to make sure the executors know what is valuable given the company's strategic objectives. Removing impediments is an especially important part of the job; if you want delivery as soon as possible, you must make it possible for executors to deliver sooner.

This management style works best with Agile and Lean approaches; it's called *servant leadership*.[5] It's based on humility, on understanding that it's the people you lead who actually matter.

Management was once thought of as a span of control issue. The number of middle management layers depended on the number of people who needed managing. This caused fracturing and siloing—with the result that many managers needed to be involved to get anything done, and their underlings stopped transferring knowledge and sharing insights with one another. Again, this may work in a world where plans are likely to lead to success; with a good plan you can divide the work among groups in such a way that interaction is minimal.* Since execution follows the plan, such fragmentation wouldn't hurt anything. But as soon as the plan needs to change, that fragmentation becomes a liability.

Instead, IT departments—as well as other business areas—are increasingly organized as a collection of small, self-contained teams with the goal of decentralizing authority. Each team is empowered, is relatively autonomous, and has all of the skills necessary to accomplish its purpose. Each can sense changes in its market and respond to them. And because it's small and communicates face-to-face, organizational complexities are reduced; its skill mix lets it make decisions independently and act quickly.

What does this mean for you if you're the leader of a large unit within the organization? What is your role if teams under your management are meant to be autonomous? For a CIO in particular, this is a vexing question, because each

---

* For philosophy geeks: This is a lot like Leibniz's point that "the monads have no windows." In Leibniz, the monads do not actually interact with each other, they simply follow their own preordained courses that happen to look like there are interactions.

team works directly with a unit of the business, which tells the team what to work on. So who needs a CIO? Is the CIO, like Napoleon, simply a harmless figurehead?

> In the battle of Borodino, Napoleon fulfilled his function as the representative of power just as well and even better than in other battles. He did nothing to harm the course of the battle; he bowed to the more well-reasoned opinions; he caused no confusion, did not contradict himself, did not get frightened, and did not run away from the battlefield, but with his great tact and experience of war calmly and worthily fulfilled his role of seeming to command.[6]

The difference between Tolstoy's view of Napoleon and the contemporary view of a business as a complex adaptive system is that a CAS *can* be guided by its leaders. To Tolstoy, Napoleon was swept up in the forces of history and was only under the illusion that he was influencing the action before him. The leader of a CAS, on the other hand, can shape its evolution and direct it toward successful outcomes. To do so, the leader has to have the humility to understand that issuing orders from a hilltop a mile away is not effective; instead, allowing the business to evolve—while guiding and gently influencing it—is what yields the best results.

In *The Biology of Business*, Clippinger could just as well have had Napoleon in mind when he wrote that leaders have no "Archimedean vantage point," and ". . . their role cannot be extricated from, or elevated above, the fray of selection and emergence."[7]

Humility is the right attitude for a leader who realizes that he or she is caught in a world that evolves by its own logic, one that is filled with complex interdependencies and unknowns, and that's driven by the needs and wants of people and the interactions that spring from these. The humble leader recognizes that he or she has a fiduciary responsibility to deliver outcomes, yet cannot just order the world to be as he or she likes. He or she works for the complex system, rather than the other way around.

Contrast this with the hubris of Napoleon:

> Napoleon rode over the field, profoundly studying the terrain, nodding approvingly to himself or shaking his head mistrustfully, and, without informing the generals who surrounded him of that profound course of thought which guided his decisions, told them only his final conclusions in the form of orders.[8]

THE OFF-BALANCE SHEET ASSET

And as every present state of a simple substance is naturally a consequence of its preceding state, so its present is pregnant with its future.

—**Leibniz**, *Monadology*

That which rules within, when it is according to nature, is so affected to the events which happen, that it always easily adapts itself to that which is possible and presented to it.

—**Marcus Aurelius**, *Meditations*

Enterprises face a very different set of challenges than startups in an environment of rapid change. Startups have no need to transform—what is there to transform? They have no history and few external expectations, other than those they set for themselves. They haven't yet perfected the craft of bureaucracy—that delicate art of constraining themselves through rules and policies and gatekeepers. They're generally funded and owned by investors who are interested in aggressive bets and understand that entrepreneurs need to test their ideas in the market and pivot frequently until they perfect their offering.

Enterprises, on the other hand, have baggage—or to use the current term in IT, a *legacy estate*. Their challenge is to unstick themselves from their legacy and move forward into the digital world. Imagine for a moment an enterprise that serves a market well. It has optimized its costs; established great relationships with suppliers, distributors, and customers; has passionate employees; manages risk; and complies with government and industry regulations. It's a paragon of S&P 500-ness and has even had a Harvard Business School case written about it.

Such an enterprise has perfected its way of doing what it did yesterday. It has structured itself to deliver yesterday's value and has hired people who are ideal for yesterday's competitive strategy. It has developed a culture suitable for yesterday's delivery, and its processes allow it to reliably create yesterday's business value. By definition, it is perfect at its legacy.

It follows logically that this perfect enterprise isn't prepared for what it needs to do tomorrow. This is all the more true the better it is at doing what it did yesterday. And the change to tomorrow is not accretive—to morph into the company it'll be tomorrow, it will need to undo some of the doing it did yesterday, not just add more doing.

This perfect enterprise needs to not only slip gracefully into the future, but learn to dance the dance of the digital age, to dubstep or pop and lock to whatever music comes up—all while the psychotic DJ with a short attention span can't settle on a style. The digital transformation requires that the enterprise embrace nimbleness as a daily dance move.

To make things more complicated, enterprises find that yesterday's doing wasn't just a set of individual practices, but rather a complex network of interrelated processes. Of course it's hard to unstick! It's not a piece of bubblegum stuck to its shoe—it's an entire vat of bubblegum that the enterprise is trying to dance Gangnam-style in. If bubblegum is made in vats.

To focus only on the difficulties enterprises face, though, is to miss an important point. Large enterprises also have advantages in the digital world— including global distribution, worldwide support systems, brand recognition, extensive ecosystems, strong balance sheets, and predictable cash flow.[1] They have strong market positions because at one time they were innovators. If the enterprise can free itself from its legacy while taking advantage of these assets, then it's in a strong position to compete in the digital economy. But to ask it to change is to recommend it stop doing that which has made it successful.

───

Sticky legacy is especially apparent when it comes to IT, for the company's systems were also designed to fit yesterday's business. There is an unfortunate law of IT system entropy: as changes are made to systems over time, they get tangled, complex, ugly, and less maintainable (unless energy is exerted to prevent that outcome). They may be based on technologies that few IT employees remember.* They were probably designed for a day when infants weren't taught to hack into computers before their first taste of organic baby food, a day when the hacking group Anonymous was also Unknown and Unpresent.

Over time, IT systems diverge from what the company really needs—let's call that *functional debt*; as a result, legacy system users develop workarounds or simply adapt themselves to the systems. And over time, IT systems diverge from the ideal internals to support what their users see—system functions work but the code is messy, the design confused, the technological underpinnings outdated. Bugs lurk, even if they're trapped under a rock for the moment; system changes risk letting them escape to bite users. This is called *technical debt*.

The debt analogy is apt. Functional debt costs the company "interest;" workarounds are inefficient and prevent the company from seizing opportunities as they arise. Technical debt also has a cost; system changes are made increasingly more difficult and take longer to implement—never mind the risk of springing loose those bugs. Eventually such debt overwhelms the systems and prevents the company from changing. That is, at least until the debt is retired, or is paid off by investing in remediating internal flaws and bringing functionality up to date. This is what companies usually mean by "modernizing."

The debt wouldn't be a burden if nothing was changing in the business environment. The company could just keep running the systems as they are, since they're adequate for supporting the status quo. But in a dynamic business climate, the enterprise feels the effect of its bubblegum vat.

Let's define agility as an organization's ability to respond quickly—and at low cost—to new circumstances. In an uncertain environment, that ability is extremely valuable. It will increase the company's revenues while reducing its expenses; it will reduce its risks and enable it to turn surprises into opportunities.

This is, simply put, the definition of an economic asset. It's not one that appears as such on the balance sheet, but nevertheless it's an intangible asset. Whatever increases the organization's agility increases the value of this asset; whatever reduces agility impairs it or creates a liability.

---

* Someday, perhaps offshoring will have to be replaced by outsourcing to a retirement community (please don't steal that idea before I pitch the venture capitalists).

IT has been one of the greatest sources of enterprise non-agility. This is ironic, because computers are general-purpose machines: the same piece of hardware will let you run financial systems, play Solitaire, catch up on the Kardashians, and email your lawyers. The difference between your financial system and *Grand Theft Auto V* is a few bits and bytes here and there. A set of directions to a computer; how hard can it be to change? Certainly not as hard as building a new factory.

The more that the company runs on software, the easier it should be to change. And even for the stuff of IT that is not software—infrastructure and networking hardware—the cloud has given us speed. Why then have IT initiatives always taken so long?

I find it helpful to think of an enterprise's total IT capabilities as a single economic asset—the *IT asset*. It includes the organization's software systems, its infrastructure, and the devices it puts into the hands of its employees. The IT asset enables a company to conduct its business—to generate revenues and to manage costs. By definition, it perfectly performs exactly what it does today, even if that means enthusiastically generating errors; functionally, it is what it is.

The IT asset's functionality that the business sees is one thing, but its inside is another. The design of the code might be elegant and simple, or convoluted and confusing. The code might be composed of reusable building blocks that can be combined in new ways, or limited to doing only what it does today. It might be rugged and resistant to hackers, or have hidden flaws that someday will become targets.

These qualities determine how agile the IT asset is, and consequently its value. As the company tries to adapt to changing circumstances, to seize opportunities and avoid hazards, the asset's agility translates into costs and lead times. Its value isn't only in what it can do today, but also in the latent value it has in its ability to adapt to the company's future needs.

Some aspects of this asset appear on the balance sheet, but some do not— the IT asset I'm proposing is a tool for managerial decision-making, not for financial reporting. Some of the software and hardware might have been capitalized, but this asset's real value—its influence on future profits or mission accomplishment (the present value of its future cash streams)—is probably not captured as such in financial statements.

What does your enterprise do to maximize this latent value? In your governance process, is there a way to justify investments that increase agility, even if they're neutral with respect to immediate functionality? Is IT encouraged to take time when building a new capability to perfect its internals and make them more flexible? In a digital world, these questions become important to your success.

IT asset quality depends largely on technical considerations—its design and overall architecture, the code's style, and its resilience when used in unexpected ways. Some of its software components might have been bought off the shelf, some developed in house by IT, and some created by contractors working from documented requirements. Assembled piecemeal over time, some components are aging while some are new. That's to say that some are immature, while others appear now and then at family gatherings and no one quite knows what they're muttering about any more.

All of these pieces fit together to support the company's day-to-day operations. The fit can be seamless and elegant, or it can be patchwork and awkward, glued together with integration code IT had to develop. Some parts of the IT asset work well; the others are unreliable, buggy, or insecure.

Even if code is written to be agile and elegant, technical debt steals in and degrades it. This decay can be reversed by *refactoring* the code to make it more agile. This is the process of improving the code without changing what the code does. A good deal of refactoring is occurring all the time as software developers groom their IT assets. They sometimes begin creating a system with one design in mind, then alter it as needs evolve. They then go back to the code that's already working and refactor it to reflect the new design. This is an everyday part of system development.

It might not have been obvious in earlier days that these asset qualities affect its value—after all, the asset did what it needed to do, even if using it annoyed its users. It therefore made little sense to invest in retiring technical debt. Enterprises often—and quite reasonably—have preferred not to invest much in maintenance spending. This might be good reasoning in an era of stability and slow change, but in times of uncertainty, such quality improvement investments can be important for future cash flows. If the asset is well structured and its architecture is simple, then it will be easier for the company to innovate and change. But if it's convoluted and coming apart at the seams, and IT spends too much time patching it, fixing emergencies, executing manual workarounds, and sitting in meetings to discuss all that's wrong, then IT won't have the focused time available to do whatever becomes important to the business. And the asset will continue to deteriorate over time.

————

Some of the technical factors that influence the value of the asset are straightforward. Code should be readable and understandable so a developer who is unfamiliar with it can quickly determine how to change it. It should be built using contemporary tools and practices.

Some large enterprises have mission-critical IT systems written in that antique curiosity of a programming language, COBOL. They can keep those things running and believe it'll be risky and expensive to try to bring them up to date. But those old systems are also holding the company back, making it difficult to innovate and serve a digital market. That in itself is a cost and a risk.

Loose coupling is an important IT design concept with business implications. Given that IT systems are a conglomeration of many component pieces, how closely together are they bound? How much difficulty would there be in removing one piece and replacing it with a similar but better one? Would you have to make many changes to other components? If so, it will be expensive and risky to make them, as the consequences of a change will ripple through other parts of the system.

By allowing developers to work quickly, *automated tests* also add agility into the IT asset and provide a safety net. Without them, developers must work slowly and carefully to make sure their changes don't break previously deployed functionality. Automated tests are so important to today's software development techniques that one author, Michael Feathers, has proposed we simply define a legacy IT system as one that doesn't have them.[2]

————

Organizational agility is determined by nontechnical factors as well. A second intangible asset, the *organizational asset*, consists of the nontechnical resources the company has for rolling out IT capabilities. It includes its investment management, budgeting, and governance processes, for example, and the people who use or create its technological capabilities.

Outsourcing has tended to impair the value of the organizational asset. During the outsourcing wave, companies believed it would make them more agile since they could add or subtract technical talent as necessary. But the need for technologists is constant, rather than project-driven. An organization that outsources critical skills must face the overhead of the contracting process whenever it needs talent, which impedes the flow of innovation and lengthens lead times. Having the right employees with the right set of skills is critical in being able to quickly respond to change.

The organizational asset includes HR capabilities and policies that make it possible to move people between roles and retrain them, along with the ability to form people into teams to work across functional silos. It includes the company's IT investment decision process. If all such investments are overseen at a coarse level, in large batches of requirements treated as a monolithic whole, then it will be hard to change course once a given investment is underway. If the governance process is slow and involved, or if the budgeting cycle locks in decisions well in advance of execution, then agility is compromised.

The company's risk posture—not its risk tolerance, but the way it perceives, prioritizes, and manages risks—is another important factor in organizational agility. An enterprise that perceives a high risk in stasis will tend to be more tolerant of change, whereas one that perceives a high risk in the new and unknown will change much more slowly.

An organization's structure also affects its agility. Functional silos slow change down, as they require cross-silo communication and handoffs. Deep hierarchies can reduce innovation. It's the front line that tends to have the ideas, because they interact with customers; it's they who experience the pain and frustration of ineffective internal processes. Even innovations formulated at the top of a hierarchy still require information to percolate upward from the front line; this takes time and risks being out of date, as with Napoleon at Borodino.

As we erase the boundary between IT and the business, new possibilities open up for improving the organizational asset. Take T-shaped people, for example. An Agile IT team has skills in coding, testing, and securing—why shouldn't it also have business skills? These can come from people who have broad technical skills but go deep into a business realm, or people who are deep in a technical area but whose broad skill set includes business savvy. Conversely, why shouldn't business teams have technical skills?

There is a third intangible asset to consider: the company's ability to use the data in its databases. There is value in those data, but only if they can be extracted and made available to employees and managers. In the old days of IT, data were used mainly to conduct transactions and were therefore organized into the types of databases that most efficiently supported transactions. But data increasingly have informational value. The agility of your *data asset*, then, is yet another source of future profits and mission accomplishment.

Let's say the company can only access its data through reports that the technologists have prepared. The data are then useful, but if employees want to pose new questions to the data, to research new topics, they have to wait until a new report is available. The data can be made more agile by setting up a flexible analytics or business intelligence system so that employees can create their own reports or conduct ad hoc analyses—perhaps using visualization tools or artificial intelligence.

As the cloud reduces the cost of storage, enterprises are able to store lots of data even before they know exactly how they'll use it. Instead of predicting how the data will be analyzed and organizing it to support those analyses, we can now take the simpler route of dumping all kinds of data into a type of repository called a *data lake*.

The data can be in virtually any form—data from Oracle databases, ERP systems, internet data sources, scanned documents, and video feeds, for example. Software tools can automatically search through text, determining what sentiments it expresses and extracting relationships between the people it mentions. Machine learning software can even scan images and ascertain which famous people appear in them.

With these increasing quantities of data come questions of privacy and security. What I'm calling the data asset includes the controls the organization puts around its data. This asset is agile to the extent that it both restricts access from those who shouldn't have it and enables access for those who should.

The IT world has been talking about "big" data for a few decades now. But what I am getting at is that big data has both an immediate value and a latent value. There is what we can do with it now, and also the agility we can build into the asset by making it available in a flexible way to support innovation and discovery.

Each of these three assets—technical, organizational, and data—has immediate value in generating cash flows today, and latent value in generating cash flows in the uncertain future. Together these assets reinforce one another to provide nimbleness that enables organizations to seize opportunities as they arise and to create opportunities through innovation.

The three assets work together in reducing lead times. The organizational asset determines how long the enterprise will spend in planning, formulation, and investment management. The technical asset determines how quickly it can create and deploy capabilities. And the data asset determines how easily it can access the data that those capabilities depend on.

Unfortunately, our traditional IT approach has often reduced the value of these assets. Agility comes from the coordination of the three assets and suffers when there are arms-length handoffs between IT and the business. There are also a few persistent beliefs we've held that have worked against agility.

The first is the conventional wisdom that using commercial off-the-shelf (COTS) software is preferable to building capabilities in house. The theory held that building software was risky; it took longer than planned, cost more than planned, and resulted in inferior products. By buying pre-existing products the company could save money, reduce its risk, acquire software that already implemented best practices, and deploy its capabilities more quickly.

But . . . the value equation has again changed as we move into the digital era, where uncertainty, complexity, and rapid change force us to think differently about that tradeoff. To understand why, we have to more closely examine what it is we're getting when we buy COTS software. In *The Cathedral and the Bazaar*, Eric Raymond makes the case that with software, its sale value (value as a final good) is much less important than its use value (value as an intermediate good).[3]

Although we often think of off-the-shelf software as if it were a final good—having the characteristics of a manufactured product like a car—all evidence shows that its value is primarily in how it's used. COTS software must be adapted to the company's needs—through configuration, customization, and additional code integrated with it—before it becomes valuable. It must also be constantly changed to keep up with changing circumstances. Raymond points out that:

When a software product's vendor goes out of business (or if the product is merely discontinued), the maximum price consumers will pay for it rapidly falls to near zero . . . the price a consumer will pay is effectively capped by the expected future value of vendor service.[4]

He concludes "software is largely a service industry operating under the persistent but unfounded delusion that it is a manufacturing industry."[5] Buying off the shelf commits us to an ongoing stream of payments to the vendor and to higher costs for making changes when we try to do it ourselves. And the vendor's roadmap for the product is unlikely to match our future needs. COTS products make our IT asset less agile.

What is really happening here is that when we buy off the shelf, we don't really own the same kind of asset that we do when we build it ourselves. We don't own the internals of the COTS product, so we cannot change them at will to keep up with changes in our business, and we can't use pieces of it as building blocks to create other capabilities. Building and buying are not two choices that refer to the same kind of product.

On the other hand, changes in software building techniques have reduced its costs and risks. When we now build software, we do so by incorporating third-party building blocks—usually open-source components or cloud services—that reduce the amount of code we have to write. We organize our code using well-understood design principles and test it using powerful test tools. We build in increments to reduce risk and gain speed.

The balance has therefore shifted to make building more attractive. But this is not to say that COTS is never appropriate. There are things that companies do that are so standard and unchanging that buying software to automate those functions is relatively low risk. Accounting software is a good example; the rate of change in accounting techniques is slow, but accounting functionality and principles remain complex.

A second area where we have often sacrificed agility is in outsourcing the delivery of IT capabilities. In many ways, outsourcing software development combines the worst characteristics of both building and buying. The elegance and simplicity—read, the agility—of the IT asset suffers as parts are created by different organizations. It's the contractor's employees who become familiar with the code and are most able to make changes to it. The contractor's incentive is not to worry much about technical debt, especially since any slowness in changing the system in the future will probably bring more revenue.

According to Forsgren and her *Accelerate* coauthors, low-performing companies are more likely to report that their software has been developed by an outsourcing provider.[6]

Perhaps the root cause of the COTS and outsourcing mistakes is that we often think of IT systems as if they were products or, as Raymond says, "manufactured goods."[7] We look at our IT asset as a collection of independent products with some glue that binds them together. We then readily think we can buy some of these products or outsource their creation, rather than building them internally.

This is one reason I suggest thinking of the entire collection of IT capabilities as a single, unified asset that lets your company run its business. When you compose this asset from independent products, you get an overall architecture that lacks the coherence, simplicity, and elegance that makes change easier. You can't reuse pieces from one of these products to create another. Each component product changes independently—there is high overhead in trying to coordinate changes. Simply put, they limit your choices.

The trend instead is to design the entire IT asset as a collection of very small, custom-built components called *microservices*, each of which can be reused as part of a number of IT capabilities. Just as DevOps lets us manage a seamless flow of capability creation, our IT systems architecture now consists of a seamless blend of components. It has become difficult to say where one product ends and another begins. The digital world is one of continuous, rather than discrete, elements.

———

IT strategy, then, is a matter of incrementally investing in these three assets— rather than one of investing in projects or products. That older way of thinking led us to make large commitments rather than seeing the value of small, incremental changes to the IT estate. It also led us to ignore the complex interactions between IT systems. Finally, it took our attention off a very important source of business value—the agility of our infrastructure and its ability to meet emerging business needs in a fast-changing environment.

Instead, digital transformation requires you to take a holistic view of your enterprise's IT and organizational states. When you do, your transformational process becomes low risk: it's incremental and consists only of improvements to assets you already own.

6

RISK AND OPPORTUNITY

Tragedies and comedies are written with the same letters.
—**Democritus** cited by Aristotle, *On Generation and Corruption*

Some white-haired old man, with many rings on his fingers, will come along and shake his head, and say to me, "Listen to me, child, yes, one ought to practice philosophy, but one should also keep one's head." This is sheer stupidity.
—**Epictetus**, *Discourses*

Risk is the possible *negative* consequences of the uncertain future, while opportunity is the possible *positive* consequences of the uncertain future. Agility is the organizational characteristic that determines whether the uncertain future becomes one or the other—or simply a benign passage of time.

For those who worry about risk, there is much to worry about. Startups arise suddenly and disrupt industries. Customers are fickle and change their tastes quickly, sometimes within the few moments it takes to read a tweet. Countries Brexit or dismiss treaties they have previously signed. Regulations are put in place and then rolled back. And technology changes in nanoseconds—when you pause for a bio-break your programmers may begin studying a new programming language you've never heard of; when you return they've already rewritten your IT systems. Both the business and technology environments are uncertain and unstable—risky, many would say.

Uncertainty, however, doesn't always lead to negative consequences. On the contrary, it also opens up opportunities. When an unforeseen event occurs, what determines whether it's an opportunity or a hazard? Yup—agility. "It is possible to prepare for unknown risks," reads a Boston Consulting Group (BCG) blog post,[1] to which I would add that it's possible to prepare for unknown opportunities as well. The post goes on: "[Our] research has demonstrated that highly adaptive companies outperform less adaptive companies in periods of economic turmoil."[2]

Let's say you spend $10 million to build a factory to produce bobblehead dolls of Sir Isaac Newton, everyone's favorite scientist. Suddenly Albert Einstein announces some theory of relativity and the market for Isaac Newton bobbleheads immediately dries up. Has your $10 million investment been sucked into the proverbial black hole?

Yes, if your factory can only produce Queen Anne-era Cantabrigian scientist dolls. But if it's agile enough to quickly retool to produce Einstein dolls, then your investment becomes worth even more: you'll be first to enter the relativity market and have a first-accelerator advantage. In other words, designing the factory to be agile from the start lowers your risk—you are able to deal with changes that take place in the uncertain future.

Given an uncertain future, anything that increases your cost of change also increases your risk. Anything that decreases the former also decreases the latter. Reducing the cost of change is the definition of agility. To put it bluntly: risk *is* lack of agility.

Another equation: "Risk management is strategy," BCG says, "and strategy is risk management."[3] In some cases, they can barely be distinguished. Let's say you choose to cross over from the bobbling head market to that of those cats waving their paws up and down—the ones you see in many Japanese restaurants. Is your decision to build a bobblepaw* cat a strategic product extension? Or is it mitigating the risk of the bobblehead market drying up? Or of competitors moving more quickly into the bobblepaw market? There really is no distinction. Risk management is just a different way of looking at strategy.

There is risk in both stasis and change; risk in competitive actions and in passively responding to competitors' actions. An analysis of the one hundred companies having the largest stock price drops from 1995–2004 showed that

---

* They're called *maneki neko*, not bobblepaws. Poetic license.

only thirty-seven were hurt by financial risks, while sixty-six were hurt by strategic risks—including competitors' actions, for example.[4]

An enterprise's goal is not to eliminate risk, but to use it for competitive advantage. If the enterprise could, say, put in place robust automated controls to reduce risk—seizing opportunities more aggressively as a result—then it could also seize market share. If it could eliminate controls that slow it down without effectively mitigating risk, it could achieve a speed and cost advantage. And if it could assess risk better than its competitors, making better bets as a result, it would wind up ahead.

The cloud, DevOps, digital transformation—all of these come with techniques for increasing business agility, thereby reducing risk. Yet enterprises sometimes hesitate to adopt them because their leaders perceive risk in the unknown. It's an interesting kind of risk: one where we don't really know what the risk is. Our fear is of a second order: the risk that there might be a risk.

In another USCIS incident, a number of us met to discuss the severe problems we were having with the performance of a large contractor. At one point, someone suggested we start a new request for proposal (RFP) to replace the contractor. "Too risky," said one of the more senior executives. "We don't know what kind of a contractor we'll wind up with or how good they'll be."

I've heard many variations of this line of thought. In this case, we had a contractor who had a 100% chance of performing poorly (since it was already doing so), yet the perceived risk of working with an unknown one somehow seemed to be higher. It's equally strange that some organizations are afraid of Agile and DevOps practices, as these were invented as a way to reduce risk. Ditto for the cloud, which eliminates the risks of managing onsite infrastructure.

I've had conversations with security experts in the government and at large commercial enterprises where someone will ask, "Is the cloud secure enough?" It is, but this is the wrong question. What they should be asking is, "Where will my security posture be better—in the cloud or in my on-site datacenter?" The framing of this question reveals a lot about fear of the new. In my role at DHS I found the decision easy, by the way. The cloud clearly enabled us to build a much more robust security architecture.

Ask any information security specialist if they're happy with their security posture in their datacenter:

"No way. Too many people have privileged access;* we have too many insecure legacy platforms; we don't patch often enough; our firewall rules are too complex; production systems aren't reviewed often enough . . ." and on and on.

"How about moving to the cloud, then?"

"Well, that would be risky . . ."

———————

There's a pattern here: we tend to attach too much weight to the risk of the new and too little weight to that of the status quo.

In fact, this is an instance of a common cognitive bias, described in a 1988 article by William Samuelson and Richard Zeckhauser, "Status Quo Bias in Decision Making."[5] The authors' experiments showed that people disproportionately decide to stick with the status quo when presented with alternatives. And in a 2016 *Psychology Today* blog, Rob Henderson wrote, "Status quo bias is a cognitive bias that explains our preference for familiarity. Many of us tend to resist change and prefer the current state of affairs."[6]

Status quo bias was further explored by Daniel Kahneman, Jack L. Knetsch, and Richard H. Thaler in their paper, "Anomalies: The Endowment Effect, Loss Aversion, and Status Quo Bias."[7] They relate status quo bias to a phenomenon called the endowment effect—the tendency of people to give a higher weighting to things they already have when making decisions.

What at first seems like fear of the new is perhaps better thought of as an emotional preference for what we already have. The effect is stronger the more choices we're confronted with (think of all the options available in the cloud!), and is stronger the longer we've held the object we may be giving up. It reminds me of those groovy old COBOL mainframe systems that have been around since hippies occupied Golden Gate Park during the Summer of Love. Hard to give up, right?

There are all sorts of risks in today's business technology environment—things for managers and leaders to worry about. There is risk that a large IT investment won't return its intended business benefits. There is risk that a dis-

---

* That is, they are given special access to systems so that they can perform administrative tasks that are not common. These people are usually IT employees, or perhaps business people who manage the access of other users.

ruptive startup will shake up the industry. Or that a hacker will steal sensitive customer data. What about a competitor thinking of a brilliant idea first? Then there's risk that costs will spiral out of control. Or that a new technology will make the current infrastructure obsolete.

I could go on and on. There are so many risks it's a wonder that an enterprise can do anything at all. But that's exactly the point—the biggest risk is not change, but stasis. Or as the Marine Corps doctrine dryly puts it, "Risk is equally common to action and inaction."[8] Unless you're sure that your enterprise is already prepared to meet all of the aforementioned risks, the status quo is a terrible place for you to be, and the risk of the new should seem negligible compared to the urgency of change.

To be very clear, I'm not suggesting that companies change their risk tolerance—if anything, I think they should be *more* risk averse. There has been persistent confusion in the literature of digital transformation, with writers suggesting that companies need to become more comfortable with taking risk, that they should consider failure to be a good thing . . . just another learning opportunity. I'm talking about comments such as, "We need to encourage risk taking and quirkiness" in Jim Highsmith's book *Adaptive Leadership*.[9] Yes, I'm all for quirkiness. But do we really want to encourage risk-taking? I think Highsmith doesn't really mean what he means. He is perhaps thinking of Xerxes, poised to invade Greece at the Hellespont:

> If you were to take account of everything . . . , you would never do anything. It is better to have a brave heart and endure one half of the terrors we dread than to [calculate] all of the terrors and suffer nothing at all . . . Big things are won by big dangers."[10]

But business leaders have a fiduciary duty *not* to take on big dangers, though there is a lot to be said for proceeding with confidence once a decision has been made (it didn't work out too well for Xerxes, by the way). The miscommunication, I think, comes from using old terminology and mental models to describe the new ideas. When a digital transformation writer says that it's important to "fail fast" and encourage failure, what they mean is that it's a good thing to try experiments and abandon them if the results aren't the desired ones, or to change direction frequently if change is warranted.

Experimentation and changes of direction, however, are tactics to *reduce* risk. Instead of committing to an investment such as building a product, choosing a technology, or launching a change to a digital service (all risky), a more Agile approach is to make a smaller commitment to an experiment first, then gauge whether the larger investment will be effective. It's a case of buying information to reduce risk. If it turns out that the larger investment isn't a good idea, then the experiment was not a failure but a success; it gave us critical information that let us avoid making a bad investment.

So please do not fail. And if not failing works out well as a strategy for you, please tell people you read about it here.

The experimental approach can also reduce the risk of fixating too early on one idea when better ideas might be available. Experiments can be rigged to try a few different innovative solutions, then compare the results. If one idea turns out to be better than the others, then testing alternatives wasn't a failure—it was a success at inexpensively buying information to reduce risk and make a good decision. As Yogi Berra said when giving directions to his house: "When you come to a fork in the road, take it." Experimentation encourages innovation by allowing ideas to be tried out, then vetted by finding Yogi's house.

Experimentation is a powerful way to avoid analysis paralysis. Since there is a cost of delay, it's often better to proceed on a small scale with a reversible decision, then quickly pivot if it doesn't work out. The cost of the effort spent going down the unsuccessful path is likely to be less than the cost of a long analysis, and the conclusion is more certain. Proceeding quickly with reversible decisions *reduces* the risk of being late to market. That's success, not failure.

You can also think of the experimental approach as a strategy of doubling down on winners. Experimentation allows us to place small bets on a portfolio of possible winners. When we find the odds on one particular idea increase, then we raise that bet.

Doubling down, by the way, is much more than a cliché—it's the actual strategy in blackjack. If you're dealt cards that add up to ten or eleven, then the only correct strategy is to double your bet. This is hard for many people to get used to—they view doubling down as optional. But in fact, over the long run, if you want your odds to come close to being even with the house, you *must* take advantage of the opportunity to double down when the cards look good. In other words, doubling down on likely winners in your "portfolio" of blackjack hands is a way of playing your cards to *reduce* risk.

The experimental, tentative decision technique is neither about failing fast nor taking more risks. As Highsmith says, "Traditional teams attempt to drive out uncertainty by planning and analysis. Agile teams tend to drive out uncertainty by developing working software in small increments and then adjusting."[11] Why then does he advise taking risks?

In a predictable world, perhaps it's right to consider anything new and unknown to be risky. In a world of uncertainty and change, however, anything old and known is risky. It's risky as well to blindly follow a plan, because we know that the world is changing and our plan is based on what we knew yesterday. This is difficult to accept, because plans have always been our way of reducing risk. Today, though, the unexpected remains unexpected even for careful planners.

The more risk-averse you are, the more excited you should be about digital transformation, even if it's frightening because it's new. Frightening isn't the same as risky.

<hr />

It turns out that people are pretty terrible at assessing probabilities and risk. In my last book, *A Seat at the Table*, I cited several examples to make this point—examples that I love because even knowing the right answer I still can't convince myself it is right.

The first example had to do with the TV game show *Let's Make a Deal*, in which the contestant is asked to choose one of three doors. Behind one, the contestant is told, is a car the contestant will win if he or she guesses correctly. Once the contestant guesses, the host opens one of the other doors to show that there's no car behind it. He then points out that two closed doors remain—the one the contestant chose and the third one—and asks if the contestant wants to switch doors. Since there are now only two doors, each seems to have a 50% chance of hiding the car, so it doesn't matter, right? But the correct strategy is *always* for the contestant to switch doors—doing so doubles his or her chances of winning.[12] Our intuition hesitates to accept that, even when it's carefully explained.

Another example that I cited looks at probability in the world of disease. Let's say you're tested for a rare disease that occurs in one out of every one thousand people. The doctor informs you that the test is 99% accurate: that is, if you have the disease, the test will be positive 99% of the time, and if you don't have it, the test will be negative 99% of the time. Unfortunately, the test comes back positive. How worried should you be? Not very, it turns out. With these parameters, the chance that you actually have the disease turns out to be only about 9%.[13]

We have a strong tendency to identify risk in all the wrong places and miscalculate the likelihood of outcomes. Traditional project management, for example, leads us to believe that projects have cost, schedule, and scope risks. A project manager following Project Management Body of Knowledge (PMBOK®) best practices will keep a risk register and make plans for mitigating those risks.

But these delivery risks are not the right risks to be concerned about. The real risks are (1) the risk of not accomplishing our business objectives, and (2) the risk of not accomplishing them in the quickest, most cost-effective way. To those I'll add (3) the risk of unintentionally exceeding the budget. Cost, schedule, and scope are at best only proxies for these real concerns.

(1) The Risk of Not Acomplishing our Business Objectives

If your goal is to increase the number of cases each employee can process in a day, say from seventy to one hundred, and you're willing to spend a million livres to achieve that objective, then the risk is that you'll spend your million livres and not achieve the objective.

If you take that objective and translate it into a set of requirements for technologists to implement, then you've added another risk—the risk that the requirements you've chosen won't actually accomplish the objective. Yet that's exactly how the traditional model proceeds; it does little to mitigate this risk, since you don't find out whether your requirements have succeeded until the project is over and you've spent all your money.

You can reduce the risk by taking the Lean startup approach and treating the so-called requirement as a hypothesis: "I believe that if we implement these features, then the result will be to increase cases from seventy per day to one hundred." Then you'll test the hypothesis, often with only a fraction of the total spend of the project. Based on the results of your test you can either modify the requirement or abandon it altogether. *That* is risk mitigation.

You can further mitigate this risk by using DevOps to quickly release one capability at a time to users. You can then see the objectives being accomplished as development proceeds; in the prior example, you can see the number of cases continually increase from seventy. With every released feature, you're decreasing the risk of not accomplishing your objective. What better risk mitigation could you ask for?

(2) The Risk of Not Accomplishing Them in the Quickest, Most Cost-Effective Way

With the old waterfall approach, it was almost certain that you were not accomplishing objectives in the quickest, most cost-effective way. The waterfall, remember, actually increased risk by encouraging feature bloat. It required costly upfront time to prepare the requirements and to plan the project before delivering any value. And it increased costs because testing came at the end, when it was the most time-consuming to fix problems (see Figure 4: Cost to Fix a Defect Versus Feedback Time).

Fortunately, your toolkit now includes a better way to manage this risk as well. With an Agile approach you can begin delivering value right away, evolving the plan as you proceed. You reduce cycle times and eliminate waste by looking at the entire value stream, both inside and outside of IT. All of these reduce the risk that you won't accomplish your objective in the quickest, most cost-effective way.

(3) The Risk of Inadvertently Exceeding Budget

In the waterfall approach, we treated scope as fixed ("required") and continued a project until either the scope had been completed or the project had been terminated as a failure. Because the project had to continue until the scope was complete, there was a high risk of exceeding budget. That was precisely what happened on many projects.

When you use the Agile approach, you get results constantly throughout the process, prioritized by their effect on the desired outcome. As a result, if the budget runs out you can simply stop the project—it has already delivered most of its value. Or you could decide to increase the budget and produce more impacts. You have the choice.

Disaster! An IT system has stopped working! Bobbleheads are bobbling in vain—they can't find their way to the people who want to buy them. The warehouse is filling up with rows and rows of grinning, nodding superheroes and politicians. The CEO, caught unprepared before his first nespresso of the day, angrily texts the CIO demanding justice for the homeless bobbleheads. Two hours later they still aren't moving—horizontally, that is. What a terrible reflection on the quality of the IT systems!

Or is it? Availability costs money and fluctuates uncertainly. At some point the company probably made decisions about how much to invest in system availability. Perhaps it was willing to accept three nines of availability (99.9%) rather than spending the incremental livres it would have cost to achieve four nines. Three nines means that the system is expected to be unavailable about nine hours a year. If the bobbleheads have been bobbling futilely for two hours now, is there an availability problem?

We simply don't know. Over the long term we're expecting about nine hours of outages, so this two-hour period may only be a part of that total duration. If today is January 25th and the system has been offline for two hours this early in the year, does that mean that it'll be down for twenty-four hours over the year (clearly unacceptable)? And does availability of three nines mean it will *predictably* be down for nine hours during the year? Wouldn't it be strange if we hit that number exactly? Shouldn't we expect some variation above and below the third nine? In that case, what if today's outage lasted eleven hours? Is that OK?

The answer to all of these questions is that, at the moment, this outage is statistical noise.* If the company reasoned correctly when it set a target of three nines, then everyone should stay calm. It merely confirms that the company saved money by not making its system more available than planned.

"Something must be done!" the CEO texts the CIO all in caps. A CIO who understands probabilities should relax and finish their breakfast.

Many risks are managed by putting controls in place. This is especially important when the organization has to fulfill compliance requirements such as SOX, HIPAA, PCI, and FISMA. Sooner or later the auditors will come around and try to verify the controls. The organization that is practicing good digital hygiene will have a good story to share with them.

In the digital world, controls are automated to the greatest extent possible. Automated controls are more reliable than manual ones and are more efficient to apply. They leave an audit trail, and we can take advantage of cheap storage to retain vast quantities of auditing information for as long as

---

* I'm over-simplifying. We can actually calculate a revised probability of exceeding our target given the new information that it has been down.

necessary. Because automated controls are applied continuously (rather than just periodically), technologists can work quickly, knowing that they're always compliant. In the DevOps world, controls, therefore, speed up work rather than slow it down.

Security controls, for example, can constantly test a system's security as it's being built. If a technologist makes a mistake that creates a vulnerability, the tests spot it right away and provide feedback with which the technologist can immediately fix the problem (and learn from it). When the system is finished, there is no need for a long period of security testing and validation; it has already passed its tests. As a result, lead times are shortened.

Automated controls can be substituted for manual ones in many more areas beyond information security. Cost controls can be put in place in the cloud to limit spending and ensure that infrastructure is tagged with accounting cost categories. Privacy controls can be used to restrict access to data. Approval workflows can be set up where necessary—although often even the approvals can be automated. In the government we had to comply with section 508 of the Rehabilitation Act, making sure that all systems were accessible for users with disabilities. We found that most checks for accessibility could also be automated.

Let me illustrate how controls can speed up delivery with an example that was at one point controversial. It involves the separation of duties between software developers and system operators (those who can make changes to production systems), previously considered to be an essential control. A developer who created code had to give it to an operations specialist, who would then validate that it was production-ready. This meant checking that testing had been completed, that users were ready to receive the new features, and that the deployment process could be completed with minimal risk.

In a mature DevOps process, however, deployments are automated. Many organizations simply permit the developer to "press the deploy button" without having to hand the code off to someone else. At first this seemed to violate the principle of separation of duties, but many auditors have realized that the automated DevOps process actually has better safeguards.

First, the automated process can ensure that the code has passed all of its tests before it's deployed. Since developers can deploy quickly and freely, they're able to deploy smaller bits of code more often. This reduces the risk of defects and the impact of changes on users. Every change is tracked in the version control system and can be audited. The testing process—which again must pass before the code is deployed—includes security and compliance tests. Many delivery teams also require code, after it's written, to be immediately reviewed by a peer developer. Better equipped to spot problems than an ops specialist, this person then provides feedback through an automated system (again, so it can be audited).

The automated controls, in this case, make for a much faster process and increase control. We can have our donuts and eat them too.*

Entering the digital world doesn't really mean taking more risks, though some people speak of it that way. It's rather a matter of correctly understanding what the risks are, then relying on fast feedback and hard data to mitigate them in a different way than we have in the past. Properly understood, fear of the new is not a risk at all.

The job of the change agent becomes much easier when you stop suggesting that your enterprise take more risks. Instead, you can carefully identify the real risks and craft an Agile strategy to manage them.

---

* If you are confused by the proverb, you are not alone. The original sense was as in the 1546 version: "Wolde you bothe eate your cake, and have your cake?" In other words, you can't continue to have it after you eat it. In Iceland they say, "You cannot both blow and have flour in your mouth." I don't understand that either.

GOVERNANCE AND INVESTMENT MANAGEMENT

Is reality exhausted by what is, or does it leave room for all that could be?
—**Susan Neiman**, *Evil in Modern Thought*

We do not desire a thing because we judge it to be good; on the contrary, we call the object of our desire good, and consequently the object of our aversion bad.

—**Baruch Spinoza**, *Ethics*

An enterprise wants to direct its resources to investments that will deliver the most value. In Chapter 4 I discussed business value in the context of the value we can expect IT investments to generate. This chapter will look at how to decide which IT activities to fund in order to garner that value.

IT investment management has been seen as a process of weighing the merits of a proposed IT initiative, as expressed in a business case, and making a go or no-go decision. But in the digital age this approach is riskier than necessary—it doesn't take full advantage of Agile and Lean revolutions. It's also too slow, as it depends on accumulating the materials to support a business case and then running that through a series of hurdles. You can instead use speed as a way to improve your decision-making and extract more value from each investment.

In the traditional model, we've seen that the business proposes initiatives, then IT uses its limited capacity to execute on them. Demand always exceeds supply, since the enterprise is filled with creative people who are constantly finding friction in their work and dreaming up improvements. There is a constantly growing backlog of IT requests waiting to be served.

Some of those are small and will be handled through some low-overhead prioritization process, often drawing on IT resources set aside in the budget for ongoing maintenance. Larger requests often take the form of a project to deliver a new IT system or make substantial changes to an old one; these are generally treated through a capital budgeting process. There may be a formal governance process to vet proposals and ensure that they're aligned with the company's strategy and business needs. For an investment large enough to cross this threshold, senior leaders are often very interested in overseeing or at least monitoring its progress. I'll refer to these more formal processes as *investment management and oversight*, and they will be the main focus of this chapter.

In *IT Governance*, authors Ross and Weill propose five archetypes for how companies might set up their governance: business monarchy, feudal, federal, duopoly, and anarchy.[1] These names offer a good feel for the legalistic spirit of their processes. They're governance in the sense of government, largely centralized (with the exception of anarchy, which, you'll not be surprised to learn, is discouraged) and heavy-handed.

Notwithstanding Weill and Ross's menu, I've found that governance decisions in an enterprise more closely fit a different archetype—something I described in *A Seat at the Table* as being like a Star Chamber.* Picture a group of hooded figures around a table in a dark room lit by a bright bulb overhead that makes it difficult to see their faces. Petitioners come with their investment proposals, and the Star Chamber renders judgment, awarding them either the boon of suffering through a large IT initiative, or condemning them to another year of workarounds and static websites.

In *Real Business of IT: How CIOs Create and Communicate Value*, George Westerman and Richard Hunter describe a classic Star Chamber process:

---

* I had to look up "Star Chamber"—it was one of those terms I vaguely knew of and that felt like it applied here. It turns out that the Star Chamber was a British court from around 1487 to 1641, which became known for its arbitrary and subjective judgments, as well as its secrecy.

The basics of the process involve project sponsors (1) developing a formal proposal that incorporates estimates benefits, risks, and resource requirements and (2) submitting the proposal to decision makers who select preferred investments from the proposals. . . . In a transparent investment process, opportunities meet a well-defined prioritization process designed to identify winning proposals.[2]

I love their use of the expression "winning proposals." It makes it clear that this is about choosing who gets rewarded—it's about passing judgment.

———————

Yet the Star Chamber has a fiduciary duty; it must decide how to deploy the organization's resources to get a good return. It must oversee each initiative, again to fulfill its fiduciary responsibility, making sure the money is well spent and stopping the initiative if it's not going well. The organization must have a well-defined process for making these decisions, as it will probably have to satisfy compliance requirements and auditors—and it will certainly have to satisfy its owners.

I'd like to suggest that there are better ways to accomplish this, if we're willing to accept that uncertainty and complexity overwhelm traditional planning and that IT is not a passive, contractor-like fulfiller of requirements. In Star Chamber governance, the hooded figures hand IT its projects, selected from among those proposals that bubble up through the business side of the organization. Each investment decision is based on a proposed battle plan that is unlikely to survive first contact with bits and bytes and changing business needs. In the digital environment, Star Chamber governance places far too much reliance on a business case and plan that are prepared in advance.

Governance is about control, and it's interesting to think about what that means in an environment of high uncertainty. In a sense, we clearly cannot control something that is subject to high degrees of chance, complexity, risk, and changing objectives. Nevertheless, intuitively we know that there is some kind of responsibility to keep the train on the tracks, to make the best possible decisions given the information at hand, to steer with an eye on getting the best outcomes for the enterprise—and that this can either be done well or done poorly.

There is a slight logical gap in the way this duty is exercised in the Star Chamber model. The governance body should be ensuring that the approved proposals are those that will do the most to advance the company's objectives. But the Star Chamber is passive. It can only pass judgment on proposals that are presented to it. Isn't it possible that some objectives, or parts of objectives, wouldn't happen to be included in proposed projects? And how do they know those projects that are proposed represent *the best way* to accomplish the objectives?

Since the Star Chamber invests in a specific plan and its business case, neither should be allowed to change during execution. That's the connection between investment management and investment oversight: the goal of oversight is to make sure a project doesn't vary much from its approved plan. Unfortunately, that also means that it resists Agile adaptation as circumstances change. You can't play Agamemnon and have your donuts too, as they say.*

Is the Star Chamber really taking the best care of the company's resources? It's certainly not lean. Since a proposal might not be selected, the work the proposers did to justify it and the work the Star Chamber does to evaluate it might be wasted. Then there is the waste of even assembling the Star Chamber to make the decisions: proposals wait until the room is set, the spooky figures are convened, and the hooded robes come back from the cleaners. Remember that wait time is a classic source of waste in Lean thinking—a step that necessarily extends lead times.

The business case the Star Chamber evaluates is for the initiative as a whole, a monolithic set of requirements. You might say it's a coarse-grained decision rather than a fine-grained one. It assumes that value is in the sum of the parts—that all those requirements add up to a single unit of value to be assessed. It's analogous to a car; you can't assess the value of its steering wheel alone—it only becomes valuable when it's combined with other parts to make a complete vehicle.

To some extent this does make sense for IT governance as well. After all, an online shopping system, for example, isn't viable unless it includes components that can take orders, handle payments, fulfill orders, and allow refunds. But you'd be surprised how minimal a product can be and still remain viable. And IT can often quickly roll out a great deal of functionality by reusing components they have already built for other purposes or by assembling components that are available in the cloud or from the open-source community.

---

* They don't really. I do. See epigraph to Chapter 3.

It's better to think of an IT initiative as delivering a number of individual capabilities, each having a different value, and some of which may need to be done in combination. Let's say that investments A and B both include a number of features. Even if we decide to prioritize investment A over its counterpart based on business case assessment, that doesn't mean every feature in investment A is more valuable than those of investment B. Perhaps we should build four features from A, two from B, another one from A, three more from B, and on from there. An Agile approach lets us do so.

Coarse-grained investment decisions sacrifice many advantages that fine-grained, Agile techniques offer. The coarse-grained approach made sense in the waterfall world that delivered a single, monolithic system at the end of each project. But in the Agile world, we can deploy individual capabilities to users as they are ready. We can work on individual requirements rather than a large batch, which we know from Lean theory will increase lead time. Coarse-grained governance results in a fixed scope, making it hard to remain flexible. It groups together work items that might individually have different priorities. As we strive to increase the agility of our IT processes, it would be a shame to forfeit their accompanying business agility.

The traditional project plan tries to manage risks by itemizing them in a register and proposing a mitigation plan for each one. Risks are mitigated to the extent necessary to bring the plan back into line—in other words, to adjust the initiative so the initial business case and plan are maintained. But the uncertainties in the IT domain go deeper—it might be that the very core of the plan needs to change.

Risks can only be itemized if they're known. The problem is that true uncertainties—unknown unknowns—are probably what will have the deepest impact on the initiative. And the number of unknown unknowns is staggering in the digital world. They range from things we can't know (Will a competitor suddenly release a new product tomorrow?) to things we just don't know (Is a hacker about to compromise our system? Is there a bad piece of code in our system that's about to be triggered when we add the next feature?).

Yes, you can incorporate risk into the traditional investment process by risk-adjusting the discount rate. But even this benign and textbook-adherent way of managing capital budgeting misses an important point. It assumes, incorrectly, that we have to make a single decision regarding our investment *right now*. But we don't; agility allows us to make an IT investment in stages. We can choose to risk a smaller amount to begin the project, then gain further information that will help us make decisions about future stages. Such an approach is called *metered funding*, *staged investments*, or more broadly, *discovery-driven planning*.

Venture capital firms practice metered funding—series A investments usually fund a startup as it develops its products, hires its first set of employees, and performs its initial marketing and branding activities. Series B usually occurs once the product is in the marketplace; it's used to scale up and establish a market position. Series C occurs when the company has been proven successful and is looking to introduce new products, grow more substantially, or prepare to be acquired or conduct an IPO. At each successive stage, investors pay more for the amount of equity they receive because uncertainty has been reduced.

In an old-style waterfall project, you wouldn't necessarily gain useful information in early project stages that you could use to reduce the uncertainty of later stage decisions. After several months of work, the developers might report that they're "15% done with component A and 13% done with component B." That doesn't give you much information about whether to invest in the next round of funding. But in the digital world you would set up the initiative to quickly deliver results, elicit feedback, and yield information about whether to fund the next stage, or what changes should be made in order to justify additional funding.

With an Agile initiative you can also get an immediate return on the early stage investments, since capabilities are constantly released to production. If the company decides not to fund the second stage, then the first stage's product is still available for people to use. As I mentioned in Chapter 4: The Business Value of IT, the return should really be modeled as a return on series A plus an option on future stages. If the option isn't exercised, there still remains the value of series A.

That's why the Agile approach makes it effective to innovate through experiments; these are economically justified because of the option value. If you make the first stage short enough and its investment small enough, sooner or later the option values start to outweigh the first stage cost. And the portfolio of ideas being tested, like a VC firm's startup portfolio, may yield a successful idea that the enterprise can later make a big bet on.

Metered funding can be used throughout the project's life, which leads to my next point: we should always cancel successful projects, not failing ones.

Here's why. If the investment decision-making process has done its work well, then the initiative is well-justified and is expected to return business value. Now let's say that we're staging our investments, which amounts to periodically remaking our investment decision—perhaps monthly. Since a successful initiative has been constantly delivering results—this is what we expect in the DevOps world—we can evaluate what it has delivered so far and what we believe will be delivered in the future. And since we've prioritized the highest return tasks and accomplished them first, we should be seeing diminishing returns. At some point our oversight process might find that enough has been achieved, so it makes sense to stop investing in the effort: resources should instead be moved to a different initiative. This would be a rational decision and one that reflects very well on the project.

On the other hand, if the project seems to be going off course—it's not returning what we truly believe it could be returning—then we shouldn't cancel it. After all, we believe it can return more. Rather, this is the moment to make adjustments to the project to get those higher returns. Is the team running into impediments that can be removed? Does it not have the resources it needs? Is this the wrong set of people to be executing the initiative? At this point we should address all of these issues.

We have often thought of project failure as being the fault of the team assigned to execute it; we cancelled their project as a sort of punishment. This makes little sense for two reasons. First, it's probably not the team's fault—after all, they were chosen for the project because we thought they could execute it best. Secondly, the justification for the project still exists; if it is a real business need then project cancellation still leaves that need unfilled.

We should instead take advantage of all the options that new IT approaches present. If we can buy additional information to reduce the risk of our investment decision, if we have the choice of stopping an initiative that has already returned sufficient value . . . well, why not? It would be irresponsible to pretend that we can make long-range, point-in-time decisions despite the uncertainty in our environment. We now have the option of staging investments, learning as we go, and adjusting plans. And if we insist on sticking to a plan that we made early—before the initiative started and when we had the least available information—then we'll likely miss out.

In Chapter 4 I suggested that instead of soliciting initiatives from around the business and prioritizing them, it would be better to start from the organization's strategic objectives and cascade down from these to the initiatives. Westerman and Hunter describe using this approach:

> We used to work with the power users in every function from the bottom up to develop the IT strategy, and it didn't necessarily connect to the business strategy. By coming from the top down, we were able to redirect IT effort on major initiatives.[3]

It might seem impractical to do this for basic maintenance work, which includes any number of small tasks that are difficult to tie to strategic objectives. But this can work for two reasons. The first is that all of the little maintenance tasks that "must" be done . . . *must they*? Has the company not been able to operate without them? It's important to focus resources on what is most essential, not on what can somehow be justified.

The second reason is that the initial development work, if done correctly, might make such small tasks unnecessary. In the DevOps model the team that launches a feature continues to monitor its success and make adjustments to it. The feature is not really finished until it's meeting all the company's needs, so there is little reason to "maintain" it later by fixing bugs and tweaking functions. That backlog of small requests should become small.

The preceding thoughts apply as long as we're governing discrete initiatives—projects, in oldspeak. We should always stage our investments and buy down risk. We should experiment freely, creating options that might become valuable. We should cascade strategic objectives into initiatives, rather than improvising initiatives that might or might not be relevant to strategic objectives. We should avoid vomiting user stories, in Pascal Van Cauwenberghe's phrase.[4] This is the Agile way to govern projects.

But we should not be governing projects. DevOps, as a Lean process, is based on minimizing batch sizes, which means processing very few requirements at a time, finishing them quickly, and moving on to the next set of requirements. Each requirement can be coded quickly and its capability delivered to users—on the order of minutes to days. DevOps can even take us close to single piece flow, where one requirement at a time can be worked on and delivered.

This is quite remarkable. It would make the IT process amazingly responsive, taking in each new mission need, immediately cranking out a solution, then quickly improving that solution until it is perfect. It would let you change course at any moment to respond to changing circumstances or to try new ideas. It would reduce delivery risk to near zero, since every item would be delivered almost as soon as work started.

But even if we have the technical ability, we often can't use it because our governance committee only meets once a year, when the Star Chamber room can be rented. And of course we can't convene the Star Chamber for every requirement. In fact, Lean principles would suggest that we avoid the wait time necessary for getting the hooded figures to make investment decisions in the first place. The only way to take full advantage of single piece flow is to decentralize governance decision-making.

But isn't the whole point of governance to centralize these decisions, to avoid the chaos of decisions made separately across the organization? Yes, but there are ways we can decentralize decision-making *and* maintain centralized direction. I know of three models for doing so: the *product model*, *budget model*, and *objective model*.

In the *product model*, teams of technologists are assigned to work as part of a particular product group. This group oversees the roadmap for their product, taking feedback from the market and input from the company's overall competitive strategy. They're generally responsible for the performance of their product, measured in whatever way makes sense to the company, but they have some freedom to develop and prioritize ideas for their roadmap. For digital products, these are largely digital features, of course. This is fairly close to the model used by Amazon Web Services, where product teams manage their own feature roadmaps in consultation with customers.

In this model the technologists become very familiar with their product and its underlying technology. Because decision-making remains within the group, communication channels are short and lean. The team works toward product objectives, which might be cascaded down from companywide strategic objectives. They also work backward from customer feedback, test hypotheses about which features will be valuable to customers, and gather additional feedback from them as they use the product.

A similar idea can be applied to "products"—business support applications—used internally by the company. The technologists align to whomever is responsible for the product and become experts in both its use and internals. For example, the technologists might align with the HR group that oversees a human resources system.

The *budget model* is the approach we use all the time for spending that isn't either "project based" or related to large capital investments. Now that we can execute our efforts at the single requirement level, why even have IT delivery projects? There's just everyday IT work, analogous to routine efforts across the rest of the enterprise. IT folks simply come to work every day and, like everyone else in the company, produce whatever needs producing. This may mean they create new IT capabilities, modify existing ones, or perhaps improve security. Some of this effort might need to be capitalized for financial reporting, but that's a topic for a later chapter.

When a company allocates budgets and cascades them through an organizational hierarchy, it's passing governance authority down to the budget holders. Why shouldn't this be done with IT initiatives as well? Some of IT's expenditures are already managed as budget items, after all—why not the rest? Such an approach is all the more plausible now that there is very little difference, execution-wise, between maintenance of existing systems and development of new ones. There is simply a rolling set of tasks that must be completed by delivery teams.

If you drop the idea of individual systems or products and consider the entire IT estate as a whole—the single large IT asset I've described—then all IT development work simply amounts to enhancements or maintenance work to this asset, whether expensed or capitalized. Investment decisions are really the assignment of budgeted teams to work streams, along with the decision as to how many teams to fund in the first place. If the company funds twenty delivery teams, for example, then the CIO can decide how many of them to put on each objective or set of capabilities, and can move those teams between work streams as deemed appropriate.

The budget approach allocates funds to the CIO to use in managing the company's technology assets. It's the approach most consistent with the Intrax CEO's message in the Introduction, as it makes the CIO responsible for the returns from the organization's IT investment portfolio. Yes, this puts a lot of responsibility in the CIO's hands—just as the enterprise places heavy responsibilities in the hands of other CXOs. They all report to the CEO or board and are managed by them. No CIO is free of oversight.

One reason why this approach has seemed out of the question is simply the traditional business/IT split—that arms-length, contractor-control model. You wouldn't give this decision power to a contractor, right?

In the *objective model*, a team is chartered with a specific business objective, cascaded from a critical company objective. The team consists of technologists together with business operations people—a group the organization believes can actually accomplish the objective. The team then owns the objective rather than a set of requirements. It does whatever it can to accomplish it: testing hypotheses, making decisions, and rolling out IT or business process changes.

I can explain this best by an example. My team at USCIS was responsible for E-Verify, an online system employers use to check whether an employee is eligible to work in the US. Although employers aren't generally required to use E-Verify, we were afraid that its use would become mandatory as part of a broader immigration reform. If so, we knew it wouldn't be able to scale up enough to handle that transactional volume.

We also realized that expanding E-Verify wasn't primarily a technical problem but a human one. The system could automatically determine the eligibility of 98.6% of the people presented to it, but a person (called a status verifier) had to research and adjudicate the remainder. In addition, observers had to monitor use of the system for potential fraud and misuse. Neither set of people would scale with increased use of the system.

So we launched an E-Verify modernization project, initially using the traditional waterfall approach. A team collected requirements, over time organizing them into about eighty-five required capabilities—including hundreds of specific features. They then began designing the system and preparing the many documents required for the DHS investment governance process. After four years, all they had produced was a stack of one-inch paper binders.

We decided to take a radically different approach. We . . . ahem . . . reclassified the one-inch binders as trash, then reduced the project to five well-defined business objectives:

1. Raise the number of cases a status verifier could process per day (about seventy at the time).
2. Increase the 98.6% of cases the automated system could process to be closer to 100%.
3. Improve the registration completion rate—a large number of companies were beginning the E-Verify user registration process, but never completing it.
4. (A goal around fraud and misuse.)
5. (A goal around technical system performance.)

We then made a very Lean investment decision. We said we were willing to spend 100 livres every three months to accomplish each of these goals, but would informally revisit the investment decision every month, and formally each quarter. Meanwhile, we also built dashboards to track metrics continuously for each objective. Because the project executors had all of the technical tools and cloud platforms already set up for them, we expected them to show results in some metrics within two weeks and continuous improvement thereafter.

Having formed a team consisting of technologists (with skills in coding, testing, infrastructure, and security) and business operational folks (status verifiers), we gave them the first objective. We instructed them to do whatever they thought best to raise that number of cases, whether by writing code or making business process changes, and that we (management) would help remove impediments.

More precisely, I said that for every case above seventy they were able to deliver, they would get a gold star. If they did any work that wasn't intended to increase that number, with a wink I said I'd take one of them outside and shoot them as an example to the others. That was our control for scope creep and feature bloat.* I also said that we would meet every two weeks to discuss the results and see what we in management could do to help.

To begin the initiative, we also brought together a broader team—managers, verifiers, technologists—to brainstorm ideas that might help the team in its efforts. We used an impact mapping technique (described in the next section) to create a "mind map" of hypotheses about what might increase

---

* Disclaimer: not official government policy, but we really have to do something about feature bloat.

that metric. But the team wasn't required to use the mind map—they were to use their judgment to prioritize tasks. We only cared about results.

Every two weeks we had a discussion to align management and the team, as well as to remove impediments, and every month we reported our results to the steering committee responsible for overseeing the investment. We were able to show immediate gains, and after several months the metric continued to improve. The steering committee chose to continue with the investment.

We did something similar with the other four objectives by assigning each to a team, then regularly checking on progress. Something interesting happened with the registration rate objective (number three). Initially the team showed improvements in the metric, but after a few months it reached a plateau. The business owners and I asked about the ideas the team was trying—the hypotheses it was testing—and agreed with the team that it was doing the right things. We concluded that the metric was not likely to improve any further, perhaps because a certain number of companies who started the registration process realized that E-Verify wasn't for them, or because people were trying it out to see what it was but weren't ever planning to sign up.

In reporting back to the steering committee, we therefore recommended that it stop investing in that objective, and instead move the budget to another one—even though we had originally planned to spend more. In other words, the team cancelled the remainder of its own project, with the consent of the steering committee.

What had been planned as a four-year project ended after two and a half years because it was so successful. Each objective had been accomplished to the extent that we all agreed it could be, so the remaining funds were returned for use in other projects. You could say that the project had achieved the Agile ideal: maximizing outcomes while minimizing output, or in other words, maximizing the amount of work not done.

To me, this shows the power of DevOps when used with an appropriate investment management process. The amount of money at risk at any given time was only one month of funding, as the investment was reviewed monthly and showed results daily. Value was delivered immediately and frequently thereafter. The teams could innovate freely but only in relation to an agreed-upon business objective. And the process had very little overhead: each month we reported the business results (obtained from our dashboard) and the amount spent to the steering committee, and each quarter we had an hour-long discussion with them.

What if the objectives hadn't been so easily quantifiable? Organizations often force themselves to find something quantifiable, even if it doesn't exactly measure what the objective intends. Instead, I would put the burden on the team to provide evidence of its results, even if the evidence isn't quantitative. Since the team is thoroughly absorbed in the effort, they are the most likely to know what impact they are having. At the biweekly meetings, management can evaluate the evidence, decide whether it is reasonable, and suggest other methods if necessary.

As I mentioned before, the objective model works especially well with impact mapping, a technique developed by Gojko Adzic. Impact mapping provides a cross-functional team with a way to visualize problems and possible solutions, such that everyone can work from a shared view of their task, a sort of mind map diagram showing possible routes to the solution. Impact mapping begins by identifying the most important goal the team should be working on. "Goals should not be about building products or delivering project scope. They should explain why such a thing would be useful . . . [they] should present the problem to be solved, not the solution," Adzic says.[5]

Team members first ask themselves the question, "Who are the actors whose behavior needs to change in order for the organization to accomplish the goal?" These are the people who can produce the desired effect or obstruct it—often employees, consumers of the product, or other stakeholders such as regulators. This becomes the first layer of the impact map.

The team then asks what behavior changes on the part of each identified actor will help achieve the goal—these become the impacts the team is trying to create. Finally, they ask what they can do as a delivery team to support those impacts—these become deliverables, software capabilities, and organizational activities.[6]

In the E-Verify project, we used impact maps to bring the team and management together to frame the problem, brainstorm alternatives, and develop a common language. For each branch of the map we estimated the amount of impact it might have on the target objective.* This gave the team some ideas about prioritization and an initial set of hypotheses they could test.

---

* Impact mapping does not include estimating the value of each branch—we added that.

A team's results are easy to measure with the impact map in hand. As Adzic says:

> The role of testing becomes to prove that deliverables support desired actor behaviours, instead of comparing software features to technical expectations. If a deliverable does not support an impact, even if it works correctly from a technical perspective, it is a failure and should be treated as a problem, enhanced or removed.[7]

What is tested is the achievement of the goal, or, to put it differently, the business value created.

Star Chamber governance is based on a mental model in which coarse-grained projects are vetted, compared, and given to IT for delivery. Oversight then focuses on making sure the plan that has been approved is executed. But this way of overseeing investment decisions does a poor job of supporting an organization's need for agility and continuous innovation.

Star Chamber governance, I would argue, doesn't provide the best stewardship of an enterprise's resources. Instead, you should stage investment decisions to deliver minimal products, learn from their results, then invest incrementally in additional capabilities. This is how you create the organizational agility you need to survive in the digital world, and at the same time gain better control over your investments.

SIDE GLANCE: *INNOVATION*

Daring ideas are like chessmen moved forward. They may be beaten, but they may start a winning game.

—**Goethe**, *Aphorisms*

A thinker sees his own actions as experiments and questions—as attempts to find out something. Success and failure are for him answers above all.

—**Friedrich Nietzsche**, *The Gay Science*

In *Capitalism, Socialism, and Democracy*, Joseph Schumpeter argued that innovation was the driving force behind change—in particular, business cycles—in capitalist economies.[1] He was trying to show that very large, industry-dominant companies were not bad for the economy, as many had believed. The conventional view at the time was that large firms would use their monopoly power to lower production and maintain a higher price, resulting in less output for the economy.

In contrast, Schumpeter believed that large companies were forced to innovate to maintain their advantage, resulting in a better outcome for all as the capitalist economy generated a constant flow of innovations. Each time it launched a new innovation an enterprise temporarily gained monopoly power and the ability to earn monopoly rents—until the advantage was competed away and the company could only earn a normal return. That incentive to constantly innovate and earn extraordinary returns was what drove the capitalist economy forward.

For Schumpeter, it was evident that large enterprises were the engines of innovation. After all, they had the financial resources, the people, the distribution channels, the market knowledge, and many other advantages over smaller, newer entrants. But innovation meant killing off their earlier, successful products and processes. Innovation depended, he said, on a continuing process of *creative destruction*.

Therein lies the challenge—and the opportunity—for enterprises trying to transform to a model of continuous innovation. An enterprise must not only create its future conditions of success but also must undo its previous ones. Edgar Schein in the *Corporate Culture Survival Guide* says, "The fundamental reason why people sometimes resist change is that the new behavior to be learned requires some unlearning."[2] Or to take Hannah Arendt out of context, "The new therefore always appears in the guise of a miracle."[3]

This is not a new idea. Hinduism, the oldest of today's large religions, posits a trinity of major deities—Brahma the creator, Vishnu the preserver, and Shiva the destroyer. Shiva destroys not only in anger—though he does plenty of that (watch out if he's opening his third eye!)—but also as part of an eternal process of re-creation. In fact, Shiva is also worshipped as a god of fertility, through the phallic image of the lingam. Some writers therefore suggest that it's more appropriate to think of Shiva as a god of transformation.[4] Although Shiva's personality and attributes are ambiguous and full of paradox, it's the resolution of these ambiguities—or perhaps the tension between them—that drives the world forward.

This cyclical aspect of Shiva's destroy-re-create-destroy activities is illustrated in representations of Shiva Nataraja, or Shiva as Lord of the Dance. The dancing Shiva is depicted inside a circle, with his foot stepping on and defeating the demon of ignorance. Shiva Nataraja is said to encompass "creation, destruction, and all things in between."[5] His dance is a "fearless celebration of the joys of dance while being surrounded by fire, untouched by the forces of ignorance and evil, signifying a spirituality that transcends all duality."[6]

Perhaps that includes the duality of IT and the business.

To anyone who has experienced the pains of a large transformation, it should come as no surprise that Shiva's son, Ganesha, is known as the Remover of Obstacles. Or that Shiva's equivalent in the Japanese pantheon,

Daikokuten,* is considered one of the seven lucky gods, particularly associated with wealth and prosperity.[7]

———————

During my last year at USCIS, I was asked to take over the leadership of a large IT program called USCIS Transformation that had until then been managed outside of the IT organization. This program was (unjustly) considered an example of a failing IT initiative, the target of many unflattering stories in the press, and audits by the Government Accountability Office (GAO) and the DHS Inspector General. I knew that the program was in better shape than people thought, but there were still issues to resolve.

I started by meeting one-on-one with each of the program's most import-ant participants. My question to each was, "What do you think we could be doing differently that would lead to better outcomes?" Each of them had great ideas. One pointed out that we were putting a lot of effort into automating a paper process, without looking at ways we could improve it to take advantage of the digital world. And he listed some new ideas along those lines. Another pointed out that we weren't talking enough to users and incorporating their ideas. She laid out some of the thoughts she'd gathered from them.

So I asked what seemed like the obvious question: "Why haven't you been doing these things? You have great ideas—why are you letting the program struggle when you know the right thing to do?" The answer, though it was worded very carefully, came down to something like this: "Do you have any idea how hard it is to get approval for a new idea? How many people can veto it? How committed the leadership is to its way of doing things?"

"Why didn't you ask me for help? I might have been able to knock down some of those barriers for you."

"We didn't think there was anything you could do."

They had learned helplessness and no longer bothered to promote their innovations.

———————

---

* Interesting note: there is a custom that whoever steals an image of Daikokuten is assured of good fortune—but only if they are *caught* doing it. So much for financial regulators.

Of course they had innovative ideas about how to make the program success-ful—they were involved every day, hands-on, struggling to bring about its success. They were deep in the smoke and mist of Borodino, making difficult tradeoffs and directing how people spent their time. The problem wasn't a lack of innovative ideas, it was that those ideas had no chance of being imple-mented. And I was implicated in the problem.

Enterprises have tried various systems for acting on new ideas. A few months ago I asked a group of CIOs how their companies encourage innovation and found that their answers followed two patterns. Some said they had cre-ated an "innovation team" and given it special powers to bypass company rules. Others talked about their "innovation boards" who reviewed new ideas from employees and decided whether to move forward with them.

"Who sits on those innovation boards?" I asked. The answers, as I recall, were along the lines of ". . . the head of product development, the VP of mar-keting, . . ." In other words, the people who had created the status quo and were heavily invested in it. These are the people—let's be honest—least likely to be open to innovative ideas.

I've already described my discomfort with this Star Chamber approach to governance; one charged with judging innovative ideas seems even less likely to succeed. But the idea of having a special innovation team that can disre-gard rules is perhaps worse, since it communicates to the rest of the enterprise, "Just do your job, don't bother trying to innovate." An innovation team is also less likely to have the constant stream of innovative ideas that others on the front lines have because they're not dealing with the everyday issues and frus-trations that breed those new ideas.

If you can let the innovation team bypass rules and bureaucracy, why can't you let everyone bypass them? "That would be chaos," one of the CIOs said. "You can't just let anyone do anything they want!"

That's true. But my point is something different. If you can set up the rules and bureaucracy such that they allow good innovative ideas to have a path to execution, then you don't need to distinguish between good ideas that come from a special innovation team from those that come from everyone else.

There was a logic to the innovation team approach, and the many gates that USCIS Transformation project employees had to go through to get approval for a new idea. That logic centers on the avoidance of risk. As the CIO pointed out, you can't just let everyone do whatever they want—that would be risky. The Important People on an innovation board apply their experience to weed out ideas that might not work. Setting up an innovation team and making it solely responsible for innovation reduces risk because ideas are fewer and come from "experts" in innovation. And the relentless series of gate reviews for the USCIS Transformation Project made sure every possible point of view was brought to bear on spotting potential risks.

But in this area too the calculus is changing as we move into the digital age. For one thing, trying out ideas has become much less risky. For another, remaining with the status quo has become much riskier.

Trying out new ideas has become much less risky because what used to require a large investment and a long lead time—developing IT capabilities to support the new idea—can now be done quickly, inexpensively, and at low risk by using DevOps, the cloud, and easily accessible open-source frameworks and components. When a new idea is proposed, instead of managing its risk by thinking of all of the things that could go wrong, remember that we can manage it by running small "experiments" that will teach us whether the idea will work, or how the idea needs to change to make it workable.

At the same time, the risk of remaining with the status quo has increased, for the simple reason that all of the enterprise's competitors have access to precisely those same tools for experimentation. The market rewards innovation and customers' expectations are constantly rising. Capital flows to startups that introduce new ideas and disrupt industries. We're living in a Schumpeterian economy where innovation drives business cycles, where the financial markets look for companies that can earn rents through continuous innovation. Both consumers and investors value innovation and progress.

An important strategy in DevOps and cloud practices is the use of automated controls, or guardrails. Instead of having a team test once to see if a system is secure before it is deployed, an organization can develop automated controls to enforce security, thereby continuously ensuring that the system always complies with security requirements. Similarly, the enterprise can develop rules that will be applied automatically in the cloud for PCI, HIPAA, and other compliance frameworks; for cost management; and for transparency and auditability.

By using automated controls, the enterprise eliminates the tradeoff between speed and innovation on one hand, and compliance, security, and quality on the other. Where an organization using manual controls must stop progress while someone validates compliance, automated controls run continuously while the work continues to flow. The manual approach is a jerky, discrete, stop-and-start, gatekeeping and remediation approach. Automated controls allow work to flow in a continuous stream.

Automated guardrails (constraints) give engineers the confidence to be creative, knowing that while the guardrails are in place, they can't go wrong. Artists have recognized that constraints are essential to their creativity as well. According to the composer Igor Stravinsky, "The more constraints one imposes, the more one frees one's self. And the arbitrariness of the constraint serves only to obtain precision of execution."[8] Painters are limited to the canvas; they cannot dance their paintings. Western musicians have only twelve notes in the scale from which to create their music; they cannot draw from oil paints. A software engineer can be inventive within the bounds of automated tests, using only the constructs of their chosen programming language.

The construction of constraints is the art of management, you might say. Constraints help direct innovation to the right objectives, which include customer needs as well as financial, compliance, and security objectives.

Innovations need not always be large—what is more important is that they address a need or an opportunity. But each innovation, according to Schumpeter, while it might give the company a temporary advantage, will wind up being competed away. Or as Drnevitch and Croson explain:

> . . . over time, even though none of the specific, individual head start advantages need be durable, the ability to create a continuous stream of these temporary competitive advantages through flexibility (as with innovation), can facilitate sustained long-term superior profitability.[9]

The challenge, therefore, is not just to create *an* innovation; it's to create a constant stream of innovations, to make innovation a normal part of doing business every day. And that can best be done if we overcome the duality of IT and the business. Innovation flows when teams have everything they need to conceive ideas *and* quickly test them—both IT and business abilities. We need to institutionalize a continuous cycle of destruction and recreation, a Shiva-esque dance of transcending duality.

An enterprise's digital goal is to build an environment where experimenting and learning can take place without impediments. The secret is in the three assets. The IT asset should be lean and flexible, to lower the risk and cost of learning. The organizational asset should be set up so that teams can quickly frame ideas and experiment with them: ideas should flow quickly and freely. And the data asset must make data accessible (subject to privacy controls) for discovering new ways to use it.

A digital company is one in which every employee has the opportunity to be an entrepreneur, as Ries puts it.[10] Instead of forming an innovation team with the privilege of breaking the rules, the enterprise should set the rules—processes, practices, bureaucracy, people, management culture, and everything else—to support all employees in being innovative. That doesn't mean a free-for-all. On the contrary, it means setting up guardrails and mechanisms within which employees can move quickly and creatively to innovate.

Innovation is encouraged when there is a continuous flow of creation, rather than a choppy, gatekeeper-controlled, stop-and-start-innovating attitude. Again, the parallel with the art world is striking.

A recent *Washington Post* article looked at improvisational arts. It interviewed GoldLink, a rapper; Jason Moran, a jazz pianist; and Andy Bustillos and Alex Song, the Upright Citizens Brigade comedy duo, about how they're able to create art on the spot in front of an audience.[11] The authors also spoke to a neuroscientist, Dr. Charles Limb, who has used fMRI technology to scan artists' brains while they're improvising. According to Limb, rappers who are freestyling actually rewire the neural networks in their brains to bypass its conscious-control, behavior-regulating parts. In other words, they achieve a state of flow where the "no saying" parts of the brain are turned off.[12]

This is similar to the improv comedy principle of always saying "yes, and." According to this principle, each comic listens carefully to what the other says and accepts it, no matter how outlandish it is, then builds on it and advances it. With digital technology and techniques, we can create a flow that supports this kind of interchange of ideas and experimentation. Instead of installing gatekeepers who say no and demand rework, we can let employees move forward with ideas knowing that guardrails are in place, letting them adjust naturally if they bump up against one of them.

The traditional duality between IT and the business is a serious impediment to innovation—virtually all of which will have an IT component, with much of that being in the digital realm. If employees need to stop, write a requirements document, put it through a governance process, contract with IT, and wait until a result is delivered, well . . . that stops the process dead—experimentation can't take place and every innovative idea again becomes a large risk. Instead, the enterprise needs to send the technologists and other employees off together on a voyage of discovery, brainstorming and testing ideas.

But even that isn't enough. Each team must have some freedom to touch the entire enterprise, and sometimes its customers as well. In *X-Teams: How to Build Teams that Lead, Innovate, and Succeed*, Deborah Ancona and Henrik Bresman make a convincing case that innovative teams must be well connected to their environments. They present the idea of an X-team, a team that's focused externally as well as internally.

> Teams that scouted out new ideas from outside their boundaries, received feedback from and coordinated with outsiders, and got support from top managers were able to build more innovative products faster than those that dedicated themselves solely to efficiency and working well together.[13]

Returning to Lean thinking where handoffs are considered waste, teams can be made more effective if they can "go and see"* for themselves, and if they can directly experience operations and promote their ideas rather than working through channels. A team that truly owns its outcomes is really responsible for achieving business results, and must be able to reach out beyond its boundaries, to learn and to affect other parts of the enterprise.

> High performing teams manage across their boundaries, reaching out to find the information they need, understand the context in which they work, manage the politics and power struggles that surround any team initiative, get support for their ideas, and coordinate with the myriad other groups that are key to a team's success.[14]

---

* *Genchi Genbutsu*, a concept from Lean manufacturing.

Not only must the teams learn from those outside, but they must advocate for their ideas. Ancona and Bresman refer to this as *ambassadorship*.[15] Ambassadors are able to sell ideas up their management chains, as well as to other stakeholders, and to link their work with the strategic objectives of the organization.

———

To encourage employees to have more innovative ideas, you have to practice and perfect the art of doing nothing. That is to say: the employees probably have good ideas already; you just need to avoid shooting them down. When the teams reach out to the enterprise with their innovative ideas, they are sure to run up against the two great demons of ignorance: bureaucracy and culture. In the next chapter, I'll show that there is no need to worry—Shiva has his foot firmly on those two. Let the dance of creation and destruction continue!

BUREAUCRACY AND CULTURE

He gains consciousness from sensuous slumber, sees that he is a man, looks around and finds himself to be living in a state. Force of need cast him there before he was capable of freely choosing this condition.
—**Friedrich Schiller**, *On the Aesthetic Education of Man*

"But I'm not guilty," said K. "There's been a mistake. How is it even possible for someone to be guilty? We're all human beings here, one like the other."
"That is true," said the priest, "but that is how the guilty speak."
—**Franz Kafka**, *The Trial*

T he enemies of digital transformation are often taken to be entrenched bureaucracy and culture. This is a misunderstanding. Bureaucracy and culture are both the starting and ending points for the transformation. In their current states they provide crucial information for anyone who wants to transform the organization. In their envisioned states, they will institutionalize the digital way of working. Moving them from the status quo to their envisioned states is the goal of transformation.

What is bureaucracy, really?

Once I was working with an Agile software development team of seven people. It held a retrospective meeting every two weeks to reflect on its performance and find things to improve. At one meeting the team pointed out to me that if they had a certain piece of documentation* easily available to them, it would make their process go faster and smoother. So as an experiment I pinned a copy of that document to a corkboard in the team's meeting room.

Several weeks later we were back in the team room for another retrospective. The document on the corkboard had been a great help, they said. But at some point it was no longer there when they went looking for it. It turned out one of them had taken the document down and forgotten to put it back. In the spirit of continuous improvement, one of the team members proposed a solution.

"How about if we put a signup sheet next to it on the corkboard? Whenever someone borrows the document they can sign it out, and put down the date and time they took it and which cubicle they're working in. That way, we can always find it."

Thus is bureaucracy born. To fix a problem and standardize an ad hoc process, the team was willing to add extra work for everyone each time they needed to borrow the document. This connection between process improvement and bureaucracy is important to understand. Bureaucracy is a natural way to solve a problem and has value if its benefits outweigh its costs. Which, unfortunately, they often don't.

I had a counterproposal: "How about if every time someone takes it they remember to return it?"

Bureaucracy wasn't always a bad word.

Max Weber, one of the founders of sociology, wrote about bureaucracy in *Economy and Society*, published in 1922.

> Experience tends universally to show that the purely bureaucratic type of organization . . . is, from the purely technical point of view, capable of attaining the highest degree of efficiency and is in this sense formally the most rational known means of exercising authority over human beings. It is superior to any other form in precision, in stability, in the stringency of its discipline, and in its reliability. It thus makes possible

---

* A state transition diagram, to be precise.

a particularly high degree of calculability of results for the heads of the organization and for those acting in relation to it. It is finally superior both in intensive efficiency and in the scope of its operations.[1]

For him, bureaucracy was an entirely rational solution to certain types of social challenges. It wasn't just Weber with this peculiar view. Sociologists Daniel Katz and Robert L. Kahn said that bureaucracy "is an instrument of great effectiveness; it offers great economies over unorganized effort; it achieves great unity and compliance."*[2] "Indeed," said Daniel Wren and Arthur Bedeian in *The Evolution of Management Thought*, "almost all the benefits we take for granted in today's society—modern medicine, modern science, modern industry—rest on a bureaucratic foundation."[3]

One reason for Weber's enthusiasm was that bureaucracy, particularly in government, replaced the arbitrariness, capriciousness, nepotism, and other undesirable characteristics of public administration that had been typical since the time of monarchies. In contrast, bureaucracy offered impartial application of rules as a protection from arbitrariness, a formal hiring process based on merit and expertise, a career orientation that was free of external pressures, and greater efficiency through the division of labor, a management hierarchy, and formal controls.

The essence of bureaucracy is that its rules are applied impartially and impersonally, or as Weber put it, *sine ira et studio*, without anger or bias, or without regard for persons, where "'without regard for persons' is also a watchword of the 'market' and all naked economic interests."[4] In other words, bureaucracy is consistent with—one might even say demanded by—the capitalist economy. As with bureaucracy, the invisible hand of the market (a core principle of capitalism) sweeps all human concerns aside and is a purely mechanical force. Firms can do business better knowing that the bureaucracy will treat them according to rules; they can predict what the results of their actions will be.

The more bureaucracy is "dehumanized," the more completely it succeeds in eliminating from official business love, hatred, and all purely personal, irrational, and emotional elements which escape calculation. This is appraised as its special virtue by capitalism according to Weber.[5]

---

* Katz and Kahn go on to point out deficiencies in bureaucracy as well.

Bureaucracy solves certain business problems: ensuring consistency across a large enterprise, establishing compliance, enforcing whatever has been discovered to be best practices, and ensuring fairness when human prejudices might otherwise interfere. The marketing function in an enterprise creates branding and style guidelines to ensure consistency in the use of the brand, so that the brand can establish trust in the minds of the consumer. Marketing's guidelines create economic value for the company because the power of the brand lets the company charge more for its products and negotiate better deals with its distributors. What are these brand guidelines other than bureaucracy?

Are impartial rules any less bureaucratic if we implement them as automated controls? Instead of having a rule that all developers must have their code reviewed by at least one other developer (definitely bureaucracy), what if we set up our systems so that a developer is automatically not able to deploy any new code until another has reviewed it (arguably bureaucracy)? Contemporary IT practice, with its automation of compliance and security controls, is in a sense a huge automated bureaucracy.

No, the problem is not bureaucracy per se. Bureaucracy is just a form of institutional memory, a way of recording good practices—and being able to establish to auditors that good practices are being followed. As Hirotaka Takeuchi and Ikujiro Nonaka wrote in their 1986 *Harvard Business Review* article (considered to be the inspiration behind many Agile ideas), "Knowledge is also transmitted in the organization by converting project activities to standard practice. . . . Naturally companies try to institutionalize the lessons derived from their successes."[6]

However, there are two problems that arise in bureaucracies that make them frustrating and destroy business value:

- They don't change easily when new best practices are discovered.
- They aren't designed to be Lean; that is, the same objectives can be met with less waste.

Are those not what drive you crazy when you bang your head against a bureaucracy?

But neither of these is an essential characteristic of bureaucracy. In his study of Toyota-influenced Lean manufacturing at the NUMMI auto plant, Paul Adler distinguishes between "compliance bureaucracies" and "learning bureaucracies"[7]—the latter of which allows rules to evolve based on employee input. The essence of bureaucracy is that it applies its rules rigidly. But just because the *application* of the rules is rigid, the *formation* and *evolution* of the rules need not be.

———————

The second problem, wastefulness, is a serious obstacle when we're trying to shorten lead times. In our IT oversight process at DHS, project teams were required to complete a document called an Analysis of Alternatives (AoA)[8] before proceeding with an initiative.* For large programs, an AoA could run to hundreds of pages and was one of a hundred or so documents that had to be approved by several oversight bodies. It was also the one that took the most time to prepare (usually about eighteen months). Its purpose was to consider program requirements and decide on the best high-level solution for meeting them—or rather, to justify a decision, since one had invariably been made before its AoA was prepared.†

An AoA was required to include a comparison of three to five alternatives. To prove its case, the document generally listed a large number of desired characteristics of the solution with a weight assigned to each. Each of the alternatives was then scored against each characteristic, usually on a scale of one to five, then the results were summed up—behold, a winner.

Since the decision had already been made before its AoA was written, it was a simple matter to adjust the weights so the chosen alternative always came out ahead. Although this sounds like cheating, it wasn't—in the sense that the decision was usually well thought out, so it was more a matter of bringing out the logic of its selection and expressing it in matrix form. So an AoA played an important role by explaining why the project team had proposed the solution it had, and by ensuring they had considered alternatives. The AoA, though a piece of bureaucracy, added value and ensured that compliance was documented—that best practices had been applied.

---

* You can find the DHS AoA at: https://dau.gdit.com/aqn201a/pdfs/Appendix_G_Analysis_of _Alternatives_(AoA)_Interim_v1_9_dtd_11-07-08.pdf.
† Note that the AoA was not intended to justify the selection of a particular product—there was a formal procurement process for that, which couldn't begin until well after the AoA had been approved. It was to justify the general approach—for example, whether a procurement would be made and for what.

Now the problem. The document cost eighteen months and generally several millions of dollars to prepare. The right question to ask is whether its benefit justified that expense, or alternatively, whether there might be a leaner, less wasteful way to get the same benefit (or a better one).

This AoA is a busy document.* It looks as if its template creators tried to think of every possible relevant factor and devise an inclusive document that made every bit of thinking apparent. That's why it often ran to one hundred pages. If instead the template simply said, "Explain why you selected this alternative and identify other alternatives you considered," I think an AoA could be written in three or four pages while still documenting all of the factors relevant to the particular decision at hand. But that's not the point. The document attempts to be self-auditing; by writing each section, the program team shows that it considered the relevant factors. It's a checklist that requires a lot of words instead of simple checkboxes.

Let's look at a few of the sections:

- **Executive Summary**—Exists only because the rest of the document is too long for anyone to read; merely repeats what's in the document.
- **Background (Section 1.1)**—Lists documents that have already been prepared; since they're all required, there is no need to list them.
- **Purpose (1.2)**—Already obvious from the document's name and its text is right there in the template, yet it needs to appear in every AoA.
- **Scope (1.3)**—Redundant with the actual analysis of alternatives below.
- **Study Team/Organization (1.4)**—If the document makes the analysis clear, it shouldn't matter who prepared it. Section exists only to prove that the analysis was done by an independent group.
- **AoA Review Process (1.5)**—Ditto.
- **Scenarios, Threats, Environments (2.1–2.3)**—Repeats information in previous documents.
- **Non-Viable Alternatives (3.2)**—Who cares?
- **Concepts (3.3–3.5), Operation Effectiveness Analysis (5.2)**—Repeats information in previous documents.

---

* I thought of filling out this template for my choice between a vanilla or a chocolate ice cream cone, but hesitated to waste the paper. That's in a book that borrows from *War and Peace*, no less.

- **Schedule (5.5)**—Irrelevant to the document's purpose.
- **Analysis, Recommendation, and Rationale (6.7)**—Says the same thing three times.

You get the idea. A section might yield interesting information now and then, but for most AoAs, the words are simply conjured up to fill the template sections. Now, there is nothing on the surface that's wrong with the template. But the AoA is deeply wrong because it's costly waste. The oversight bodies should demand that the program team fill out this form as briefly as possible, ignoring any sections that would add little value, because otherwise they're creating waste—anything that doesn't add enough value to justify its cost (in time or dollars). And waste is really what the oversight bodies are there to prevent.

Okay, it's easy to toss out a government process as an example of bureaucracy gone wild. But what would it look like if you took a Lean scalpel to all of your own company's bureaucracy and cut out the waste? Think of it as a bureaucracy-buster's version of Occam's razor.

Occam, a 13th–14th century friar and philosopher, is often credited with the principle, "Don't overcomplicate things." That's not actually what he said—it was more like, "Don't posit more entities than necessary to explain things."

What he had in mind was something like this: If person A said, "That rock is falling toward Earth because objects with mass attract each other," and person B said, "That rock is falling toward Earth because objects with mass attract each other, so seeing two objects with mass, an invisible chorus of bobbleheads sings the gravity song to encourage the Earth to attract the rock" . . . well, of those compelling explanations we should prefer person A's.

Bureaucracy is not the enemy of digital transformation. It's merely a codification of how an enterprise has operated until now. Bureaucracy has evolved along with the enterprise in order to solve problems it has encountered, to provide necessary controls, and to enforce what the enterprise has found to be best practices. Yes, bureaucracies often require singing the gravity song when they should instead be subject to Lean Occam's turkey carver. They generally have tons of waste—extremely damaging when we're trying to speed the flow of work for digital transformation. And yes, they should be better at changing over time.

But if you're willing to accept my broad definition of bureaucracy, the purpose of digital transformation is to build a new bureaucracy—one that's highly automated and consequently Lean, and that enforces the good practices we're trying to put in place.

Similarly, organizational culture is not an obstacle—it's another form of institutional memory that provides good information about how a company has chosen to solve problems. Our goal is not to eliminate its culture, but to reset it so as to support our transformed world. We can't mandate culture change, but we can provide better solutions and let them be naturally incorporated into a company's culture.

Edgar Schein has written extensively about corporate culture. He explains it as an organization's interpretation of what works:

> Culture is a pattern of shared tacit assumptions that was learned by a group as it solved its problems of external adaptation and internal integration that has worked well enough to be considered valid and, therefore, to be taught to new members as the correct way to perceive, think, and feel in relation to those problems.[9]

The organization as a group has learned which strategies, values, protocols, and behaviors work in its environment to support its aims, whether these are maximizing shareholder value or accomplishing mission objectives. People have had to learn what leads to success within the organization. Such learning forms the basis of tacit assumptions and norms, an organization's collected wisdom about which behaviors are valuable.

How, then, should we go about changing culture for the digital age? Speaker and author Christopher Avery, in his work on organizational change, talks about using an Agile approach to transformation. Citing organizational psychologist Kurt Lewin, he argues that we can never understand an organization until we try to change it. He therefore suggests a "provoke and observe" approach:

> We can never direct a living system, only disturb it and wait to see the response. . . . We can't know all the forces shaping an organization we wish to change, so all we can do is provoke the system in some way by experimenting with a force we think might have some impact, then watch to see what happens.[10]

Avery's provoke and observe approach is analogous to the Agile principle of "inspect and adapt." Through it we can learn where resistance is—which aspects of the culture are hard to change and why. But remember that cultural change follows transformational activities, not vice versa. It occurs when employees find new behaviors that lead to success. In John Shook's retrospective look at NUMMI's cultural change, he says, "[What my] experience taught me that was so powerful was that the way to change culture is not to first change how people think, but instead to start by changing how people behave—what they do."[11]

As an enterprise changes its way of working with digital technology, it will come up against resistance from both culture and bureaucracy. Such resistance is a necessary part of transformation, since both culture and bureaucracy are simply forms of institutional memory. In digital transformation, you'll replace today's bureaucracy and culture with improved versions of themselves that institutionalize the practices that work well in the digital world.

SIDE GLANCE:
SECURITY

The law is not thrust upon man; it rests deep within him, to waken when the call comes.

—**Martin Buber**, *Israel and the World*

Do not weep. Do not wax indignant. Understand.

—**Baruch Spinoza**

I was once accidentally given some classified information in my government job. I had been at a breakfast meeting where one of the attendees had passed around copies of a presentation that inadvertently included something that was classified. Since most of us at the meeting didn't have a need to know that information, and since in any case it wasn't appropriately marked as classified, this was considered a spill and had to be cleaned up immediately.

An hour or so later, two men showed up at my office in dark suits and carrying briefcases. They asked me to hand over the slide deck, asked a few questions about whether anyone else might have seen it, carefully slid the material into a briefcase, and left without—I noticed—smiling or making any jokes. This incident fit my stereotype of what information security would be like. It was the only incident in my career that did.

Yes, information security is a major risk today. But it's important to go beyond the hype and the disaster stories. These can easily activate an availability bias—that is, a bias that the examples that come quickest to mind are more representative than they actually are. The newspaper articles and some email news blasts you read might give you the wrong impression of how big the risks are or what exactly is at risk. To Spinoza's advice at the beginning of this chapter, I would add: do not panic.

As for how big the risks really are—well, actually they are very big. Your technologists probably don't tell you every time a hacker tries to break into your systems, because it's probably happening dozens of times a day.* Fortunately, most of their attempts don't succeed.

But I can't emphasize this enough—you're under constant attack, whether you're a charity, a scholar of Napoleonic military campaigns, a bank, or the Department of Homeland Security. This means that you must constantly be taking steps to stay secure. Security is not something you can add whenever threats arise. Every bit of digital technology you deploy must be built to be secure, and every business process must be examined carefully with an eye toward its security.

Now for the good news. Most successful break-ins are not sophisticated. The security vulnerabilities they exploit come from stupid stuff. Many can be solved through what amounts to basic hygiene or simple automated controls. While the digital age exposes you to more threats, it also provides tools for dealing with them. The difficulty comes when you try to address new threats with old tools or when you consider security to be the job of a few supergeeks in IT, an issue no one else needs to worry about.

Since bad actors generally attack us over the internet, traditional security models have often focused on the point at which the enterprise's network is connected—thinking of it as a door that must be locked tight and monitored at all times. Or, in the militaristic lingo that's used, the place where you conduct your "perimeter defense"—often by building a demilitarized zone between your network and the internet.

One challenge of perimeter defense is that it's hard to tell the difference between malicious traffic coming from the internet and the valid traffic that constitutes your business. Another is that such a defense doesn't provide ade-

---

* According to an IBM study, forty-six times per day.[1]

quate protection against malicious insiders—employees or contractors, for example—who legitimately have internal network access. Ultimately you want to always be prepared to deal with any dangerous case—if somehow a bad actor does sneak through your DMZ and into your network, what then? Are you helpless?

———

I'm going to propose a simple program for becoming secure in the digital age.

1. Create a culture where security is considered important.
2. Stop doing things that make it easy for bad guys to attack you.
3. Rely heavily on automation, because people make mistakes.
4. Be prepared to respond quickly to new threats and bad activities.
5. Then have the security geeks take care of the complicated stuff.

That's all, but please make no mistake about it: security is your job and everyone else's, not just something the IT department deals with.

———

Let's start with some basic concepts. Generally, we think in terms of three goals for information security, easily remembered by the acronym CIA: confidentiality, integrity, and availability.*

Confidentiality—The information in your systems should only be available to those you want it to be available to. Bad guys want to steal your confidential information—your customers' credit card numbers, your secret product designs and business strategies, and details of your IT infrastructure that they can use to cause additional mischief.

Integrity—The information in your databases should remain accurate and your systems should continue to do what they were meant to do. The bad actors would like to make your IT systems do bad things or change your data, have money sent to their bank accounts, allow terrorists to get green cards, remove evidence of their criminal convictions, deface your website.

---

* A fourth is sometimes added—nonrepudiation. This means that if someone "signs" a transaction they can't later deny that they did so.

Availability—Your systems should function and be available for legitimate users to use. Hackers want to interfere with your systems, delete your data unless you pay them a ransom, bombard your servers with traffic so they're too busy to do legitimate work, block you from communicating with partners and customers.

Your goal is to secure confidentiality, integrity, and availability. As a side note, it's not only the actions of external attackers that can keep you from this goal. Someone in your organization might accidentally email confidential information to people who shouldn't have it. Bugs in your code can send money to someone who doesn't deserve it. A flood might wipe out your datacenter. Or a system might crash when you have no backups and thereby keep you from doing business. You should consider all of these events—anything that can affect CIA—as security threats.

It's useful to divide the bad guys into two main groups: the so-called script kiddies and the professionals. Or, more accurately, the hackers who look for easy victims, and those who are absolutely *determined* to do whatever it takes to hack into *your* company. The latter category is often referred to as advanced persistent threats (APTs).

By far the majority of hackers are in the first category, and their job is pretty easy. There are so many internet-connected networks that they can just use easily available automated scripts to search for the companies that have made things easy for them by exposing vulnerabilities.

Hackers of this sort are constantly scanning the gates of your network looking for a way in. They might, for example, be checking to see if you're running an old version of a software product known to have vulnerabilities.* Defending against them is a matter of hygiene—that is, adopting good practices that are widely known.

But the APTs are a different breed. They're brilliant problem solvers, sometimes state-sponsored, and the problem they are trying to solve is how to break through your security controls. They're willing to put considerable effort into it. They might, for example, research your company's executives—perhaps

---

* You are. See Figure 7: Vulnerable Downloads per Month.

even spy on them. Then they might use information they gather to craft very legitimate looking spear-phishing emails that seem to come from a friend or spouse and relate to a topic relevant to them. That email might have a link that appears plausible but when clicked installs malware onto the computer that, in turn, throws open the door to your network. You get the idea.

The APT is in it for the long haul, willing to do research, stealthily and slowly exploiting opportunities, and leveraging any foothold it gets on your network so it becomes a large-scale breach. And they are adept at covering their footprints as they do this.

You want to completely stop the wannabe hackers, make things really difficult for the APTs, then make a business decision about how much more expense and effort to put into guarding yourself against the most dedicated and smart hackers, and in which areas.

———————

Security is part of the service that you deliver to your customers and a responsibility you have to shareholders. It's a requirement of doing business. It's the job of marketing and sales, who are making an implicit promise to customers that they (you) will safeguard their personal data while providing a service that continues to function. It's the job of the CFO, who is managing risk for the company. It's the job of operations, for the company must be able to continue to do business. And, of course, it's the job of the CIO and CISO.

It's tempting to think of security as something that is outsourced to the IT department, but in fact everyone must participate and be willing to devote effort. Investments in security are not investments to meet "IT's needs"—they're to meet your business's needs, with IT acting as a steward. Employees understandably squirm at constraints on their freedom, with their natural inclination being to resist any security rules. But in the digital world, security absolutely must be part of doing business, implicitly written into every employee's job description. Everyone in the enterprise should collaborate in building a culture of security.

Enterprises are remarkably good at doing things that hackers can exploit. At USCIS, we had our auditors call employees, pretending to be from the IT helpdesk and asking for their passwords. Many obliged. The auditors wandered around our office in the evening, finding sticky notes with employee passwords and documents with personal information on their desks. Think about this: hackers can easily find exploitable information by "dumpster diving" through your company's trash or by reading your employees' Facebook posts.

Dumb mistakes are common within IT as well. There is a well-known, top-ten software vulnerabilities list, yet developers continue to include these types of defects in their code. They also often don't patch old versions of open-source software with vulnerabilities (see Figure 7: Vulnerable Downloads Per Month). And it's easy for an IT employee making manual changes to "fat finger" a mistake that creates a vulnerability. Worse, IT organizational silos have led even developers and operators to think of security as a job only for the security specialists.

We must reduce the number of these mistakes by creating a culture of security across the entire enterprise.

<hr>

The good news is that a lot of what makes for good security is free, or nearly so. It just requires intent. It also helps to think of security as an aspect of quality, a security vulnerability being just like any other defect that needs to be fixed. Instead of reactively dealing with security threats as they arise, the enterprise should be building its systems and conducting its operations with security built in, just as it strives to build in quality.

The Rugged Software movement promotes such an approach for software development. In its manifesto (of course it has a manifesto!), the rugged way of thinking is defined this way:

> "Rugged" describes software development organizations which have a culture of rapidly evolving their ability to create available, survivable, defensible, secure, and resilient software. Rugged organizations use competition, cooperation, and experimentation to learn and improve rather than making the same mistakes over and over. Rugged organizations also actively seek out threats and create defenses before they are a problem.[2]

The Rugged movement proposes that organizations change their way of thinking about security. Instead of reacting when threats and vulnerabilities are discovered, a rugged organization makes its systems defensible against any kind of threats that might emerge in the future.

While this might sound impossible, Rugged points out that it's largely a matter of commitment. Much of security is simply about developing good habits, like washing your hands. It might seem inconvenient at first, but it quickly becomes ordinary hygiene and, when it does, it can be virtually costless.

In the spirit of erasing boundaries between IT and the rest of the enterprise, I suggest that we extend the idea of rugged software to everything your enterprise does. Security should be built into business processes as well as IT systems. It should be a way of doing business, not a set of defenses that are added.

———

Automation helps solve many security issues. Code can be tested automatically for security flaws. Open-source products with known vulnerabilities can be identified by automated scans. Automated controls can be placed in cloud environments to enforce security policies and check for common vulnerabilities. Automating certain business processes can also improve security: for example, when an employee leaves a company, all of their IT accounts should automatically and immediately be deactivated.

When a security incident does happen, your organization must be able to detect and respond to it quickly. In the traditional approach, security experts sat in front of screens with dashboards and monitoring information, looking for evidence of break-ins. Increasingly, this kind of monitoring and detection is automated, as is the response to detected incidents.

Information security is indeed a complex area, and you need the help of the supergeeks to master it. But all of their efforts are in vain if the rest of the organization isn't committed to customer security and doesn't take basic steps to preserve it. The company must also be willing to invest in security—not because IT asks for it, but because it is essential.

The goal of the organization isn't just to enforce security and compliance, but to remain fast and nimble while doing so. With automated controls in place, employees can work quickly, secure in the knowledge that controls are keeping the enterprise safe and compliant. Once again, speed and agility are the important risk mitigators. But let's not allow that arms-length relationship between IT and the rest of the business fool us into thinking that security is something only IT worries about, because that opens a huge gap through which the bad guys can slip.

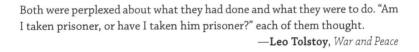

9

PLANNING AND REPORTING

Both were perplexed about what they had done and what they were to do. "Am I taken prisoner, or have I taken him prisoner?" each of them thought.
—**Leo Tolstoy**, *War and Peace*

Once the decision has been made, close your ear even to the best counterargument: sign of a strong character. Thus an occasional will to stupidity.
—**Friedrich Nietzsche**, *Epigrams and Interludes*

In Chapter 4 I suggested that IT spending cannot be considered in isolation; it affects other budget categories and depends on an organization's strategic intentions. A marginal dollar spent on IT might result in more than a marginal dollar of revenue in one business unit or cost reduction in another. Dollars spent in IT might also have consequences for future revenues and costs. A marginal dollar to reduce technical debt or build some other kind of agility might create an option that has much more than a dollar of impact later on.

So how can an enterprise know how much to spend? How can it reduce costs, or make sure that every dollar it spends earns as much value as possible? And how can it measure and report on the results of its IT investments?

Reducing IT Costs

The main driver of IT spending should always be the company's operational and strategic needs. This point is easily neglected when we think of IT as separate from the business, a painful and unavoidable cost. In that case it makes sense to consider reducing its total budget to drive efficiencies within IT. But as we pull IT deeper into the heart of the enterprise, our focus needs to shift. Instead of just cutting total costs, our goal is to eliminate waste so that every dollar spent on IT is as effective as possible, and then to adjust spending based on the organization's business goals. The IT financial strategy for the digital age is to focus on leanness.

A good place to look for waste is in administrative overhead. With large initiatives that don't produce product until late in the effort—the traditional approach—there is a lot of risk to manage, resulting in a lot of administrative overhead. Documents are produced, discussions conducted, statuses reported, decisions signed off on, steering groups convened, and fingernails bitten. This risk-mitigating administrative activity is expensive. And when budgets are tightened, this activity isn't the part that is cut—after all, with a tight budget, we have even more need to make sure that every dollar is well spent.

But in an environment where leanness is prized, such activities have a painful impact on lead times and cost. I'm not suggesting that we stop over-seeing our investments responsibly. What I am suggesting is that we make the oversight lean, that we remove any ineffective activities from it, and that we make sure the cost of oversight is appropriate given the amount of risk. And then we find ways to reduce risk, so we can reduce administrative overhead.

In Chapter 8: Bureaucracy and Culture, I showed how the DHS Analysis of Alternatives document was wasteful. It was only one of about one hundred documents that are prepared for a project. The thirteen required gate reviews included one to make sure there was an actual need for the project, another to verify that the plan was in place, one to make certain the requirements had been locked down, yet another to make sure the system design had been completed . . . you get the picture. Each document required signatures from a number of stakeholders and every gate review had dozens of attendees.

Since much of our work was done by contractors, we also spent time nego-tiating contract terms to protect us against performance risk. Overly cautious stakeholders wanted applications to be tested in ways that were barely effec-tive in finding defects. Program reviews were conducted by the GAO—and by the Inspector General, the Office of Management and Budget, the DHS CIO's office, assorted consultants, and of course, the financial auditors.

These are expensive mechanisms, especially in terms of lead times. They're the obvious costs of risk management—for that is their intention, right?—but there are more subtle costs as well. These include the frequent meetings to discuss the status of the project, its requirements, the project plan, when exactly to deploy the system, whether the stakeholders are ready, and whether the system has been tested thoroughly. When projects are going poorly, the length and frequency of these meetings increases, thereby worsening the problem.

Altogether, I'm fairly certain that in government IT we were spending about ten dollars to mitigate the risk of every one dollar of actual engineering spend.* That's the government. But how much is your enterprise spending? What is the right proportion to spend on risk management, and how much effect should we let it have on lead times? And, more importantly, how much of it goes to mitigate the risk that IT won't behave, as the contractor-control model fears?

<hr/>

There is a vicious circle in heavy-handed oversight. Large projects incur heavy oversight because they're risky. The oversight then becomes so much of a burden that everyone tries to avoid it. More and more is added to each project so that employees won't have to go through the oversight process more than once. The result is that each project becomes larger and riskier.

The best way to reduce the cost of oversight is to break this vicious circle—to conduct only small initiatives that return value quickly, thereby reducing risk and requiring less oversight. The risk-reducing practices I've discussed throughout this book—staging investments, using fast feedback cycles to test ideas, deploying automated controls—all are cost-effective ways to accomplish the same goals.

Because these oversight costs aren't confined to the IT budget but spread across the entire enterprise, it can be difficult to identify the potential savings. It's only by looking at IT delivery holistically, rather than looking at organizational budget categories, that we can spot the potential for eliminating waste.

One of the metrics I think is most important for gauging the efficiency of IT processes is the ratio of administrative overhead to actual creation work. Product creation and operation—engineering work—is what actually adds value for the enterprise. All other effort is just there to support it and can be thought of as overhead, whether it's performed by the engineers or others. Not

<hr/>

* I made up that number, but it is consistent with my intuitions and seems fair to others in the government I have mentioned it to.

all overhead can be eliminated, but it's the part of the IT budget that should be purposefully minimized.

Remember the sources of waste that come from managing IT as if it were an independent contractor. There is the overhead of negotiating schedules with IT; documenting requirements in a bulletproof, no-scope-creep-allowed way; managing change requests when requirements are discovered to be unsatisfactory; not to mention the effort IT spends justifying its value and administering chargeback models, for example. Each is a cost that increases that important ratio of administrative costs to total costs. All are costs we've assumed we have to bear because of an old mental model about how enterprise IT works.

———

The largest area for savings is in removing feature bloat; that is, in following the Agile principle of "maximizing the amount of work not done." In the model where IT is handed a set of requirements and told to deliver on it, IT cannot take part in reducing this cost. Remember that the amount of waste in unneeded features and features that don't actually accomplish their goals can be tremendous—as much as two-thirds of the spending on IT delivery.*

The best way to eliminate feature bloat is with a Lean Startup approach:

1. First build a bare-bones minimum viable product.
2. Add to it incrementally, prioritizing the features that will contribute most to accomplishing the goal.
3. Continue with step 2 until diminishing returns suggest that you stop.

Jim Highsmith's advice is:

Do less: cut out or cut down projects, cut out overhead that doesn't deliver customer value, cut out or cut down features during release planning, cut out or cut down stories [requirements] during iteration planning, cut down work-in-process to improve throughput. At the same time, focus on delighting the customer by frequent delivery of value.[1]

---

* Based not just on the Standish study, which I have my doubts about, but on the Microsoft study that I referenced in Chapter 1 that showed that one third of ideas don't affect the metric they were intended to improve, one third make it worse, and only one third succeed.

A popular IT metric is the percentage of its spending used to create or acquire new capabilities ("innovation") versus the spending necessary for "keeping the lights on (KTLO)." This metric is often promoted by CIOs and IT leaders to explain the constraints they face in a statement like, "Well, we couldn't accomplish that much this year because we needed 70% of our budget just for keeping the lights on."*

KTLO is assumed to be something akin to waste; it is the remainder of the budget that is not thought to be adding business value. I have trouble accepting this. KTLO generally includes items such as maintenance of existing software systems, licensing or maintenance fees for using off-the-shelf software and hardware, network and telecom costs, and cloud computing charges. These are the costs of actually doing the company's work—a good thing! Existing systems account for the company's current revenue and operations—they run the company day-to-day. Paying for them is a joyous thing; we know they work (the company is running today) and we can use them as a springboard for new capabilities.

It's true that many of the items in this bucket we would like to manage downward for a given level of operating capability. But in my experience, "maintaining" software often turns out to be making changes to its capabilities—enhancements, improvements, or changes to keep up with changes in the business. These changes are really innovation work, and are in fact some of its most cost-effective sources, since the enterprise builds them incrementally on an existing system rather than having to create a new one from scratch.

In truth, there is no such thing as "maintaining" a piece of software. After you buy a new car, you must continue to spend money so it continues to function as it did when you bought it. But software continues to function as purchased even without maintenance spending. The problem is we don't *want* the software to continue to function as it did when purchased; we want it to change as the enterprise changes. The costs for those changes are often in the KTLO bucket, although they deserve to be in the innovation bucket.

The belief that we should maximize the non-KTLO percentage comes from thinking that KTLO spending is non-discretionary, something the company is

---

* According to Peter Weill and Jeanne W. Ross, the average KTLO spend in 2007 was 71% of the IT budget.[2]

stuck with. But that is a sunk cost fallacy. That we have bought a piece of software doesn't mean we have to keep paying licensing or maintenance or support fees for it. We can stop using it. The decision to continue spending on it is a positive affirmation of its value to the company—or spending that should be discontinued. As in many cases it should be.*

<hr/>

Not only do we often build unnecessary features but we also over-constrain solutions. In our requirements documents we used to say things like, "The system must be available 99.3% of the time," or "Response time must be less than 2.4 seconds." Or we established service level agreements (SLAs) with the IT department. Yes, if we're contracting work out, we need to have criteria for non-performance. But when we're working with an internal IT organization, the calculus is different.†

In theory, the 99.3% availability requirement is calculated in a business case showing how much it'll cost the company if the system is down more than 0.7% of the time—how much business will be lost, how far operations will be set back. Even if we could have confidence in this calculation, it's missing an important component: the marginal cost. The relevant calculation is *the marginal cost* for achieving 99.3% availability over whatever level we have versus the benefit. In other words, if we get to 99.2% and discover that it'll cost an additional $10 million to get to 99.3%, is it worth it? And what if it only costs an additional penny to get it to 99.99%? Shouldn't we "require" that?

When we're planning an initiative it's virtually impossible to calculate marginal costs in advance. Does anyone really know exactly what will be needed to achieve 99.3% availability rather than 99.2% or 99.4%? It's only through continuous feedback and adaptation that we can make a good decision on marginal costs and benefits.

<hr/>

* For the philosophy geeks out there, you might say that the enterprise continuously chooses what it wants to be, IT-wise. See Sartre, *Being and Nothingness*, and take the sunk cost fallacy as analogous to Sartre's idea of bad faith.
† I'm not saying don't do it, because many people I respect are practitioners of the ITIL framework, which considers service level agreements (SLAs) between the business and IT to be important. They are wrong, but I still respect them.

Cloud infrastructure is an interesting case for managing costs. If you're not working in the cloud, you have to buy a fixed amount of infrastructure based on your projections of how much usage your system will get. But your usage will vary over time—all the more so if we're talking about an internet-facing site. Tax software gets used a lot in tax season, but rarely otherwise.[3] Fitness apps are used a lot in January, after New Year's resolutions.* To avoid a fiasco like Healthcare.gov,† you have to buy the amount of infrastructure needed to handle your peak usage, plus some. Most of that infrastructure will be underused most of the time, and there will still be a risk of larger peaks than you've planned for.

In the cloud, on the other hand, you pay for exactly the amount of infrastructure you need at any given moment. If your employees go home at night, you can turn off some of the servers that were running during the day and stop paying for them. If your software is only used during tax season, then you can turn off servers during the rest of the year.

This is optimal from the cost standpoint, but seemingly less predictable from the budget standpoint. It isn't really, because you can set spending limits in the cloud. But what if you've reached your budget and suddenly get an unexpected surge in usage? What if your digital service is doing better in the marketplace than you had budgeted for? Do you want to stick to your budget and have the system crash, or exceed your budget and serve the customers? Probably the latter.

The unpredictability doesn't really come from using the cloud, but from the unpredictability of the market itself. At least you have the choice to respond to that unpredictability, whereas if you had bought fixed infrastructure, there would be no practical way to quickly expand it. Spending more on cloud infrastructure often just means that you're successful with your product. Although there has been a lot of talk about how the cloud turns capital expenditures (CAPEX) into operational expenditures (OPEX), the more interesting point may be that it turns a fixed cost into a variable cost. When paying by the drink

---

* Yes, really. Ask UnderArmour about the use of their Fitness Connect mobile app, for example.[4]
† The Obama Administration's signature health insurance initiative was set back after its launch in October 2013 when usage was five times the expected volume.[5]

in the cloud, you don't know how many drinks you'll be taking. That is a good thing, as you want to be free to decide—responsibly, of course.

The theme here is making incremental or marginal spending decisions. With an Agile project, you can make a decision at any time to continue past the originally planned cost if there are still value-adding features to be built. Or you can decide not to finish a planned scope of work if the marginal value of remaining work is too low. With staged investments, you can determine whether a marginal commitment is worthwhile. With cloud infrastructure, you can decide to increase or decrease infrastructure from where it is at any given moment, depending on which direction has marginal value. This is business agility: most of the interesting decisions are made at the margins.

Budgeting and Planning

Considering the IT budget independently from the rest of the business can lead to inefficiency. If IT's budget is constrained so it can't make a one hundred dollar investment that will reduce marketing's costs by twice that amount, or if IT is constrained so that the internals of a system aren't as flexible as they should be, then business value is destroyed. Once we agree that IT is no longer just a simple cost of doing business, its interrelationships with other parts of the enterprise become important in choosing spending levels.

How should you budget for IT? One way is to base your budget on empirical data, where historical spending levels represent the company's actual lived experience. Let's say that the company funded twenty cross-functional delivery teams last year, and they were allocated among its work streams. Based on last year's experience, you know approximately what that amount of capacity can accomplish. Given your best guesses and the company's objectives this year, do you need more capacity? You can make your best estimate and finance to that level, then IT can allocate its teams to work streams.

Sometimes it may be possible to "do more with less," but an empirical, data-based approach would suggest that you can do "the same amount with the same amount." That said, IT and the rest of the business should constantly be looking for ways to make processes leaner and negotiate better prices with suppliers.

I'm a little uncomfortable with the idea of setting capacity, then managing demand for it, because I have trouble with IT constantly going to the rest of the business and saying, "Sorry, we can't do everything you need. You'll have to prioritize." I hear this often and it doesn't feel right to me. The organization should *want* what it has the capacity to do, and IT must generally be able to meet *all* of the company's needs. I suspect this really is an artifact of a model where IT provides customer service to competing parts of the enterprise.

In Chapter 4 I proposed that IT's efforts should be cascaded from high-level, enterprise-wide objectives. Demand for IT services should, in that case, be more or less what the enterprise decided at the outset it was going to try to accomplish and what it budgeted for. Excess demand would imply that managers are asking for things that aren't necessary for meeting the objectives. If the enterprise doesn't budget enough for IT to support its objectives, that's a failure of leadership and the budgeting process.

I've also pointed out that when it comes to financing IT projects, traditional project management makes it unlikely that an initiative will stay within its planned costs. That's because projects start with an immutable set of requirements and continue spending until the requirements are complete. If we really care about budget, we must hold the budget fixed and vary the requirements. The case for doing so are especially strong because we know that some of the requirements are less valuable than others, and some have no value at all. After all, that's the way we treat budgets in most corners of the organization—if we don't have enough money to do all the things we want to do, we just do less of them. But IT projects have been treated differently, because we have assumed that requirements are . . . required.

A vicious circle can occur in the annual planning process, as Boston Consulting Group (BCG) has pointed out.[6] The uncertainty in the environment sometimes leads enterprises to plan more carefully, especially if plans have gone awry in the past. As a result, they start the planning process earlier. But forecasting earlier just extends the period they must forecast for, which increases the amount of uncertainty, which makes the plan less accurate, which causes them to spend even more time on planning the following year. Once the volatility of the digital world sets this dynamic in motion, the costs of planning increase and the plans become less useful.

Instead, BCG says "the overall focus for planning must move away from precise forecasting and toward more strategic, top-down ambition-setting that is validated with bottom-up business insight."[7] They suggest that companies plan in less detail so they can retain more flexibility, set targets top-down, and remain nimble and adaptable.

An annual budgeting process necessarily limits agility during the year. In *Implementing Beyond Budgeting*, Bjarte Bogsnes explains the alternative planning practices he implemented at companies such as Equinor, Scandinavia's largest company. The problem with budgets, he says, is that they're entirely focused on what you put in, not what you get back.[8] In other words, the budgeting process puts a cap on what a division can spend, without reference to what return it would get from any marginal spend—which could be substantial. "What we want is not necessarily the lowest possible cost level," he says. "What we want is the optimal cost level, the one that maximizes value creation."[9]

The problem isn't just that budgets prevent managers from spending when they should, but that they also allow managers to keep spending until their budget is exhausted, whether the spending is worthwhile or not. The budget number is viewed as an entitlement, and it's rare for a manager to "return" unused money, especially since the unspent money will probably be taken out of the following year's budget.

The Beyond Budgeting movement, whose ideas are practiced worldwide by companies large and small across a range of industries, recommends a number of ways to make the budgeting process more agile, including planning on shorter horizons, doing rolling planning through the course of the year, and fostering extreme transparency into budgets and spending. The idea is to give the company agility to deal with uncertainty and change, while at the same time setting motivating targets, providing good forecasts, and effectively allocating scarce resources.[10]

I've pointed out the persistent confusion in IT between estimates and commitments, or between forecasts and execution plans. Fundamentally, a budget is a way of turning forecasts into targets. In an environment of uncertainty, we have to ask, "How reliable are our forecasts that reach eighteen months into the future?"

Eric Ries offers an amusing account of forecasting at a startup:

> I found out that some investors actually believed the forecast. They would even try to use it as a tool of accountability—just like Alfred

Sloan. If a startup failed to match the numbers in the original business plan, the investors would take this as a sign of poor execution. As an entrepreneur, I found this reaction baffling. Didn't they know that those numbers were entirely made up?[11]

It might be an exaggeration to say that the numbers are made up, but his point is that what good investors look for in a startup is not meeting forecasted targets, which are created under conditions of great uncertainty, but adapting well to market conditions. A startup is well managed if it conducts good tests and adapts to what it learns; it's a good investment if it proves that there is customer value and a ready market.

We try to use budgets to control spending based on our forecasts. But spending in the digital world isn't always amenable to that sort of control; it should instead be determined by actual, evolving circumstances. Control can still be established through continuous transparency and adaptation. You can't have it both ways—encouraging employees to innovate and adapt while also asking them to make a plan and stick to it. Clayton Christensen, in *The Innovator's Dilemma*, explains that this is why enterprises miss out on innovation opportunities:

> Companies whose investment processes demand quantification of market sizes and financial returns before they can enter a market get paralyzed or make serious mistakes when faced with disruptive technologies. They demand market data when none exists and make judgments based upon financial projections when neither revenues or costs can, in fact, be known. Using planning and marketing techniques that were developed to manage sustaining technologies in the very different context of disruptive ones is an exercise in flapping wings.[12]

CAPEX and OPEX

In that old world, we thought of an IT system as a product—something you either built or bought, and rolled out for use as a whole. It fit neatly into our mental model of what a capital asset looked like. But today we build systems incrementally and put each piece into use as it's completed, possibly on the order of a hundred times a day. Determining when a system is "finished" has also become difficult; IT systems continue to evolve throughout their lifetimes, as we maintain a continuous backlog of further work and continue drawing from it. In theory, an IT system can survive forever—if the company keeps making changes to it, replacing it piece by piece, changing its functionality as the business changes, and changing its internals as necessary to fight entropy.

It is becoming less and less clear what that asset is that we are capitalizing. Its boundaries are now difficult to identify, since IT systems are increasingly made by combining small components—called microservices—each of which is reusable and forms part of other systems as well. Its infrastructure can be difficult to identify since it may be ephemeral and exists only in the cloud where it is obtained on demand from a cloud provider and can be changed, supplemented, reduced, or disposed of as the company's needs change. It might, moreover, consist of services provided by the cloud, also on an on-demand basis, such as artificial intelligence, analytics, or even call center capabilities.

All of these changes have occurred because they are improvements. That systems are amorphous and constantly changing helps ensure they support the business as it evolves. The ability to consume infrastructure and services on demand reduces costs and risks. Breaking down systems into microservices saves money, increases reliability, and speeds time to market. And the fact that systems are delivered incrementally and continuously reduces the risk inherent in large projects and also lets the company harvest the value of IT work more quickly.

But it does complicate the picture from an accounting point of view, doesn't it? Our old model of capitalizing systems for internal use or external sale fits awkwardly with these new developments. We have always expensed our costs for establishing feasibility of a new system, capitalized the costs of building or buying it, then depreciated that asset and expensed the maintenance costs associated with it. How does that fit with today's IT practices?

I'm not an accountant and cannot offer any accounting guidance. I can only wonder about how these developments will affect the accounting treatment of IT costs. Some questions suggest themselves:

- If what we called maintenance is really adding capabilities and altering the system to keep it aligned with the changing business, are we not adding to the value of the asset? Shouldn't we therefore be capitalizing these costs?
- If we begin using a capitalized capability as soon as it's been developed, shouldn't we also start depreciating it at that moment rather than waiting for the rest of the "asset" to be delivered?

- If the system is constantly updated, evolved, transformed, improved—and its lifecycle is therefore effectively infinite—over how many years of its useful life is it to be depreciated?
- If some parts of the system, including features it offers, are actually paid for "on demand" from the cloud, are they not part of the asset, while those features built inhouse are?
- If throughout the system lifecycle we're constantly trying experiments and sometimes backing away, how do we distinguish "establishing feasibility" from "development?"

Measuring Success

If we're no longer assessing our IT department by its cost and schedule adherence, cost reduction, IT budget as a percentage of revenue, customer satisfaction, percentage of KTLO spending, or any of the other metrics I've rejected throughout this book, then how do we assess it?

Primarily, IT's success is measured by that of the company. Since IT is meant to support business initiatives and operations, it's successful to the extent that it supports them well. If business objectives are cascaded down to multi-functional teams that include both business and IT people—as I've suggested—then it's the success of these teams that really matters. That's hard to break down into its IT component. And since IT is responsible for maintaining the agility of its systems and processes so the company can be agile in the future, it's the long-term success of the company that reflects IT's performance.

When we look at improving IT processes, the important metric to focus on is lead time from concept to delivery. Notice that much of that is external to IT or at the boundary where IT meets the rest of the business. Then again, why should that matter, since it's internal to the business as a whole and IT is an integral part of the business?

Lead time is a very important metric because reducing it:

- means removing waste from processes (this leads to cost reduction and improved employee morale);
- reduces time to market for new products, and time to value for investments that affect internal users;
- lets a company quickly try out ideas and get feedback on them, thereby increasing innovation and fit-to-need;

- means coming closer to delivering as soon as possible;
- reduces risk by reducing work-in-process (the amount of investment risk at any moment);
- and helps keep systems more secure (the IT team will be able to respond to emerging threats more quickly, patch software more quickly, and respond to incidents more quickly).

Lead time tells us how efficient a company is at processing each requirement once it's identified. It's a replacement for, and an improvement over, on-time delivery as a metric. It applies not just to software, but to IT capability delivery in general—for example, provisioning a laptop for a new employee, resetting a forgotten password, or coming to the rescue when audiovisual equipment isn't working in a conference room.

Lead time is speed, and speed is essential in an environment of uncertainty.

The IT performance construct created by DevOps Research and Assessment (DORA) is an excellent way to assess IT performance, especially since DORA showed it to predict business success. Their construct includes metrics that are easily measurable, very much actionable, and relevant to success in the digital environment. DORA's software delivery and operation (SDO) construct includes:

- **Frequency of deployments.** This is closely related to throughput and overall lead time.
- **Lead time from finishing code to deploying it.** This is also related to throughput and overall lead time. It's the portion of overall lead time that should be relatively stable and amenable to immediate improvement.
- **Change failure rate.** When new capabilities are deployed, how often do they fail? This is a measure of quality and of the stability of delivery processes.
- **Mean time to repair (MTTR).** When a problem occurs in live systems, how long does it take to fix? This also determines how long it takes to respond to a security incident or to implement a security patch.

Availability—the percentage of time IT systems are operational and available to be used—is another important metric studied by DORA in its latest report. Availability standards are now very high, as customers and employees have become used to the "always on" availability of services from such providers as Amazon and Google.

Other metrics could be useful but may be more difficult and more expensive to measure. *Escaped defects* are bugs that make their way into production and affect users. Since code is vetted by automated tests throughout its lifespan, only its undetected defects pose a problem; in any case, they're the ones that result in costly rework.

Process agility is a more abstract performance metric. If the company decided to stop producing bobbleheads and start producing toenail clippers tomorrow, how quickly could IT adjust? If IT is working on project A when project B suddenly becomes a higher priority, how quickly could it change focus and how much waste would there be?

Then there is the amount of *technical debt*—how much gunk there is in the IT asset that will slow down future work.

These metrics serve as a basis for continuous improvement. They're not intended for assessing any one person's performance or that of a particular group. For one thing, there is no correct value for any of the metrics. For another, they can be gamed if used for performance measurement. For example, the number of deployments per day can be increased by deploying increasingly smaller changes (which, fortunately, is a desirable behavior anyway!). No, there are too many interacting, determinant factors for them to be useful in attempting to allocate blame or award praise.

How then can you measure your IT organization's productivity, or that of, say, a given software developer within that organization? In the old waterfall contractor-control model, on-time performance was considered a productivity measure. I hope I've convinced you that it is not—if anything, it's a measure of how stubborn the technologists were in sticking to the original plan and how much padding existed in the original estimates. But Agile and DevOps approaches seem to remove even that as a way to gauge productivity.

Jim Highsmith is on target when he says, "Productivity measures in general make little sense in knowledge work."[13] Designing good software and infrastructure, solving business problems, and creating IT strategies are knowledge work.

That doesn't mean they can't be done poorly or too slowly. Highsmith's comment aside, how do you measure the performance of other knowledge workers in the enterprise? In fact, how do you measure the performance of most employees? Generally, it's not by measuring delivery against a pre-planned schedule. Managers evaluate the performance of their employees by staying close enough to their activities to observe their productivity, quality of work, quality of communications, and so on. The same holds in IT—managers *manage* their employees.

Ultimately, the performance of the IT organization is reflected in a company's business results. This should be what motivates and incentivizes the employees of IT. If it isn't, then any improvement in lead times, escaped defects, availability, and other measures I listed are beside the point; even if these show a good trend, the organization won't become more successful. Notice—it's *business* results that should motivate IT, not any internal IT metrics. You could almost take that to be the definition of a digital enterprise.

SIDE GLANCE:
THE CLOUD AND
THE FUTURE

How long, then, should we hold to these rules and not break up the game? As long as the game is going nicely.

—**Epictetus**, *Discourses*

A sublime thought, if happily timed, illumines an entire subject with the vividness of a lightning-flash.

—**Longinus**, *On the Sublime*

It's very difficult to keep a computer busy all day. A billion times a second it's looking around for a new task. No matter how many cat videos you watch, the computer still spends most of its time waiting for you to tell it which cat video you want to see next. This restlessness has been the driver of much of the recent innovation in technology.

I would be undermining my point that uncertainty dominates the digital arena if I were to write a chapter telling you what I think is coming next for enterprise IT. Instead, I'd like to point out some of the important trends of the moment that should influence the way we think about the future.

I'll start with the cloud, the impact of which is already deeply felt. A logical extension of the cloud is serverless computing. Artificial intelligence, and in particular machine learning, has become practical for general business use and changes our fundamental ideas about computing. All three of these developments have deep implications for the way enterprises use IT and what IT is capable of contributing to the enterprise.

There is an enormous amount of restless computer processing capacity in the world today, and cloud providers are adding more of it. The trends I'll discuss are ways of keeping our processors from getting bored with us.

———————

The impact of the cloud is deeper than you may think. It's leading toward the demise of the hardware that has run our enterprise systems, at least as a concern for IT departments. This change is happening at the same time that consumer devices are replacing the desktop and laptop computers we use every day, the devices we actually put our hands on. Computing power, in other words, is in our pockets and in the cloud, and less in the offices and datacenters of our companies.

The cloud's magic is that it turns computing power into a service. Like electricity in your home—flip a switch and it's on, flip it again and it's off. You pay the electric company for what you use. You have no need to burn coal or set up a hydroelectric dam to get your electricity—presumably someone else is doing that, although in any case you have no reason to concern yourself with it.

In the past, enterprises acquired computing power by doing the equivalent of generating their own electricity. They bought computing hardware, installed it in racks in a datacenter, and set it up following the manufacturer's instructions. They connected it to electricity and to the internet, and provided enough air conditioning to keep the hyperactive, restless computers cool. They set up physical security to prevent bad guys from sneaking into the datacenter. And they provided the labor to manage the computer, upgrade its software, and diagnose its problems.

Organizations using the cloud don't have to do any of these things. When they need computing power, they use their cloud provider's website or run an automated script to request it and it's immediately available. When they're done computing, they release the computing power and stop paying for it. If they need data storage, that is also immediately available—and just as immediately disposable when it's no longer needed. In fact, as of the end of 2018 Amazon Web Services (AWS), the pioneer in cloud computing, offers a menu of more than 165 different services an enterprise can consume at any time as a utility—from computing power and storage to networking, security, databases, analytics, machine learning, and even automated call center services. Flip a switch and they're on, flip it again and they're off.

One consequence of the cloud's rise is that information technology, once a matter of both hardware and software, is now increasingly about software only. The IT organization can set up infrastructure in the cloud by writing automated scripts—in other words, by programming it—rather than by fiddling around with hardware. In this book I've made the case that agility is critical for digital enterprises; imagine now how much nimbler the transition from hardware to software can make you. Software is something you can change in seconds by entering keystrokes at a keyboard, while hardware can only be changed by replacing it with new hardware.

Another consequence is that organizations can rapidly adjust the amount of computing power they consume. If your website suddenly gets a surge of user traffic, then you can increase the amount of infrastructure you use until the surge dies down. If your employees only work during daylight hours, then you can reduce the amount of infrastructure you're paying for at night. If you have a seasonal business, then you can reduce your infrastructure spending out of season. Intuit, for example, can save five-sixths of its TurboTax AnswerXchange infrastructure costs by turning off infrastructure when tax season ends.[1]

Again, the cloud is a lot like that electrical utility company. Cloud providers such as AWS achieve tremendous economies of scale and pass the savings on to its customers. AWS and other providers have put a lot of restless computing capacity in the cloud, and enterprises can use it to make themselves nimbler.

To explain how and why the cloud works, I'll dive briefly into its history. It starts with the fact that most of the computers permanently connected to the internet are *servers*, which means they wait for another computer to ask them to do something, do it, and then resume waiting. For example, when your browser displays a web page, your laptop communicates over the internet with a server, which transmits the bits that make up the web page. Other servers handle the company's HR systems, databases, email, and fantasy football pools.

Even while one of these servers is working, it's often just one part of the computer that's busy, while the rest are twiddling their thumb drives. In the 1990s, technologists came up with a solution for all of this wasted computer capacity. They created a piece of software called a *hypervisor* that lets one server act as if it were many, each called a *virtual machine (VM)* or an *instance*. Since each VM would get somewhat busy handling the tasks it was assigned, overall they were able to keep a single physical server reasonably busy most of the time.

This was all possible because the server hardware, it turned out, was pretty much ignored once it was installed in a datacenter rack. Even systems administrators responsible for the servers rarely saw the hardware—they sat in a different room, perhaps even at different geographical location, and communicated with the server over a network, just like everyone else. So as the single physical server morphed into many VMs, no user was any the wiser.

The actual work you want the computer to perform—the software you want it to run—is called the *workload*. If you had a number of VMs running on a number of servers, and a number of workloads to task them all with, all you had to do was distribute the workloads among the VMs and let them work.

This was the way that Amazon.com had set up its infrastructure, and in 2006 the company had the idea of offering extra VMs to other companies to use for their workloads. It launched something it called the Elastic Compute Cloud, or EC2. Any company could use Amazon's automated tools to set up a VM on one of Amazon's servers, load a workload into it, and set it running. No one could tell that the server was in an Amazon facility, since everyone using it was located somewhere else anyway. Your web pages appeared to your customers just as if your web server were in your own headquarters, in a datacenter, or under Gerald's desk.

———

The cloud developed from there. In addition to VMs, cloud providers also began to offer data storage for a fee. Each started replicating its infrastructure in multiple locations so that workloads would be resilient in the face of disasters. And the cloud providers began offering software capabilities in addition to infrastructure, with fees again based on usage.

Cloud infrastructure is now globally distributed. AWS alone has infrastructure in twenty locations as of the end of 2018, each consisting of at least three separate datacenters to provide resilience against disasters. Businesses benefit from the effort AWS puts into ensuring that its infrastructure is reliable and secure. Among its users today are federal agencies, such as the Department of Homeland Security and intelligence agencies; banks and financial services firms such as JPMorgan Chase and Capital One; and highly trafficked consumer companies such as Netflix and Expedia.[2]

The next phase in cloud evolution is called *serverless computing*. Since providers have abstracted away physical infrastructure into the virtual world, the next step is to altogether eliminate the concept of infrastructure. With serverless computing, which is already available but will likely become more common in the future, IT folks no longer need to explicitly provision infrastructure in the cloud. Instead they can simply provide some code and specify under what conditions it should run—that is, when compute power should be applied to it. The cloud takes care of the rest. Serverless computing brings us one step closer to computing as a utility.

Many companies are already using serverless computing, but the wave of innovation it will bring, I think, is just starting. As it develops, the IT budget will continue to move toward compute as an operational resource that is consumed, rather than an investment in hardware as a fixed asset.

The cloud is one of the drivers of the digital revolution. It has reduced barriers to entry across industries, since new entrants no longer have to invest in hardware and datacenters before becoming operational. The infrastructure they need is immediately available and their costs—based on volume of use—remain low while their businesses have a chance to grow.

The cloud helps provide the agility that enterprises need if they're to succeed in their digital transformation. In addition to cost advantages and the ability to quickly scale up and down based on demand, it promotes agility by letting them try out innovative ideas, all the while decreasing their lead times and making it easy for them to scale globally.

Innovation. When used together with DevOps, the cloud helps an enterprise innovate and find new opportunities for growth, as it can try out ideas with little risk and minimal cost. If an innovative idea doesn't work out, the enterprise can simply stop paying for the infrastructure and services it used to launch it.

Velocity. The cloud shortens lead times by eliminating the need to acquire and set up hardware. It gives an enterprise immediate access to powerful capabilities it can include in its applications, such as machine learning, identity management, and analytics.

Global reach. With twenty regional datacenter clusters and 160 other global points of presence where it has infrastructure, AWS makes it easier for an enterprise to serve a global market. It maintains fast performance in each region and satisfies data sovereignty requirements of different countries (rules that data has to stay within a given country's borders).

The easy availability of electricity led to the explosion of innovation and creativity that resulted in all of the household appliances we use today. We don't yet know what the easy availability of computing power will make possible. But we can already see that organizations are taking advantage of it to do things that would have been impossible a few years ago.

McDonald's, for example, runs its global point of sale (POS) systems on AWS, including 200,000 registers and 300,000 other POS devices serving sixty-four million customers a day.[3] When it decided to develop a mobile home delivery application, it was able to create and deploy it to customers in only four months.[4] GE Oil & Gas was able to speed up its application development time by 77%.[5] BMW was able to develop its car-as-a-sensor app (CARASSO) for its 7 Series cars in a matter of six months.[6] Such is the speed of the digital world.

- Clemson University has done research in natural language processing that involved spinning up 1.1 million concurrent processors for a brief period.[7] Before the cloud, it would never have been possible to buy a million computers, set them up, use them, then return them for a refund.
- The International Centre for Missing and Exploited Children (ICMEC) is able to compare photos of missing children against those found on social media to generate leads for investigators.[8]
- FINRA, the Financial Industry Regulatory Authority, is now able to look for fraud patterns in stock transactions by making available to its analysts petabytes of information (each petabyte is 1024 terabytes, or over one quadrillion bytes), gathering up 37 billion financial transactions a day.[9]

These are not just examples of performing tasks on an exceptionally large scale, but of doing things that simply would not have been possible before.

Around since the 1950s, *artificial intelligence* is the science of giving computers human intelligence-like abilities. Scientists have tried to solve a range of problems—playing chess, recognizing objects in photos, understanding human languages, controlling robots, and the like—using a variety of software engineering techniques. Of those, machine learning has become practical for business use, partly because of advances in the field and partly because new, fast, restless hardware has made practical the intensive computing that is required.

Machine learning also opens up for solution a whole new class of problems that would otherwise have been too complex. As an example, consider the task of recognizing handwritten numerals. Since everyone's handwriting is different, creating a computer program able to scan an image and identify the number it represents would be practically impossible. But with machine learning, we can show the machine a large number of handwritten numeral examples and inform it what each number is. This process is called supervised training. The computer uses that training data to construct a model it can apply to subsequent images. When you think about it, this is also how people learn to distinguish handwritten numbers—by seeing lots of examples and generalizing from them.

Machine learning is a complex subject and an endless source of topics for PhD dissertations. But in its quest to "democratize" machine learning, AWS has pre-trained models for common tasks that can be used by anyone—even those totally unfamiliar with machine learning. These pre-trained models can be used to recognize images in still photographs or video; to synthesize human-like speech in a number of languages; to understand text written in natural languages like English; to translate between languages; and to transcribe speech into text.

C-SPAN uses machine learning to recognize politicians in its video footage, then index the footage for easy access.[10] Stanford University uses it to scan retina images to diagnose diabetic blindness before the human eye would be able to.[11] Fraud.net, a collaborative effort of online merchants, uses it to spot instances of potential fraud,[12] and Hudl uses machine learning for predictive analysis on sports plays.[13]

The cloud, serverless computing, and machine learning make possible entirely new categories of applications, businesses, and IT processes. As technical advancements that also have deep business implications, I'm choosing these as good examples of how you can realize business benefits when the technologists play a role in mapping out your enterprise's future. It's the combination of technology and business savvy that is so important, and it's difficult to realize unless you bring the technologists and "business" people together to innovate.

PART III

Prescriptions

ACTION PLAN

When a craftsman repairs a timepiece he can still its wheels; but the living clockwork of the state has to be repaired while it continues to strike, the turning wheel has to be replaced while still in motion.

—**Friedrich Schiller**, *On the Aesthetic Education of Man*

Take time to deliberate, but when the time for action comes, stop thinking and go in.

—**Napoleon Bonaparte**

The preceding chapters have laid out what I believe is the best way to think about the role of enterprise IT in the context of digital transformation. Now we'll address the digital transformation itself. We have at our disposal the new techniques and mental models of IT—DevOps, Lean startup, Agile. How can we use them to get better value from our technology?

Beginning with this chapter, you'll notice that I am writing in imperatives, offering prescriptions rather than concepts. I'm doing so because of the urgency of getting started, and the difficulty in getting traction I've seen many enterprises face. Let's go—it's time to seize the initiative. Napoleon's army is poised . . . wait a minute, forget that. It didn't work out for him.

———————

The Agile approach, remember, is both lean and incremental. It's about moving quickly to avoid overplanning while constantly learning and adapting. It's about immediately and frequently delivering chunks of success, provoking and observing, experimenting and then either pivoting or persevering. The best way to succeed at digital transformation is to start right now, with a sense of urgency. Minimize risk by working in small increments, yet keep moving toward the vision. Learn through action where the impediments lie, then focus on removing them.

Starting immediately doesn't mean starting to *plan* immediately—it means starting to *do* immediately. Immediately means getting results within two weeks or so. They don't need to be big results, but they need to be actual results. An example of something that is *not* a result is holding a meeting. There won't be time for many meetings anyway. Other examples of things that aren't results (quoting directly from self-assessments by some of my former employees) are "worked with stakeholders," "drafted a plan," and "discussed options."

Instead, think big and execute small. Have a very clear vision that sets a direction, communicate it, then find the smallest thing that will move the enterprise in that direction. Instead of mitigating risk by planning, mitigate risk by taking small steps that produce results, then adjusting as necessary. Provoke, observe, repeat.

Just because someone is afraid of what is new doesn't mean that what is new is risky. As I said in Chapter 6: Risk and Opportunity, the status quo bias leads us to perceive risk lurking in that which is new. But it's riskier today to stick with the old ways of doing things—waterfalls, commanding from a remote redoubt, erecting barriers in the way of innovation. The digital way of working is now standard in countless enterprises across all industries. It is effective. It is not just a superpower of cutting-edge technology companies, but is also the way of large, old, sometimes stodgy (previously stodgy, that is) enterprises in retail, financial services, manufacturing, healthcare, media, government, nonprofit, and any other industry where companies use computers.

There are four objectives of the early transformation stages. Proceed toward these four in small steps, but proceed relentlessly. Your objectives are:

- Tie IT initiatives to business outcomes.
- Shorten lead times.
- Emphasize delivery and results.
- Treat requirements as hypotheses.

Tie IT Initiatives to Business Outcomes

An IT initiative should not be organized around a fixed set of requirements, but rather an intended outcome. Requirements should be used only to the extent that they're useful, and should be ignored if the team executing the initiative finds better ways to achieve the outcome. "Better" ways, in this context, means ways that accomplish the outcome more successfully or more simply. Minimize the amount of work done to accomplish the goal—the watchwords are lean, simple, fast, inexpensive.

To put this into action, you can charter a small team with an objective. The team should be self-contained. It should have all of the skills it needs to accomplish its objective and should have all the requisite tools and authorities. All management layers above it should be dedicated to removing impediments as they arise.

I'm starting with this objective because I think every organization can put it into action immediately. Don't try to reorganize your entire enterprise into objective-oriented teams; create one or two and focus on making them successful. There is something in every enterprise that is waiting to be done. Start there.

An objective is a business result. It's not something like "write x piece of software." It may be what answers the question, "Why do we think we need x piece of software?" It may or may not be quantitative, but it must be well-defined and there must be a way to see how well it is being accomplished. A full business case isn't necessary. Instead, cascade the objective down from a high-level strategic objective. You'll control the initiative by frequently reviewing its progress and assessing whether it's worth continuing to invest in. Clear time on your calendar.

The team charged with the objective should not know exactly how to accomplish it. If they do, then have them read the earlier Side Glance: Humility and Hubris. They're on a journey of discovery together to generate hypotheses and test them, then implement the ideas that actually work. Together they're responsible for the results. The team may include employees from IT and a business unit, perhaps from marketing or finance. The team should value good contributions no matter which team member they originate with. Good business ideas might come from the technologists and good technical ideas might come from a non-technologist.

Impact mapping, which I described in Chapter 7, is an excellent tool for the team to use. The technique works backward from the objective to formulate hypotheses about what might accomplish it. The team's work will also be made easier if IT provides tools to work with, such as DevOps automation and cloud infrastructure.

Eventually you want to orient much of IT around objectives rather than requirements that have been tossed over the wall from the business. But getting started requires only a single objective and a single team.

Remember:

1. Choose a few objectives for trial.
2. Assign each to a cross-functional business/IT team that is fully empowered to execute.
3. Use impact mapping to brainstorm with the team.
4. Remove impediments.
5. Review progress often and make adjustments.
6. Celebrate success.

Shorten Lead Times

Focus on the one important metric: lead time. Don't get bogged down in the complexities of measuring it. Just take parts of the process—of introducing a change or innovation such as a new IT capability—map them out, and begin questioning every step.

Lead time is the time from when the organization conceives of an *objective* to the time that it is met. But it's useful to start with a subset, such as the lead time from when a *specific task* or action item is conceived to when the corresponding capability is given to people to use. If we decide, say, that we're going to deliver a web page to customers that will let them use a home camera to check on their bobbleheads when they're out at the office, how long will it be until the bobblecam page is available?

Each step in the process of going from bobblecam requirement to bobblecam rollout should be identified, questioned, removed if possible, and otherwise shortened. Many of the steps won't involve technology at all.

Perhaps the requirement has to find its way into a larger project. Does the governance process for funding the bobblecam take two months? Why? Does a meeting have to be convened that includes people whose schedules are hard to coordinate? Can it be done instead by a different group of people? A smaller group? Can you set aside a regular weekly time for them to meet? If the investment is small enough, can you skip the governance process? Can you then make the bobblecam investment small enough? Or can you stage the investment so that the initial commitment is small enough? If it takes time to put together a team to would work on the project, perhaps you can have standing teams that are ready to take on new projects.

Within the IT part of the process, adopting DevOps and cloud practices will reduce the technical lead time. It may require some new skills on the part of the technologists, but I'd suggest they learn primarily by doing. It's easy enough to set up a sandbox in the cloud where they can play with the required new tools. The most difficult skill to learn for engineers used to older practices, you'll find, is how to write robust automated tests.

If the bobblecam would normally have to go through a security review, perhaps you can eliminate it by incorporating security controls as the product is being built. Particular attention should be paid to setting up automated controls that function as guardrails. These take a short time to set up and will thereafter speed up work as well as improve quality, security, and reliability.

For quick improvements to lead time, use the cloud rather than physical infrastructure. Be relentless in reducing the size of projects and make sure that only a small group of requirements is worked on at any given moment. Make sure that the technical people aren't getting distracted, but are able to focus on the work at hand. Try delegating authorities and eliminating sign-offs; you'll be surprised by how dependent lead time is on waiting for Important People to deal with papers sitting on their desks. And for any step that will have to be repeated, find a way to automate it.

With just that paragraph-worth of tactics, most organizations can realize a dramatic speedup in lead time.

Remember:

- Emphasize urgency and fast delivery.
- Your goal is not to make people work faster or harder, but to improve workflow. Make that clear.
- Take advantage of the cloud.
- Ask IT to speed up the portion of delivery that is technical. This will probably involve implementing DevOps, creating reusable components, and designing secure "landing zones" in which new work can safely be done.
- Find bureaucracy that isn't adding value or that could be made leaner with Occam's turkey carver. Often this includes sign-offs required from people who have no good basis for making the sign-off decision,

forms that ask for unnecessary information, or controls that could be automated.

- Becoming lean means reducing calendar time. Wait time, for example, should be eliminated, even though no effort is being spent.
- Task switching is a source of waste and defects. Organize work so that everyone can focus. You can make this easier by keeping tasks small so they can be finished quickly.

Emphasize Delivery and Results

Raise the bar. The only measure of progress in the digital land is *finishing* things that add business value. Nothing should be 47% complete or "on schedule." In the software world there is an expression, "Always be shipping." Products rarely need to be "shipped" any more—CDs and floppy disks have pretty much vanished as delivery vehicles—but the concept has remained. The goal of a software engineer is to keep finishing things. The goal of everyone else in the organization should also be to keep finishing things.

If a task cannot be finished quickly, it's too big. Bite off something small, finish it, give it to users, get feedback, incorporate the feedback, move on. Reflect frequently to see what can be improved.

I hear enterprises transitioning to the digital world say things like, "We have a plan to move quickly on this project. We've designed a prototype that is scheduled to be delivered in six months and then a version 1.0 that will ship a year later." I usually suggest that they go back to the whiteboard and figure out what small thing they can deliver to customers or internal users in two weeks, then move on from there.

I know their response will be, "That's impossible." Sometimes it is. But very rarely. In those few cases where it's impossible, my next question is, "What needs to change so that it can become possible?"

- If it's a technical limitation, then often a good implementation of DevOps will remove the barrier. Automated testing and controls may help.
- If the problem is that there are lots of checkpoints around the business that prevent products from being deployed quickly, then those checkpoints can often be eliminated, especially if each delivery is small.
- If the difficulty is that the market won't accept partial delivery of what they consider to be a large, monolithic product, then creativity can

sometimes save the day. Can this new idea be attached to an existing product that already has users, to let them try it out and see what they think?

There *is* a way to deliver small—many companies, of all sizes and lifecycle stages, are doing it across their various industries.

I've chosen this objective—finishing results quickly—as one of the four places to start because it forces everyone in the enterprise—IT and business—to work together creatively to make it possible. To succeed in the digital world is to move at much higher speed than anyone is used to or comfortable with.

A good way to bring people together in accomplishing this objective is to expose a lead time metric that depicts their progress. You can create a dashboard that measures it, then help people focus their enthusiasm on seeing results there. The metric won't budge unless products ship.

Remember:

- Ensure that work is organized into very small units, work toward minimum viable products, and experiment to learn and test ideas.
- Monitor *results* starting immediately.
- Remove organizational impediments that resist quick shipping.
- It may be easier to begin "working small" by modifying an existing system.
- "Shipping" means that people start using the product. Prototypes and demos aren't shipping (although they might be valuable steps on the way).
- Don't be afraid of disruption from shipping quickly. The idea is that by shipping quickly and frequently, each shipment is very small, and is consequently low-risk.

Treat Requirements as Hypotheses

This is the most difficult of the initial changes, but it'll drive the remainder of the transformation. It's the ultimate step in coming to grips with uncertainty. It's also the embodiment of humility in the sense I mentioned in the Side Glance: Humility and Hubris. The enterprise must stop thinking of its ideas as *requirements* to be given to IT. Instead, it must treat its ideas as hypotheses about what will accomplish business goals. It's very tempting to assume that these hypotheses are correct. But they must be tested and refined, or possibly abandoned. The testing should be done as inexpensively as possible.

The first step is to identify what these (often hidden) hypotheses are. This takes practice. A requirement that "the system shall display data from the x database" is probably a hypothesis that "if the user had data from the x database, they could make higher quality decisions about whether to extend credit," where making better decisions is the objective at which they're aiming.

Once the hypothesis is explicit, the next step is to define how the outcome will be measured. How do we know whether the quality of the decisions is improving? Once we decide this, we can set up a way to measure it.

The next question is, what is the smallest experiment that will let us know whether building this capability will accomplish the goal? This can be a trivial experiment. What if we put a link on the adjudicator's screen that offers to provide the information from database x? We could see how many clicks it gets, then give the adjudicator a message reading "Coming soon" when they click it. Next, we might try getting some of the information we think is most important and see if it makes a measurable difference. We do all of this before we fully implement the feature.

With each experiment, the risk of investing in the feature goes down. But with each one we also open ourselves up to surprises. Perhaps data item n is more important than data item p, although we thought the opposite. That may change how we eventually display them. Perhaps data item q is obtained from a third party and we have to pay every time we obtain it. Maybe we can learn in which cases to request it and in which it won't be useful.

Users always surprise us. Operational situations also surprise us—something that seemed valuable in the lab might be unusable under real-world operational circumstances. Or perhaps it turns out that a feature we thought was extremely valuable is actually only somewhat valuable. In that case, maybe we decide not to invest in it after all. For this reason, the team that is creating the IT capability should work directly with customers or internal users to determine what they're trying to accomplish, test ideas on them, and discover what works best for them.

The notion that a requirement is an IT command has cost us a lot—in building unnecessary or imperfect features, in missing perhaps even more compelling opportunities, or in taking unnecessary risks. By testing hypotheses, we get a tighter fit between what is built and what is needed, while opening up possibilities for learning and innovation.

Remember:

- Read the Side Glance on humility!
- Question assumptions by asking how they can be tested.
- It's better to put effort into testing an idea than to risk not testing it.
- A/B testing (where some users are shown version A, some version B, then the results are compared) is very effective and might be easy to set up.
- Be sure that the test subjects are the same people who will be using the product—not, for example, managers or people within the product team.

These four principles are both a large part of the ultimate vision and a good starting point. Starting along these four paths holds very little risk. They are all matters of degree. There is no reason we cannot begin working toward all four, pushing for results right away while accepting that they are techniques we'll get better at.

What is a small thing you can do right now to reduce lead times? Do it! What is a small initiative you can govern through objectives rather than requirements? Launch it! What is an important assumption you're making and how can you test it? Test it! Agile transformations should be conducted agile-ly.

With these four directions set and the changes in motion, it's time to begin working on the other transformations I've laid out. Here they are.

Make Projects Smaller . . . Or Nonexistent

The hallmark of the old approach to IT was the large project. Requirements were collected and assembled into a single initiative. To avoid later scope creep, an increasing number of them were packed into the initial scope. As each project became larger, administrative overhead, management overhead, and risk mitigation were added. Results were not delivered until the end of the project.

In Lean theory, large batch sizes (of requirements, in this case) result in longer lead times and greater variability. Essentially, the project requirements are being held "in inventory" and are also in danger of "becoming stale" while they're waiting to be addressed. Instead, work in small initiatives that build on one another incrementally, thereby reducing risk, enhancing organizational agility, and speeding value delivery. In turn, break each initiative into small pieces and deliver each piece independently and quickly. Alternatively, lose the notion of projects entirely and build incremental capabilities in a steady flow.

Value Agility

In an environment of uncertainty, complexity, and rapid change—the digital world—agility has high business value. It's the most powerful reducer of risk, since it determines whether unexpected events become hazards or opportunities. It gives the enterprise freedom to innovate and drive the market forward, or to respond to competitors' actions. IT is one of the enterprise's most important sources of agility. Software is easier to change than physical assets; hardware can be replaced by cloud infrastructure to gain agility and speed.

Because agility is valuable, always consider it when making decisions. Buy call options to give yourself flexibility in the future. Make sure that any contracts you sign are flexible. When building new IT capabilities, see that they're built with agility in mind, both in design and in the effort devoted to making certain the code is clean. Invest in paying off technical debt to increase agility. Simply put, invest in agility because it's valuable.

The cloud is a powerful source of agility. Operating your own datacenter draws away resources that could be otherwise employed. The cloud lets you provision infrastructure, change it, increase it, or decrease it—virtually instantaneously. It's the foundation for fast technical delivery processes.

Strive for Continuous Innovation

The digital world is about the continuous, unobstructed flow of innovation. Instead of shooting for rare, big innovations, created by special innovation teams or approved by an innovation Star Chamber, think of innovation as a process of constant idea generation and testing, and part of everyone's day-to-day work.

When an idea shows promise, double down on it. Encourage employees to try out many small ideas, which will create a portfolio of small successes and possible big bets.

Establish a Culture of Security

Security is everyone's job. Sales and marketing owe it to their customers to keep their data private, and they have a stake in whether the company's products are able to continue operating. The CFO owes it to the owners and other stakeholders to manage security risk. Every employee should consider security an essential part of their job, not something that is forced on them or is something that only IT takes care of.

Among its other requirements, Europe's General Data Protection Regulation (GDPR)—to which any organization touching any personal data of any European citizen must adhere—requires that every organization practice "privacy by design." This means the organization should plan how it will treat personal data to keep it private, and build privacy into everything it does. This is a great idea, and not just for companies doing business with European citizens.

Much of security is inexpensive or free, but funds are sometimes required. Be prepared to support these investments, understanding that they're difficult to justify formally when they contend with investments in new features. Security is the foundation of what you do, not an optional add-on.

Make Data Available

Data is an asset whose value is often underexploited. The old way of managing it has been far from agile—we placed it in a database that was structured based on how we *thought* it would be used. As a consequence, it might not have been available for ad hoc or new and innovative analyses, nor available to the right people at the right time with the right tools. Data were held in different silos in the enterprise, or perhaps not integrated when a new company was acquired.

Supported by the cloud, a contemporary technique is to create a data lake that has data drawn from across the company's databases, including those of newly acquired subsidiaries. A variety of tools, including visualization software and ad hoc querying functions, can be used to analyze and report on the data contained within the data lake, even if it's a hodgepodge of different formats and provenances. Machine learning techniques are also now widely available in the cloud and provide new ways to analyze the data.

Automate Controls

In the digital world, you want to automate as many controls as possible. The goal is to replace gatekeeping with constant assurance—in other words, instead of having periodic reviews or reviews just before an IT system is deployed to users, use automated controls to continuously enforce compliance. That way, problems are discovered and fixed immediately, and lead time is shortened because you can eliminate the review and remediation steps at the end of a delivery process. Teams can move very quickly once you've made sure automated guardrails are in place.

Use automated controls to enforce security policies and to manage compliance with PCI, HIPAA, and other compliance frameworks. Make sure the controls are not only applied unfailingly, but that there is an audit trail to show that they were applied. Use automation to enforce financial controls as well. For example, in the cloud you can:

- Set up controls that limit spending or warn the comptroller when spending thresholds are reached
- Ensure that every piece of infrastructure is tagged with an accounting cost category
- Ensure that infrastructure that isn't being used is turned off
- Notify someone if an employee tries to violate a security policy

Look for Self-Service Opportunities

One way to get more leverage from scarce IT resources is to set up self-service models that make it possible for employees to get what they need without help from IT. For example, many organizations now have an automated password reset screen, since forgotten passwords can take up more of the helpdesk's time than anything else.

You can go well beyond password resets, though, for the principle is widely applicable and powerful. To draw another example from the IT world, software developers have often had to wait for system administrators to set up infrastructure for them. But today it's common for the infrastructure operators to set up a platform for the developers to help themselves. Another area where self-service can be powerful is with data and analytics—some organizations have made it possible for data scientists to self-provision the tools and data they need to do each analysis. Self-service models are empowering and can free your colleagues to be more innovative and agile.

Reduce Reliance on COTS Products and Outsourcing

Off-the-shelf software can appear to offer best-in-class capabilities at a reasonable price, with none of the risks of custom-developed software. Sometimes it does—typically for accounting systems, generally for ERP systems, and frequently for tools such as analytics systems and office utilities. These are all areas where there is substantial common ground across businesses, where features don't generally need to change based on company tactics or operational strategies, and where well-supported products exist in the marketplace. By all means, use COTS products for these types of applications.

But for other needs, be skeptical of the conventional wisdom that buying off the shelf is better than building. COTS software takes effort to configure, to customize, and to integrate with other enterprise systems. It reduces your flexibility when you need to make changes. It locks you in to a particular vendor—its contract terms, its product roadmap. At a time when good IT practice suggests that you should be working with users to design software around their needs, COTS software instead forces users to adapt to its designs.

Despite that conventional wisdom, you should be creating IT systems in house whenever possible. Use open-source frameworks and building block services available in the cloud to reduce the amount of building necessary and to be able to move more quickly. But tailor the software to your needs. Buying off the shelf is not the right solution in times of uncertainty and fast change—times when you need agility.

Along the same lines, outsourcing particular IT functions (e.g., testing, development) is not generally effective, especially when you're trying to build long-term agility into your organization.

Deal with Accounting Issues

Discuss with your accounting experts how to best deal with capitalizing and expensing costs as you move into the digital world. The questions are both complex and case-specific.

Raise the IT Bar

Empower IT to take ownership of business outcomes, rather than just its product output. IT should be accountable for the results of the IT portfolio, not only for delivering according to requirements documents. IT should contribute to business strategy and be the enterprise's guide to the digital world.

Hire T-Shaped People

Businesses have tended to undervalue generalist skills. This was a consequence of organizing the company into functional, specialist silos. But as you move toward cross-functional teams to support digital initiatives, specialized generalists—that is, T-shaped people—become increasingly important, as they multiply the power of their teams. Such employees are good at many things, but are especially deep in a given area. And as we erase the boundary between IT and the rest of the enterprise, you should be hiring people whose skills cross those boundaries as well.

———

The surest way to fail at a digital transformation is to let it languish while you try to make risk vanish by planning. A hesitant, slow approach to transformation sends mixed messages when you're trying to encourage your organization to move to a fast-paced, continuously innovative way of doing things. As John Kotter says in *A Sense of Urgency*:

> "What is the single biggest error people make when they try to change?" After reflection, I decided the answer was that they did not create a high enough sense of urgency among enough people to set the stage for making a challenging leap into some new direction.[1]

Employees will be nervous in the face of transformational change. You can help overcome that nervousness with a steady hand, a clear vision, and a commitment to the urgency of transformation.

THE LEADERSHIP TEAM

The image of the human species in each of us has been enlarged, shattered and scattered as shards, not in proportioned admixtures; so that one has to go from one individual to another to reconstitute the totality of the species.
—**Friedrich Schiller**, *On the Aesthetic Education of Man*

Inscrutably involved, we live in the currents of universal reciprocity.
—**Martin Buber**, *I and Thou*

Throughout this book I have made the case that IT should be drawn more deeply into the heart of the enterprise, rather than held at arms-length as if it were a contractor. I've also noted that the fracturing into functional roles occurs in other areas as well. The transformation to the digital world opens up the opportunity, and perhaps the demand, to reconsider how all of the functional areas of the enterprise work together.

This chapter is about the enterprise leadership team. I'd like to open with a question: *Is* the leadership of the enterprise a team? I've described how cross-functional DevOps teams have become essential to contemporary IT. Other operational parts of the enterprise work in teams, especially in those organizations influenced by the Toyota Production System. But the organization's leadership team—the CXOs and the other most senior leaders—do they actually make up a cross-functional team?

They are certainly cross-functional—there is a CFO with expertise in finance, a CMO with expertise in marketing, and a CIO with technology expertise. But do they operate as a team of colleagues sharing accountability? Or are they really a collection of functional leaders, each operating in their own silo and accountable only for their own domain? It seems to be the latter in my experience. When they do come together, it's to negotiate and try to get each other's cooperation . . . or, in dysfunctional cases, to point fingers and distribute blame.

This might be an exaggeration. But I suspect that there is a lot of opportunity we're leaving on the table. What if we thought of the leadership team in the same sense that we think of operationally focused teams, such as an IT DevOps team?

A team has shared accountability for an objective, not individual accountability for separate functions. Because the accountability is for shared outcomes, team members can't just think about what is best for their functional areas. For example, software developers now have to design for operations; they not only have to produce features, but also make sure those features are easy to operate and will perform well. In earlier days, those were concerns of the operations team, not development. But with DevOps, the developers are as accountable as anyone else for the operational success of the code.

On a DevOps team, T-shaped people are the ideal; that is, generalists who also have a specialty competence. When you put the right blend of these people together, you not only have a team with all of the requisite specialties, but all members can contribute in each other's areas. They can help each other, back each other up, and understand one another's concerns. There is more diversity, in the sense that more than one person can contribute on each issue.

A team works face-to-face, passing ideas around and collaborating on experiments. They actively work to make each other more effective, coach one another in areas where they're strong, and freely ask for help when they're stuck or their workload is unmanageable. Team members can challenge one another at any moment, asking, "Is that idea the best one for accomplishing our shared goal?" Finger pointing becomes far more difficult, because any member's failure belongs to the entire team.

To achieve agility, it's desirable for teams to be responsible for both production and stability of new features, as they can move quickly and respond rapidly to change. Teams can take advantage of the diverse skills and points of view of their members. They can innovate by brainstorming together and testing out ideas on a small scale before committing to them.

Today the leadership team challenge is not how to run each function well as a standalone unit. Rather, it's how to benefit from the interactions between functions. A digital service might be replacing other company activities that run within the COO's span of control. But at the same time its function may be to deepen customer relationships so as to meet the CMO's objectives. The new service might be based on tools, provided by the CIO's team, that offer constant monitoring of customer interactions. Meanwhile, the CFO oversees the application of capital to ongoing improvements to the service and monitors its compliance controls, and the CEO and board can scout for growth opportunities enabled by the service. In other words, each C-suite member empowers the others in achieving the shared objectives of the enterprise.

Taking the DevOps team concept and applying it to the executive team would cause us to lead the enterprise quite differently, perhaps in a way that's more appropriate for a digital enterprise seeking to act quickly and flexibly. The leadership team would have the shared goal of accomplishing the enterprise's highest-level objective: to increase shareholder value, prevent terrorist incidents, or eradicate malaria.

In its strategy-setting process, the leadership team would translate this high-level goal into a set of cross-functional objectives that could be cascaded down through the organization. Each might involve marketing, IT, and operations, for example. The delegation of work would be rather different: the leadership team would try to find ways to run fast experiments that cross organizational silos to elicit feedback and buy down risk. Because the whole team would be accountable for outcomes, it would constantly adjust, changing and improving plans and making resource allocation decisions together.

Ideally, the leadership team would be composed of T-shaped people and take advantage of that diversity. This bears some thought. If the CMO, for example, had IT expertise, would the team as a whole take advantage of that expertise, or would it provoke a turf war between IT and the CMO? If the CIO brings some financial expertise, would the CFO take advantage of it or feel threatened?

I think an ideal leadership team would always defer to the member having the deepest functional experience related to each decision. That member would happily accept input by all, valuing the generalist skills of the other members.* That this might feel uncomfortable to many who read this (including me) is a sign that we don't currently treat the leadership team as a real team.

When I joined USCIS, I found that our IT group faced a problem with "shadow," or "rogue" IT. The problem was exacerbated by the agency's geographical dispersion, as individual offices would have their own "IT people"—not necessarily true experts—build local applications to handle local business processes. The patchwork of applications was out of control; none were "industrial strength," for they were both insecure and unreliable. The field offices were stepping on IT's sensitive toes and, as the new CIO, I had to resolve the situation.

My thinking went something like this: The field offices were building applications themselves because central IT was unable to support their needs, or because the process of working through central IT was cumbersome and time consuming. If someone outside of IT was willing to do the work and could do a good job with it, the agency would better accomplish its goals. That would be a good thing! Should I care if it were someone within my IT department who did the work? The real challenge was to ensure that the work was done well.

We wound up permitting the field offices to develop rogue applications as long as they used a standard set of tools we provided. These building blocks (reusable components built to the highest standards) could be used to speed up their efforts and included automated tests that would ensure security and compliance.

We also set up rapid-response IT teams we could dispatch to field offices to quickly solve problems (as well as pitch in on creating applications) using a localized governance process that didn't require a lengthy central approval.

Then we doubled down on the approach. We held hackathons and invited everyone within the agency to participate, whether they were in IT or not. Even employees with no technical skills could participate as designers, testers, sub-

---

* If you are familiar with software development, think of this as a pull request. Everyone can contribute, but only one of the team members owns the function and has to do a peer review on all contributions.

ject matter experts, and so on. On average, each two-day hackathon produced eight new, small applications that quickly met business needs. Every one of them passed our security and reliability requirements. Each could be reviewed by IT experts to make sure that standards were being upheld.

What I'm getting at is that we all shared the goal of getting business results, and that it didn't matter which unit the creators came from, as long as they were producing work that met the agency's needs with respect to all applicable controls. All the while IT used its expertise to keep the results bar high.

Now imagine that your leadership team shared these principles.* The CXOs would not need to be territorial; they could instead focus on shared goals and visions. But importantly, each would have domain expertise considered to be decisive. Mutual respect and an unwavering focus on the enterprise's objectives would ensure that there is no stepping on proverbial toes.

It's in the coordination of leadership team activities that strategy and competitive advantage arise.

Let's look at how the digital world affects this coordination.

Chief Financial Officer (CFO)

Napoleon achieved competitive advantage through clever application of his financial resources. He took care of his soldiers well, setting aside the "contributions" received from conquered territories for the exclusive use of the army. He paid his soldiers in coins rather than in the depreciated paper money (*assignats*) that the French Directorate had ordered him to use, thereby winning his soldiers' loyalty. He adopted the principle that "the war should feed the war," essentially financing his activities out of cash flows.[1]

Finance in the digital world is similarly a driver of competitive advantage; the CFO's role is strategic. There is little distinction between risk and opportunity, or risk and strategy, in the fast-changing digital environment. The CFO ensures that resources and capital flow to activities that need them for carrying out strategic intent; in many cases, this means responsible use of small

---

* I say "imagine" because I have not really tried this. Each leadership team I have been part of has had some of these characteristics; that is why intuitively I believe it to be possible.

experiments to reduce risk. Innovation requires that the enterprise invest in ideas that have yet to prove themselves via a formal business case, but that can easily be tested through everyday processes. Investments are managed as options, not just as projected cash flows.

It's not a simple matter to continually direct resources to the right opportunities, or to be prepared to double down on successful ideas. But when the finance group can do that, it creates competitive advantage and the ability to earn rents until the advantage gets competed away; in the meantime, the CFO has already moved on to additional opportunities.

It goes beyond funding opportunities, though. Eighty-one percent of CFOs believe their responsibilities include identifying and targeting new areas of value across the enterprise.[2] CFOs must find and cultivate new sources of growth. As Jeannette Wade, CFO of the Office of Technology Services & Security, says, "The role of the CFO has changed from being the keeper of the financial information to the driver of business change with financial information."[3]

The role is no longer backward-looking—analyzing and presenting historical data—but forward-focused—prospecting for and investing in opportunities and monitoring leading indicators and key performance indicators (KPIs). To play this role, the CFO must gain transparency across enterprise silos and surface, analyze, and present indicators of the company's operational performance, ultimately acting as the steward of the company's performance and sustainability. All of this requires that the leadership group become a cross-functional, mutually supporting team.

The CFO is focused not on how to reduce costs per se, but on how to spend wisely. The analog to controlling costs in the digital world is running lean. Becoming lean not only reduces costs by eliminating waste—it also speeds up lead times. Leanness doesn't come from eliminating productive activities to reduce costs but from eliminating unproductive ones to reduce waste. The Lean CFO targets wasteful spending, such as investing in unproven hypotheses (e.g., feature bloat), excessive bureaucracy, overly constrained problems, and processes that involve waiting time. (Remember that feature bloat is managed by producing minimal releases and then adding to them incrementally, analyzing what works and what doesn't while investing in stages.)

The CFO manages risk. Importantly, this means steering the enterprise through its cognitive biases and misperceptions of risk—particularly the status quo bias that causes inappropriate fear of that which is new. A digital world CFO is focused on a different set of risks—most critically, the risk that the company won't be able to respond to change quickly and effectively. The CFO plays a part in making sure that the company is agile in its three assets: the IT asset, the organizational asset, and the data asset. Investment must flow toward maintaining agility.

The CFO is responsible for providing data and actionable business intelligence to the rest of the leadership team. Increasingly, this includes not just financial data but performance data and operational metrics. BCG's report on the changing role of the CFO says that,

> CFOs are being called upon not only to get the numbers right but also to be the chief custodian of shareholder value and a genuine strategic advisor to the business. In this respect, the chief financial officer is becoming the corporation's "chief performance officer."[4]

Finally, the CFO, along with the CEO, is responsible for telling the company's story to the capital markets. This requires communicating its digital activities—including those that are primarily future-oriented and designed to promote agility and flexibility—in a way that clarifies their purpose and effectiveness. The CFO manages investor relations so as to create the flexibility the company needs to remain agile. A good example is Jeff Bezos's annual letter to the Amazon shareholders.

The CFO works with the CIO and leaders of other functions to fulfill these mandates. It's in the integration of functions, both inside and outside of finance, that business value lies. According to a Grant Thornton report,

> The tension that the CFO is experiencing between priorities inside and outside of the finance function increases the need to streamline processes through technology, which, in turn, promotes more integration between finance, risk, treasury and operations.[5]

Chief Marketing Officer (CMO)

The digital world generally requires deeper relationships with customers. Expectations are high, set by companies that are already very successful at digital interaction. This poses challenges, but also opportunities for the CMO. For example, frequent digital contact with customers lets the CMO test ideas and get feedback, find problems and quickly fix them, and gather market data. As your enterprise designs new products and the CMO interacts more deeply with its customers, prepare to be surprised. As the voice of the customer, the CMO should present these surprises to the rest of the leadership team.

The CMO is aware of changes in customer buying patterns and their implications for company strategy. As the digital world evolves rapidly, it's the CMO who senses change so that the enterprise can react quickly and appropriately. The CMO sorts through the confusion and complexity of the marketplace to provide actionable insights for the entire leadership team.

The CMO contends with global market complexities, tailoring interactions to particular geographies and managing huge numbers of price points. There are new distribution channels to oversee and new venues for communication and advertising. Through these channels the CMO works to shape the company's public profile, to build a global brand and communicate it effectively.

In all of these areas the CMO is supported by, and supports, the entire leadership team. As McKinsey puts it, "Marketers must work more intensively than they have in the past with colleagues in other functions to develop, deliver, and communicate value propositions to consumers."[6] The CIO, for example, is the source of data and digital capabilities for customer interaction in addition to the tools to help cut through complexity.

Chief Executive Officer (CEO)

CEOs need to grow the business while at the same time sustaining current core businesses. Until recently this was seen as a matter of balance and tradeoffs. I suggest that growth and stability can come together. Think of growth and innovation as a part of every activity. By making processes lean and removing impediments to innovation, the enterprise can unlock growth opportunities that have been passing below its radar. It's now possible to do so at minimal cost and risk, using the techniques described in this book.

The CEO doesn't just grow the business this quarter or this year, but sets it up for sustained growth. Or in those rare cases where the company doesn't intend to grow, the CEO sets it up to survive future waves and increments of disruption. In the case of a nonprofit or a government agency, the leader strives to make the enterprise continually improve at fulfilling its mission. The only way to sustain growth and mission improvement—if we accept that the future is uncertain—is to make the enterprise lean and adaptable; that is to say, agile. The organization must not just adapt today, but continue to be adaptable to survive and prosper in an unknown future.

Building agility is not glamorous in the short term; both the CEO and CFO will need to communicate its value to the capital markets. Much of the enterprise's agility comes from its IT function, so the digital CEO brings IT into the very core of the enterprise and takes advantage of its technology expertise in organizing for the future. By erasing the boundary between IT and the rest of the enterprise, the CEO discovers opportunities to make the enterprise lean—to reduce costs while growing and innovating.

Board of Directors and Audit Committee

Is the company survivable? Is it future-ready? Is it transparent and auditable? Is it secure and resilient? Can it continue to innovate and grow? Building the nimbleness to respond to market change requires investments, the benefits from which will be felt in the future. These sometimes take the form of options rather than "certain" cash flows, so support of the board is crucial. More than that—the board should *insist* that the leadership team take the necessary actions to make the company future-ready.

In many cases this doesn't require extra investment, but is more a matter of making the right choices, weighing future flexibility more heavily than we have in the past. For example, putting its IT infrastructure in the cloud, where it can scale up and down as needed, enables the enterprise to build its future on a resilient and secure foundation. It's likely that doing so will also yield favorable short-term results.

A best practice in the digital world is to use automated guardrails that let the company move quickly to seize opportunities, while at the same time ensuring that it remains secure, compliant, transparent, and under centralized control where necessary. The more speed, the more control, since adjustments can be made quickly to reestablish compliance when it's momentarily lost. The audit committee should verify that the company has put in place effective automated controls, and that it's collecting data proving that each control is continuously providing the desired level of enforcement.

Information security and privacy controls have become critical. Security and privacy are no longer "add-ons" to company systems and processes. Instead, they need to be designed into every system and process from the start. Rather than reacting to every new threat, the company should set up its systems and processes to be rugged—to be resistant to both known and unknown threats it can face at any time. The audit committee is charged with seeing that the entire company has a culture of security—that protecting customer and employee data, all the while making sure company systems continue to operate, is understood throughout to be everyone's job.

The digital enterprise's board of directors broadly interacts with the leadership team. The CIO, for example, is now an important voice in implementing controls, enabling innovation, and ensuring security. The board also plays an essential role in transforming the enterprise for the digital world by adding urgency to the effort.

Chief Information Officer (CIO)

The CIO brings IT expertise to the senior leadership team. Let me loudly shout my message: enterprises in general are not taking enough advantage of their CIOs. Having held the title myself, I believe CIOs should be held to a higher standard, that they should be accountable for contributing much more to the enterprise. And I believe other CIOs would agree with me.

That higher standard has little to do with on-time delivery of projects, continual IT budget reductions, or friendly customer service provided to the rest of the enterprise. Rather, it has to do with continually delivering valuable IT capability (in incremental small pieces), and contributing their expertise in IT and the digital world to support and influence the other CXOs.

The CIO is a driver of business outcomes and strategy, as are the other CXOs. And likely more so, since moving the enterprise into the digital age requires technical leadership. Your CIO should be responsible for business revenues and costs, competitive strategy, and caring for the IT asset to make sure it remains agile, cost-effective, lean, secure, and resilient. Your CIO should be the voice of technology.

What kind of a CIO do you need? Again, I think the conventional wisdom has been mistaken; "Run IT like a business" has led organizations to think that even a generalist business leader can lead IT, that technical skills are a nice-to-have. But if your CIO is to be the technology expert sitting at the strategy table, then technical skills become much more important. All CXOs should be T-shaped, generalists who also go extremely deep in one area. For a CIO, that area is information technology.

Alas, the CIO can be none of these things given the mental model enterprises have had for the role. If IT is separate from the business, providing it good customer service, accepting requirements documents and grinding out IT capabilities, with the CIO as the general of IT, then, like Napoleon at Borodino, the CIO can coordinate soldiers and cannons and even win battles, while the company thoroughly and catastrophically loses the war. For an enterprise to succeed in the digital age—the age of IT—IT must be a driver of the business, a formulator of business strategy, a pioneer in innovation, a . . . well, IT must *be* the business.* And as IT becomes the business, it awakens additional superpowers for the other CXOs as the entire leadership team assumes responsibility for making the enterprise future-ready and sustainable.

* Thanks to Martha Heller, author of *Be the Business*, for this way of wording it.

AFTERWORD

Need one say more? For it may easily be guessed.

—**Epictetus**, *Discourses*

Let be be finale of seem
The only emperor is the emperor of ice-cream.

—**Wallace Stevens**, "The Emperor of Ice-Cream"

The digital way of thinking is different from the way that we have traditionally thought about technology in the enterprise. To arrive at it we have to
overcome a number of dualities: IT and the business; control and speed; agility
and pre-planning; complexity and leadership; legacy and innovation; Napoleon
and Kutuzov. The image of Shiva and his dance of destruction and re-creation,
with one foot firmly on the demons who oppose us, should encourage us to
move forward with confidence and humility. Despite Napolean's hubris—
well, the only emperor is the emperor of ice cream. And through it all, smiling
bobbleheads.

Good luck with your enterprise transformation.

ACKNOWLEDGMENTS

Every day, I learn from my colleagues at AWS: Jonathan Allen, Thomas Blood, Ashley Brown, Joe Chung, Miriam McLemore, Stephen Orban, Phil Potloff, Clarke Rodgers, and Xia Zhang. Many of the ideas here were developed with their feedback, and many more will be tested with them as we try to help AWS customers transform. Also at AWS, Adrian Cockcroft has been a great supporter of all my books and I thank him for it. A five-minute conversation with Adrian makes me rethink my ideas or see them in a different light.

One of my main points in this book is the importance and power of humility in the digital world. I'm sure I had Gene Kim in the back of my mind as the model of the humble leader. Gene brings out the best in everyone through his supportive, curious, open-minded community-building. I owe a lot to him as does the rest of the DevOps community.

Thanks to my editor, Anna Noak, who is almost always right, and is then right the rest of the time too, and to Leah Brown, who sees what I am trying to say and makes sure I'm saying it. And to Margueritte and the rest of the IT Revolution folks.

My formative years—really—were the time I spent at USCIS, where I learned from pretty much everyone, but in particular Keith Jones, Larry Denayer, Luke McCormack, Margie Graves, Mike Hermus, Josh Seckel, Sarah Fahden, Tammy Meckley, Kath Stanley, Tracey Renaud, Lori Scialabba, Chip Fulghum, Greg Rankin, David Blair, Yemi Oshinaiye, Norm Palmer, Rafaa Abdalla, and the late Mark Caldwell. And everyone else—all of them doing the impossible work of the under-appreciated civil service.

And thanks to Jenny who supplied me with yogurt, oatwa, and Nespresso pods, and lots of encouragement, love, and support.

BIBLIOGRAPHY

A

Adler, Paul S. *The "Learning Bureaucracy": New United Motor Manufacturing, Inc.* Los Angeles, CA: University of Southern California, School of Business Administration, 1992. https://www.marshall.usc.edu/sites/default/files/padler/intellcont/NUMMI%28ROB%29-1.pdf.

Adzic, Gojko. *Humans vs Computers*. London: Neuri Consulting, 2017.

———. *Impact Mapping: Making a Big Impact With Software Products and Projects*. Surrey, UK: Provoking Thoughts, 2012.

Agile Alliance. "Manifesto for Agile Software Development." Agile Manifesto. February 11–13, 2001. http://agilemanifesto.org.

Ancona, Deborah and Henrik Bresman. *X-Teams: How to Build Teams that Lead, Innovate, and Succeed*. Boston: Harvard Business Review Press, 2007.

Anderson, Philip. "Seven Levers for Guiding the Evolving Enterprise," in Clippinger.

Avery, Christopher M. "Responsible Change." *Cutter Consortium Agile Project Management Executive Report* 10, no. 6 (2005): 1–28.

B

Bogsnes, Bjarte. *Implementing Beyond Budgeting: Unlocking the Performance Potential*. Hoboken, NJ: John Wiley and Sons, 2009.

Brooks Jr., Frederick P. *The Mythical Man-Month: Essays on Software Engineering, Anniversary Edition*. Boston, MA: Addison-Wesley, 1995.

C

van Cauwenberghe, Pascal. "How Do You Estimate the Business Value of User Stories? You Don't." Nayima blog, December 30, 2009. http://blog.nayima.be/2009/12/.

Christensen, Clayton. *The Innovator's Dilemma: When New Technologies Cause Great Firms to Fail*. Boston, MA: Harvard Business Review Press, 1997 and 2016. Kindle Edition.

von Clausewitz, Carl. *On War*. Edited by Michael E. Howard and Peter Paret. Princeton, NJ: Princeton University Press, 1976. Kindle Edition.

Clippinger III, John Henry, ed. *The Biology of Business: Decoding the Natural Laws of Enterprise*. San Francisco, CA: Jossey-Bass, 1999.

D

DeMarco, Tom. *Why Does Software Cost So Much?: And Other Puzzles of the Information Age*. New York: Dorset House Publishing Company, 1995.

Denning, Stephen. *The Age of Agile: How Smart Companies Are Transforming the Way Work Gets Done*. New York: AMACOM, 2018. Kindle Edition.

Dixit, Avinash K. and Robert S. Pindyck. "The Options Approach to Capital Investment." *Harvard Business Review* (May–June 1995).

Drnevitch, Paul and David Croson. "Information Technology and Business-Level Strategy: Toward an Integrated Theoretical Perspective." *MIS Quarterly* 37, no. 2 (June 2013): 483–509.

Dyche, Jill. *The New IT: How Technology Leaders are Enabling Business Strategy in the Digital Age*. New York: McGraw-Hill Education, 2015.

E/F

Feathers, Michael. *Working Effectively with Legacy Code*. Upper Saddle River, NJ: Prentice Hall PTR, 2005.

Financial Accounting Standards Board (FASB). Publication 350. https://law.resource .org/pub/us/code/bean/fasb.html/fasb.350.2011.html.

Forsgren, PhD, Nicole, Jez Humble, and Gene Kim. *Accelerate: The Science of Lean Software and DevOps: Building and Scaling High Performing Technology Organizations*. Portland, OR: IT Revolution Press, 2018. Kindle Edition.

G

Gaddis, John Lewis. *On Grand Strategy*. New York: Penguin Press, 2018. Kindle Edition.

Gawande, Atul. *The Checklist Manifesto: How to Get Things Right*. New York Metropolitan Books, 2009.

Gray, A. M. *Warfighting*. New York: Doubleday (Currency Books), 1989. Kindle Edition.

H

Hackman, J. Richard. *Leading Teams: Setting the Stage for Great Performances*. Boston, MA: Harvard Business Review Press, 2002.

Heller, Martha. *The CIO Paradox: Battling the Contradictions of IT Leadership*. Brookline, MA: Bibliomotion, 2012. Kindle Edition.

Highsmith, Jim. *Adaptive Leadership: Accelerating Enterprise Agility*. Boston, MA: Addison-Wesley, 2014.

Highsmith, Jim. *Agile Project Management: Creating Innovative Projects*, 2nd ed. Boston, MA: Addison-Wesley, 2009.

Hope, Jeremy and Robin Fraser. "Who Needs Budgets?" *Harvard Business Review* (February 2003). https://hbr.org/2003/02/who-needs-budgets.

Hubbard, Douglas W. *How to Measure Anything: Finding the Value of "Intangibles" in Business*, 3rd ed. Hoboken, NJ: Wiley, 2014.

Humble, Jez, Joanne Molesky, and Barry O'Reilly. *Lean Enterprise: How High Performance Organizations Innovate at Scale*. Sebastopol, CA: O'Reilly, 2015.

Hunter, Richard and George Westerman. *The Real Business of IT: How CIOs Create and Communicate Business Value*. Boston, MA: Harvard Business Review Press, 2009.

I/J/K

Kahneman, Daniel and Amos Tversky. "On the Psychology of Prediction." *Psychological Review* 80, no. 4 (July 1973): 237–251.

Kaufman, Sarah L., Jayne Orenstein, Sarah Hashemi, Elizabeth Hart, and Shelly Tan. "Art in an Instant: The Secrets of Improvisation." *Washington Post*. June 7, 2018. https://www.washingtonpost.com/graphics/2018/lifestyle/science-behind-improv-performance/?noredirect=on&utm_term=.3eba35169f21 or http://wapo .st/improv?tid=ss_email.

Kierkegaard, Soren. *Either/Or, Part One*. Princeton, NJ: Princeton University Press, 1987.

L/M

McChrystal, General Stanley. *Team of Teams: New Rules of Engagement for a Complex World*. New York: Portfolio, 2015.

McGowan, Brendan. "Communication Between IT and Non-IT Workers in a State of Crisis." *CIO Magazine*, May 18, 2015. https://www.cio.com/article/2923452/it -organization/communication-between-it-and-non-it-workers-in-a-state-of-crisis .html.

Mlodinow, Leonard. *The Drunkard's Walk: How Randomness Rules Our Lives*. New York: Vintage Books, 2009.

Moore, Geoffrey A. *Zone to Win: Organizing to Compete in an Age of Disruption*. New York: Diversion Books, 2015. Kindle Edition.

N

Narayan, Sriram. *Agile IT Organization Design: For Digital Transformation and Continuous Delivery*. Boston, MA: Addison-Wesley, 2015.

O/P

Patton, Jeff. *User Story Mapping: Discover the Whole Story, Build the Right Product*. Sebastopol, CA: O'Reilly, 2014.

Paulos, John Allen. *A Mathematician Reads the Newspaper*. New York: Basic Books, 1995.

Poppendieck, Mary and Tom Poppendieck. *Lean Software Development: An Agile Toolkit*. Boston, MA: Addison-Wesley, 2003.

Q/R

Raymond, Eric S. *The Cathedral and the Bazaar: Musings on Linux and Open Source by an Accidental Revolutionary*. Sebastopol, CA: O'Reilly, 2008.

Reinertsen, Donald G. *The Principles of Product Development Flow: Second Generation Lean Product Development*. Redondo Beach, CA: Celerita Publishing, 2009.

Ries, Eric. *The Lean Startup: How Today's Entrepreneurs Use Continuous Innovation to Create Radically Successful Businesses*. New York: Crown Business, 2011.

———. *The Startup Way: How Modern Companies Use Entrepreneurial Management to Transform Culture and Drive Long-Term Growth*. New York: Currency, 2017. Kindle Edition.

Rosenthal, Casey, Lorin Hochstein, Aaron Blohowiak, Nora Jones, and Ali Basiri. *Chaos Engineering: Building Confidence in System Behavior Through Experiments*. Sebastopol, CA: O'Reilly, 2017.

Ross, Jeanne W., Peter Weill, and David C. Robertson. *Enterprise Architecture as Strategy: Creating a Foundation for Business Execution*. Boston, MA: Harvard Business Review Press, 2006.

Rugged Software. *Rugged Handbook: Strawman Edition*, August 2012. https://www.ruggedsoftware.org/wp-content/uploads/2013/11/Rugged-Handbook-v7.pdf.

S

Schumpeter, Joseph A. *Capitalism, Socialism, and Democracy*. Start Publishing LLC, 2012. Originally published 1942. Kindle Edition.

Schwartz, Mark. *The Art of Business Value*. Portland, OR: IT Revolution, 2016.

Standish Group. "The Chaos Report (1994)." 1995.

Stravinsky, Igor. *The Poetics of Music in the Form of Six Lessons*. Cambridge, MA: Harvard University Press, 1947.

T

Takeuchi, Hirotaka and Ikujiro Nonaka. "The New New Product Development Game." *Harvard Business Review* (January 1986).

Tolstoy, Leo. *War and Peace*. Translated by Richard Pevear and Larissa Volokhonsky. New York: Vintage Classics, 2007. Kindle Edition

U/V/W

Weber, Max. *Economy and Society: An Outline of Interpretive Sociology*. Edited by Guenther Roth and Claus Witch. Berkeley: University of California Press, 1978. First published 1922.

Weill, Peter and Jeanne W. Ross. *IT Governance: How Top Performers Manage IT Decision Rights for Superior Results*. Boston: Harvard Business Review Press, 2004.

———. *IT Savvy: What Top Executives Must Know to Go from Pain to Gain*. Boston: Harvard Business Review Press, 2009.

Westerman, George, Didier Bonnet, and Andrew McAfee. *Leading Digital: Turning Technology Into Business Transformation*. Boston: Harvard Business Review Press. 2014.

Wiegers, Karl E. "Seven Truths About Peer Reviews." *Cutter IT Journal* (July 2002). http://www.processimpact.com/articles/seven_truths .html.

Wren, Daniel and Arthur Bedeian. *The Evolution of Management Thought*. 6th ed. Hoboken: John Wiley and Sons, 2009.

X/Y/Z

NOTES

INTRODUCTION

1. Alexander Roos, James Tucker, Fabrice Roghé, Marc Rodt, and Sebastian Stange, *CFO Excellence Series: The Art of Planning* (Boston, MA: Boston Consulting Group, 2017) http://image-src.bcg.com/Images/BCG-Art-of-Planning-Apr-2017_tcm30 -153928.pdf.
2. Kasey Panetta, *Gartner CEO Survey*, Gartner.com, April 27, 2017, https://www .gartner.com/smarterwithgartner/2017-ceo-survey-infographic/.
3. Gartner, "Gartner Survey Reveals that CEO Priorities are Shifting to Embrace Digital Business," Gartner.com, May 1, 2018, https://www.gartner.com/newsroom /id/3873663.
4. Nicole Forsgren, PhD, Jez Humble, and Gene Kim, *Accelerate: The Science of Lean Software and DevOps: Building and Scaling High Performing Technology Organizations* (Portland, OR: IT Revolution Press, 2018), Kindle locations 348–351.
5. Ankur Agrawal, Brian Dinneen, and Ishaan Seth, "Are Today's CFOs Ready for Tomorrow's Demands on Finance?" McKinsey.com, December 2016, https://www. mckinsey.com/business-functions/strategy-and-corporate-finance/our-insights/ are-todays-cfos-ready-for-tomorrows-demands-on-finance.
6. Julien Ghesquieres, Jeff Kotzen, Tim Nolan, Marc Rodt, Alexander Roos, and James Tucker, "The Art of Performance Management" (Boston, MA: Boston Consulting Group, 2017), https://www.bcg.com/en-us/publications/2017/finance -function-excellence-corporate-development-art-performance-management.aspx.
7. Ghesquieres et al., "The Art of Performance Management."
8. Kimberly A. Whitler, Neil A. Morgan, D. Eric Boyd, and Daniel McGinn, "The Trouble with CMOs," *Harvard Business Review*, July 1, 2017, https://hbr.org/product /the-trouble-with-cmos/R1704B-HCB-ENG.
9. David Court, "The Evolving Role of the CMO," *McKinsey Quarterly*, August 2007, https://www.mckinsey.com/business-functions/marketing-and-sales/our-insights /the-evolving-role-of-the-cmo.
10. Ideas in this paragraph are paraphrased from: EY Reporting, "10 Priorities for Boards and Audit Committees in 2018," *EY*, February 7, 2018, https://www.ey

.com/gl/en/services/assurance/ey-reporting-10-priorities-for-boards-and-audit
-committees-in-2018.

11. Pedja Arandjelovic, Libby Bulin, and Naufal Khan, "Why CIOs Should be Business-Strategy Partners," McKinsey.com, February 2015, http://www.mckinsey.com /business-functions/digital-mckinsey/our-insights/why-cios-should-be-business -strategy-partners.

12. Arandjelovic, Bulin, and Khan, "Why CIOs Should be Business-Strategy Partners."

13. KPMG as cited in Workday Staff Writers on Finance, "6 Priorities CEOs Care Most About," Workday.com, April 12, 2016, https://blogs.workday.com/6-priorities-ceos -care-most-about/.

14. Geoffrey A. Moore, *Zone to Win: Organizing to Compete in an Age of Disruption* (New York: Diversion Books, 2015), Kindle locations 113–134.

15. C. K. Prahalad and Gary Hamel, "The Core Competence of the Corporation," *Harvard Business Review*, May-June 1990: 79–91, https://web.archive.org/web /20140714112311/http:/km.camt.cmu.ac.th/mskm/952743/Extra%20materials /corecompetence.pdf.

16. Joseph A. Schumpeter, *Capitalism, Socialism, and Democracy* (New York: Harper Perennial, 1942).

17. Stephen Denning, *The Age of Agile: How Smart Companies are Transforming the Way Work Gets Done* (New York: American Management Association, 2018), Kindle locations 175–176.

18. George Westerman, Didier Bonnet, and Andrew McAfee, *Leading Digital: Turning Technology into Business Transformation* (Boston, MA: Harvard Business Review Press, 2014), 157.

19. Brendan McGowan, "Communication Between IT and Non-IT Workers in a State of Crisis," *CIO Magazine*, May 18, 2015, Results from the CEC's 2015 Power of Effective IT Communication Benchmark Survey." https://www.cio.com/article/2923452 /it-organization/communication-between-it-and-non-it-workers-in-a-state-of -crisis.html.

20. Steve Tack, "15 Ways to Bridge the Gap Between IT and Business," *APM Digest*, November 19, 2012, https://www.apmdigest.com/apm-bridge-gap-between-it-and -business.

21. "Bimodal," Gartner.com, accessed on November 26, 2018, https://www.gartner. com/it-glossary/bimodal/. Jez Humble talks about the problems with Gartner's bi-modal approach in https://continuousdelivery.com/2016/04/the-flaw-at-the -heart-of-bimodal-it/.

22. D. L. Nelson, "The Economics of Bobbleheads," *Athletics Nation*, June 13, 2013, https://www.athleticsnation.com/2013/6/13/4420506/the-economics-of-bobble heads.

CHAPTER 1

1. Stephen Denning, *The Age of Agile*, Kindle locations 917–918.
2. Laura Noonan, "JP Morgan's Requirement for New Staff: Coding Lessons," *Financial Times*, October 7, 2018.
3. Jeff Patton, *User Story Mapping: Discover the Whole Story, Build the Right Product* (Sebastopol, CA: O'Reilly, 2014), 26.
4. Jez Humble, Joanne Molesky, and Barry O'Reilly, *Lean Enterprise: How High Performance Organizations Innovate at Scale* (Sebastopol, CA: O'Reilly, 2015), 179.
5. Jim Highsmith, *Adaptive Leadership: Accelerating Enterprise Agility* (Boston, MA: Addison-Wesley, 2014, Kindle locations 1042–1043.
6. Samuel Greengard, "Tackling the High Cost of Unused Software," *CIO Insight*, November 18, 2014, https://www.cioinsight.com/blogs/tackling-the-high-cost-of-unused-software.html#sthash.XjTc9Ukr.dpuf.
7. Agile Alliance, "Manifesto for Agile Software Development," AgileManifesto.org, 2001, http://agilemanifesto.org/.
8. Westerman, *Leading Digital*, 233.
9. Pascal van Cauwenberghe, "How Do You Estimate the Business Value of User Stories? You Don't." *Thinking for a Change* blog, December 30, 2009, http://blog.nayima.be/2009/12.
10. Richard Hunter and George Westerman, *The Real Business of IT: How CIOs Create and Communicate Value* (Boston, MA: Harvard Business Review Press, 2009), Kindle locations 154–156.
11. Moore, *Zone to Win*, Kindle locations 765–770.

CHAPTER 2

1. Leo Tolstoy, *War and Peace*, trans. Richard Pevear and Larissa Volokhonsky. (New York: Vintage Classics, 2007) 799–800.
2. Tolstoy, *War and Peace*, 800.
3. Carl von Clausewitz, *On War* (Create Space Publishing Platform, 2012), 101
4. Atul Gawande, *The Checklist Manifesto: How to Get Things Right* (New York: Metropolitan Books, 2009), 23.
5. Gawande, *The Checklist Manifesto*, 24.
6. Gawande, *The Checklist Manifesto*, 24.
7. John Henry Clippinger III, ed., *The Biology of Business: Decoding the Natural Laws of Enterprise* (San Francisco, CA: Jossey-Bass, 1999), 10.
8. Clippinger, *The Biology of Business*, 5.
9. Peter Weill and Jeanne W. Ross, *IT Savvy: What Top Executives Must Know to Go from Pain to Gain* (Boston, MA: Harvard Business Review Press, 2009), Kindle locations 1822–1825.
10. Clippinger, *The Biology of Business*, 2–3.
11. Clippinger, *The Biology of Business*, 133.

12. A. M. Gray, *Warfighting* (New York: Crown, 1995), 82–83.

13. Tolstoy, *War and Peace*, 772–773.

14. John Lewis Gaddis, *On Grand Strategy* (New York: Penguin Press, 2018), 212–213.

15. Paul Drnevitch and David Croson, "Information Technology and Business-Level Strategy: Toward an Integrated Theoretical Perspective," *MIS Quarterly* 37, no. 2 (June 2013): 498.

16. Christopher Avery, "Responsible Change," *Cutter Consortium Agile Project Management Executive Report* 6, no. 10 (2005): 22–23.

CHAPTER 3

1. Gray, *Warfighting*, 11.

2. Gray, *Warfighting*, 79.

3. Mary Poppendieck and Tom Poppendieck, *Lean Software Development: An Agile Toolkit* (Boston, MA: Addison-Wesley, 2003), 4.

4. Forsgren, Humble, and Kim, *Accelerate*, Kindle locations 604–605.

5. Forsgren, Humble, and Kim, *Accelerate*, Kindle locations 1500–1503.

6. Forsgren, Humble, and Kim, *Accelerate*, Kindle locations 2734–2735

7. The first known reference seems to be from David Guest, "The Hunt is on for the Renaissance Man of Computing," *The Independent*, September 17, 1991. The idea was popularized by Tim Brown of IDEO.

8. Forsgren, Humble, and Kim, *Accelerate*, Kindle locations 2738–2740.

9. Forsgren, Humble, and Kim, *Accelerate*, Kindle locations 434–436.

10. Forsgren, Humble, and Kim, *Accelerate*, Kindle location 925.

11. Forsgren, Humble, and Kim, *Accelerate*, Kindle locations 1079–1080.

12. Eric Ries, *The Lean Startup: How Today's Entrepreneurs Use Continuous Innovation to Create Radically Successful Businesses* (New York: Crown, 2011), 61.

13. Eric Ries, *The Startup Way: How Modern Companies Use Entrepreneurial Management to Transform Culture and Drive Long-Term Growth* (New York: Currency, 2017), 86.

14. Ries, *The Startup Way*, 89–94.

SIDE GLANCE: THE GRAPHS

1. Adapted from Fred Brooks Jr., *The Mythical Man-Month* (Boston, MA: Addison-Wesley, 1995), figure 2.4, 19.

2. Adapted from Forsgren, Humble, and Kim, *Accelerate*, figure 5.1, 65.

3. Adapted from Maurice Dawson, Darrell Norman Burrell, Emad Rahim, Stephen Brewster, "Integrating Software Assurance into the Software Development Life Cycle (SDLC)," *Journal of Information Systems Technology & Planning* 3, no. 6: January 2010, Figure 3, p. 51, https://www.researchgate.net/figure/255965523_fig1 _Figure-3-IBM-System-Science-Institute-Relative-Cost-of-Fixing-Defects.

4. Adapted from Elizabeth Hendrickson, *Agile Quality and Risk Management*, SlideShare .net, August 6, 2013, slides 9 and 11, https://www.slideshare.net/ehendrickson /to-aqarm-sm?next_slideshow=1.
5. Adapted from Sonatype, *2018 State of the Software Supply Chain* (Fulton, MD: Sonatype, 2018), 7.
6. Adapted from Donald G. Reinertsen, *The Principles of Product Development Flow: Second Generation Lean Product Development* (Redondo Beach, CA: Celeritas Publishing, 2009).

CHAPTER 4

1. *The Standish Group Report: Chaos* (Boston, MA: The Standish Group, 1995), https:// www.projectsmart.co.uk/white-papers/chaos-report.pdf.
2. Bob Sullivan, "Agile, Waterfall, Brooks' Law, and 94% Failure Rates—There's Lots to Learn from HealthCare.gov Troubles," BobSullivan.net, October 22, 2013, https:// bobsullivan.net/cybercrime/technology-run-amok/agile-waterfall-brooks-law-and -94-failure-rates-theres-lots-to-learn-from-healthcare-gov-troubles/.
3. IBM, *Making Change Work*, (Somers, NY: IBM Corp, 2008), 9, http://www-935.ibm .com/services/us/gbs/bus/pdf/gbe03100-usen-03-making-change-work.pdf.
4. *KPMG New Zealand Project Management Survey* 2010 (New Zealand: KPMG, 2010), http://www.beconfident.co.nz/files/events/Project-Management-Survey-report %20copy.pdf; italics added.
5. Michael Bloch, Sven Blumberg, Jürgen Laartz, "Delivering Large-Scale IT Projects On Time, On Budget, and On Value," McKinsey.com, October 2012, https://www .mckinsey.com/business-functions/digital-mckinsey/our-insights/delivering-large -scale-it-projects-on-time-on-budget-and-on-value.
6. Bloch, Blumberg, Laartz, "Delivering Large IT Projects."
7. "Why up to 75% of Software Projects Will Fail," Geneca.com, January 25, 2017, https://www.geneca.com/why-up-to-75-of-software-projects-will-fail/.
8. Bloch, Blumberg, Laartz, "Delivering Large-Scale IT Projects On Time."
9. Tom DeMarco, *Why Does Software Cost So Much?: And Other Puzzles of the Information Age* (New York: Dorset House Publishing Company, 1995), 3.
10. DeMarco, *Why Does Software Cost So Much?*, 4.
11. Peter Weill and Jeanne W. Ross, *IT Governance: How Top Performers Manage IT Decision Rights for Superior Results* (Boston, MA: Harvard Business Review Press, 2004), 16.
12. Dan Strumpf, "U.S. Public Companies Rise Again," *Wall Street Journal*, February 5, 2014, http://www.wsj.com/articles/SB1000142405270230485110457936327210 7177430.
13. Mary Ellen Biery, "4 Things You Don't Know About Private Companies," *Forbes*, May 26, 2013, http://www.forbes.com/sites/sageworks/2013/05/26/4-things-you -dont-know-about-private-companies/.

14. Bill Javetski, Cait Murphy, and Mark Staples, eds., *Perspectives on Founder- and Family-Owned Businesses* (New York: McKinsey and Co., 2014), 4.
15. Belén Villalonga, "Growing, Financing, and Managing Family and Closely Held Firms," Harvard Business School Course Number 1402 description, accessed October 18, 2018, http://www.hbs.edu/coursecatalog/1402.html.
16. *National Venture Capital Association Yearbook 2015* (Washington, DC: Thomson Reuters, 2015).
17. Brice S. McKeever and Sarah L. Pettijohn, *The Nonprofit Sector in Brief 2014*, (Washington, DC: Urban Institute Center on Nonprofits and Philanthropy, 2014), http://www.urban.org/sites/default/publication/33711/413277-The-Nonprofit-Sector-in-Brief--.PDF.
18. Drnevitch and Croson, "Information Technology and Business-Level Strategy," 496.
19. Moore, *Zone to Win*, Kindle location 156.
20. Clayton Christensen, *The Innovator's Dilemma: When New Technologies Cause Great Firms to Fail* (Boston, MA: Harvard Business Review Press, 2015) Kindle locations 2025–2029.
21. Drnevitch and Croson, "Information Technology and Business-Level Strategy," 484.
22. Drnevitch and Croson, "Information Technology and Business-Level Strategy," 486.
23. Drnevitch and Croson, "Information Technology and Business-Level Strategy," 497.

SIDE GLANCE: HUMILITY AND HUBRIS

1. Mental Floss UK, "17 Famous Authors and Their Rejections," *Mental Floss*, May 16, 2017, http://mentalfloss.com/article/91169/16-famous-authors-and-their-rejections.
2. Joshua Moraes, "20 Famous People Who Faced Rejection Before They Made it Big," SchoopWhoop.com, June 23, 2015, https://www.scoopwhoop.com/inothernews/famous-people-rejected/#.3l2ysbcfu.
3. Highsmith, *Adaptive Leadership*, Kindle locations 2000–2001.
4. Ries, *The Startup Way*, 115.
5. Coined by Robert K. Greenleaf, *Servant Leadership: A Journey into the Nature of Legitimate Power and Greatness* (Mahwah, NJ: Paulist Press, 1977).
6. Tolstoy, *War and Peace*, 785–786.
7. Clippinger, *The Biology of Business*, 22.
8. Tolstoy, *War and Peace*, 781.

CHAPTER 5

1. Moore, *Zone to Win*, Kindle locations 301–304.
2. Michael Feathers, *Working Effectively with Legacy Code* (Upper Saddle River, NJ: Prentice Hall PTR, 2005), xvi.

3. Eric S. Raymond, *The Cathedral and the Bazaar: Musings on Linux and Open Source by an Accidental Revolutionary* (Sebastopol, CA: O'Reilly, 2001), 117.
4. Raymond, *The Cathedral and the Bazaar*, 119.
5. Raymond, *The Cathedral and the Bazaar*, 120.
6. Forsgren, Humble, and Kim, *Accelerate*, Kindle locations 1029–1031.

CHAPTER 6

1. Ulrich Pidun, Marc Rodt, Alexander Roos, Sebastian Stange, and James Tucker, *CFO Excellence Series: The Art of Risk Management* (Boston, MA: Boston Consulting Group, 2017), https://www.bcg.com/en-us/publications/2017/finance-function -excellence-corporate-development-art-risk-management.aspx.
2. Pidun et al., *The Art of Risk Management*.
3. Pidun et al., *The Art of Risk Management*.
4. Pidun et al., *The Art of Risk Management*.
5. William Samuelson and Richard Zeckhauser, "Status Quo Bias in Decision Making," *Journal of Risk and Uncertainty* 1, no. 1 (1988): 7–59.
6. Rob Henderson, "How Powerful Is Status Quo Bias?" *Psychology Today* blog, September 29, 2016, https://www.psychologytoday.com/blog/after-service/201609 /how-powerful-is-status-quo-bias.
7. Daniel Kahneman, Jack L. Knetsch, and Richard H. Thaler, "Anomalies: The Endowment Effect, Loss Aversion, and Status Quo Bias," *The Journal of Economic Perspectives* 5, no. 1 (1991): 193–206.
8. Gray, *Warfighting*, 8.
9. Highsmith, *Adaptive Leadership*, Kindle locations 1638–1639.
10. Xerxes quoted in Gaddis, *On Grand Strategy*, 3.
11. Highsmith, *Adaptive Leadership*, Kindle locations 1782–1784.
12. Leonard Mlodinow, *The Drunkard's Walk: How Randomness Rules Our Lives* (New York: Vintage, 2009), 53–56.
13. Mlodinow, *The Drunkard's Walk*, xx.

CHAPTER 7

1. Ross and Weill, *IT Governance*, 12.
2. Hunter and Westerman, *The Real Business of IT*, Kindle locations 1216–1217.
3. Hunter and Westerman, *The Real Business of IT*, Kindle locations 941–943.
4. Cauwenberghe, "How Do You Estimate the Business Value of User Stories?"
5. Gojko Adzic, *Impact Mapping: Making a Big Impact with Software Products and Projects* (Woking, UK: Provoking Thoughts, 2012), Kindle locations 162–164.
6. Adzic, *Impact Mapping*, Kindle locations 207–209.
7. Adzic, *Impact Mapping*, Kindle locations 270–273.

SIDE GLANCE: INNOVATION

1. Joseph A. Schumpeter, *Capitalism, Socialism, and Democracy* (New York: Harper Perennial, 1962).
2. Edgar Schein, *The Corporate Culture Survival Guide* (San Francisco, CA: Jossey-Bass, 2009), 105.
3. Hannah Arendt, *The Human Condition* (Chicago, IL: University of Chicago Press, 1958), 9.
4. Jan Gonda, "The Hindu Trinity," *Anthropos* 63/64, no ½ (1968): 212–226. https://www.jstor.org/stable/40457085?seq=1#page_scan_tab_contents.
5. James G. Lochtefeld, *The Illustrated Encyclopedia of Hinduism: A-M* The Rosen Publishing Group. p. 147, entry for Chidambaram. ISBN 978-0-8239-3179-8. Cited in Wikipedia (Nataraja).
6. James G. Lochtefeld (2002). *The Illustrated Encyclopedia of Hinduism: N-Z* (New York: The Rosen Publishing Group, 2002), 464–466.
7. Jeremy Roberts, *Japanese Mythology A to Z* (New York: Chelsea House, 2010), 28.
8. Igor Stravinsky, *Poetics of Music in the Form of Six Lessons* (Cambridge, MA: Harvard University Press, 1942), 65.
9. Drnevitch and Croson, "Information Technology and Business-Level Strategy," 498.
10. Ries, *The Startup Way*, 37–38.
11. Sarah L. Kaufman, Jayne Orenstein, Sarah Hashemi, Elizabeth Hart, and Shelly Tan, "Art in an Instant: The Secrets of Improvisation," *The Washington Post*, June 7, 2018, https://www.washingtonpost.com/graphics/2018/lifestyle/science-behind-improv-performance/?noredirect=on&utm_term=.6f05d5e77fa1.
12. Kaufman, et al., "Art in an Instant."
13. Deborah Ancona and Henrik Bresman, *X-Teams: How to Build Teams that Lead, Innovate, and Succeed* (Boston, MA: Harvard Business Review Press, 2007), Kindle location 267.
14. Ancona and Bresman, *X-Teams*, Kindle location 667.
15. Ancona and Bresman, *X-Teams*, Kindle locations 673–794.

CHAPTER 8

1. Max Weber, *Economy and Society: An Outline of Interpretive Sociology*, ed. by Guenther Roth and Claus Witch (Berkeley, CA: University of California Press, 1978), 223.
2. Daniel Katz and Robert L. Kahn, *The Social Psychology of Organizations* (New York: Wiley, 1966), 222.
3. Daniel Wren and Arthur Bedeian, *The Evolution of Management Thought*, 6th ed. (Hoboken, NJ: John Wiley and Sons, 2009), 233.
4. Weber, *Economy and Society*, 975.
5. Weber, *Economy and Society*, 975.

6. Hirotaka Takeuchi and Ikujiro Nonaka, "The New New Product Development Game," *Harvard Business Review*, January 1986, https://hbr.org/1986/01/the-new-new-product-development-game.

7. Paul S. Adler, *The "Learning Bureaucracy": New United Motor Manufacturing, Inc.* (Los Angeles, CA: University of Southern California, School of Business Administration, 1992), 64. https://www.marshall.usc.edu/sites/default/files/padler/intellcont/NUMMI%28ROB%29-1.pdf.

8. *Analysis of Alternatives*, DHS Acquisition Instruction/Guidebook #102-01-001: Appendix G, Interim Version 1.9, November 7, 2008. https://dau.gdit.com/aqn201a/pdfs/Appendix_G_Analysis_of_Alternatives_(AoA)_Interim_v1_9_dtd_11-07-08.pdf; A 56-page explanation of how to use it may be found at https://www.anser.org/docs/reports/AOA%20Methodologies%20Considerations%20for%20DHS%20Acq%20Analysis.pdf.

9. Schein, *The Corporate Culture Survival Guide*, 27.

10. Avery, "Responsible Change," 22–23.

11. John Shook. "How to Change a Culture: Lessons from NUMMI," *MIT Sloan Management Review* 51, no. 2 (2010): 63.

SIDE GLANCE: SECURITY

1. "These Cybercrime Statistics Will Make You Think Twice About Your Password: Where's the CSI Cyber Team When You Need Them?," *CBS*, March 3, 2015, https://www.cbs.com/shows/csi-cyber/news/1003888/these-cybercrime-statistics-will-make-you-think-twice-about-your-password-where-s-the-csi-cyber-team-when-you-need-them-/.

2. Rugged Software, *Rugged Handbook*, https://www.ruggedsoftware.org/wp-content/uploads/2013/11 /Rugged-Handbook-v7.pdf, 6.

CHAPTER 9

1. Highsmith, *Adaptive Leadership*, Kindle locations 1558–1560.

2. Peter Weill and Jeanne W. Ross, *IT Savvy*, Kindle locations 860–893.

3. "AWS Case Study: Intuit," AWS website, accessed February 12, 2019, https://aws.amazon.com/solutions/case-studies/intuit-cloud-migration/.

4. "Under Armour Case Study," AWS website, accessed February 12, 2019, https://aws.amazon.com/solutions/case-studies/under-armour/.

5. Tim Mullaney, "Obama Adviser: Demand Overwhelmed HealthCare.gov," *USA Today*, October 5, 2013, https://www.usatoday.com/story/news/nation/2013/10/05/health-care-website-repairs/2927597/.

6. Alexander Roos, James Tucker, Fabrice Roghé, Marc Rodt, and Sebastian Strange, "The Art of Planning," *BCG* blog, April 30, 2017, https://www.bcg.com/en-us/publications/2017/strategic-art-planning.aspx.

7. Roos et al., "The Art of Planning."

8. Bjarte Bogsnes, *Implementing Beyond Budgeting: Unlocking the Performance Potential* (Hoboken, NJ: Wiley & Sons, 2009), Kindle locations 542–543.

9. Bogsnes, *Implementing Beyond Budgeting*, Kindle locations 547–548.

10. Bogsnes, *Implementing Beyond Budgeting*, Kindle locations 195–196.

11. Ries, *The Startup Way*, 26–27.

12. Christensen, *The Innovator's Dilemma*, Kindle locations 382–386.

13. Highsmith, *Adaptive Leadership*, Kindle location 877.

SIDE GLANCE: THE CLOUD AND THE FUTURE

1. "AWS Case Study: Intuit," AWS website.

2. See the following case studies: "Mark Schwartz, DHS, CIS CIO Shares How Agencies are Modernizing and Accelerating the Pace of IT," YouTube video, 9:40, posted by Amazon Web Services, July 20, 2015, https://www.youtube.com/watch?v=Whbed 3dAxiU; Kim S. Nash, "J.P. Morgan Set to Run First Apps in Public Cloud," *Wall Street Journal*, March 30, 2017, https://blogs.wsj.com/cio/2017/03/30/j-p-morgan-set-to -run-first-apps-in-public-cloud/; "Capital One Case Study," AWS website, accessed February 12, 2019, https://aws.amazon.com/solutions/case-studies/capital-one /; "Netflix Case Study," AWS website, accessed February 12, 2019, https://aws .amazon.com/solutions/case-studies/netflix/; "Expedia Increases Agility and Resil- iency by Going All In on AWS," AWS website, accessed February 12, 2019, https:// aws.amazon.com/solutions/case-studies/expedia/.

3. "About McDonald's," AWS website, accessed February 12, 2019, https://aws .amazon.com/solutions/case-studies/mcdonalds/.

4. "AWS Case Study: McDonald's Home Delivery," AWS website, accessed February 12, 2019, https://aws.amazon.com/solutions/case-studies/mcdonalds-home-delivery/.

5. Jeff Barr, "GE Oil & Gas—Digital Transformation in the Cloud," AWS News Blog, May 2, 2016, https://aws.amazon.com/blogs/aws/ge-oil-gas-digital-transformation -in-the-cloud/; "GE Oil & Gas Saves Millions with AWS," *PolarSeven*, accessed Febru- ary 12, 2019, https://polarseven.com/ge-oil-gas-saves-millions-with-aws/.

6. "AWS Case Study: BMW," AWS website, accessed February 12, 2019, https://aws .amazon.com/solutions/case-studies/bmw/.

7. Jeff Bar, "Natural Language Processing at Clemson University—1.1 Million vCPUs & EC2 Spot Instances," AWS News Blog, September 28, 2017, https://aws.amazon .com/blogs/aws/natural-language-processing-at-clemson-university-1-1-million -vcpus-ec2-spot-instances/.

8. "International Centre for Missing & Exploited Children Case Study," AWS web- site, accessed February 12, 2019, https://aws.amazon.com/solutions/case-studies /icmec/.

9. "FINRA Case Study," AWS website, accessed February 12, 2019, https://aws .amazon.com/solutions/case-studies/finra/.

10. "C-SPAN Case Study," AWS website, accessed February 12, 2019, https://aws .amazon.com/solutions/case-studies/cspan/.

11. "An Eye on Science: How Stanford Students Turned Classwork into Their Life's Work," AWS Government, Education, & Nonprofits Blog, October 4, 2016, https://aws.amazon.com/blogs/publicsector/an-eye-on-science-how-stanford-students -turned -classwork-into-their-lifes-work/.

12. "Fraud.net Case Study," AWS website, accessed February 12, 2019, https://aws .amazon.com/solutions/case-studies/fraud-dot-net/.

13. Derek Hernandez, "Hudl raises $30MM to Bring Cutting-Edge Sports Analytics to Teams around the World," Hudl blog, July 6, 2017, https://www.hudl.com/blog /hudl-raises-30mm-to-bring-cutting-edge-sports-analytics-to-teams-around-the -world.

CHAPTER 10

1. John P. Kotter, *A Sense of Urgency* (Cambridge, MA: Harvard Business Review Press, 2008), Kindle Edition.

CHAPTER 11

1. Pierre Branda, "Did the War Pay for the War? An Assessment of Napoleon's Attempts to Make His Campaigns Self-Financing," *Napoleonica La Revue* 3, no. 2 (2008): 2–15. https://www.cairn.info/revue-napoleonica-la-revue-2008-3-page-2.htm.

2. "CFOs Play a Major Role in Digital Investment Decisions Across the Enterprise, According to Latest Accenture Research," Accenture news release, September 12, 2018, https://newsroom.accenture.com/news/cfos-play-a-major-role-in-digital-in vestment-decisions-across-the-enterprise-according-to-latest-accenture-research .htm.

3. Amanda Houston, "Expert Interview: Jeanette Wade, CFO, Executive Office of Technology Services & Security," *Innovation Enterprise Channels*, accessed on November 26, 2018, https://channels.theinnovationenterprise.com/articles/expert-interview -jeanette-wade-cfo-executive-office-of-technology-services-security.

4. Ghesquieres, et al. "The Art of Performance Management."

5. "Today's CFO Strategic Role: Changing the Game Plan for Tomorrow," GrantThorn ton.com, March 27, 2017, https://www.grantthornton.com/library/survey-reports /CFO-survey/2017/changing-game-plan-for-tomorrow.aspx.

6. David Court, "The Evolving Role of the CMO," *McKinsey Quarterly*, August 2007, https://www.mckinsey.com/business-functions/marketing-and-sales/our-insights /the-evolving-role-of-the-cmo.

ABOUT THE AUTHOR

Mark Schwartz is an iconoclastic CIO and a playful crafter of ideas, an inveterate purveyor of lucubratory prose. He has been an IT leader in organizations small and large, public, private, and nonprofit.

As an Enterprise Strategist for Amazon Web Services, he uses his CIO experience to advise the world's largest companies on the obvious: time to move to the cloud, guys. As the CIO of US Citizenship and Immigration Services, he provoked the federal government into adopting Agile and DevOps practices. He is pretty sure that when he was the CIO of Intrax Cultural Exchange, he was the first person ever to use business intelligence and supply chain analytics to place au pairs with the right host families.

Mark speaks frequently on innovation, change leadership, bureaucratic implications of DevOps, and using Agile practices in low-trust environments. With a BS in computer science from Yale, a master's in philosophy from Yale, and an MBA from Wharton, Mark is either an expert on business value and IT or just confused and much poorer.

Mark is the author of *The Art of Business Value* and *A Seat at the Table*, and the winner of a *Computerworld* Premier 100 award, an Amazon Elite 100 award, a Federal Computer Week Fed 100 award, and a *CIO Magazine* CIO 100 award. He lives in Boston, Massachusetts.